A HISTORY OF SOCIAL DEMOCRACY
IN POSTWAR EUROPE

The Postwar World
General Editors: A.J. Nicholls and Martin S. Alexander

As distance puts events into perspective, and as evidence accumulates, it begins to be possible to form an objective historical view of our recent past. *The Postwar World* is an ambitious new series providing a scholarly but readable account of the way our world has been shaped in the crowded years since the Second World War. Some volumes will deal with regions, or even single nations, others with important themes; all will be written by expert historians drawing on the latest scholarship as well as their own research and judgements. The series should be particularly welcome to students, but it is designed also for the general reader with an interest in contemporary history.

Decolonization in Africa
J. D. Hargreaves

The Community of Europe:
A History of European Integration since 1945
Derek W. Urwin

Northern Ireland since 1945
Sabine Wichert

A History of Social Democracy in Postwar Europe
Stephen Padgett and William E. Paterson

A History of Social Democracy in Postwar Europe

Stephen Padgett
William E. Paterson

Longman
London and New York

Longman Group UK Limited
Longman House, Burnt Mill, Harlow,
Essex CM20 2JE, England
and Associated Companies throughout the world.

*Published in the United States of America
by Longman Inc., New York*

First published 1991

British Library Cataloguing in Publication Data

Padgett, Stephen
  A history of social democracy in postwar Europe.
  I. Title   II. Paterson, William
  320.5
  ISBN 0-582-49173-8
  ISBN 0-582-49174-6 PBK

Library of Congress Cataloging-in-Publication Data.

Padgett, Stephen, 1951–
  A history of social democracy in postwar Europe /
Stephen Padgett, William Paterson.
      p. cm. — (The Postwar World)
  Includes bibliographical references and index.
  ISBN 0-582-49173-8.—ISBN 0-582-49174-6 (pbk.)
  1. Socialism—Europe—History—20th century.
  2. Europe—Politics and government—1945-
  I. Paterson, William   II. Title.   III Series.
HX238.5.P33   1991   91-10130
320.5'315'094—dc20   CIP

Set in 10/12pt ITC New Baskerville

Produced by Longman Singapore Publishers (Pte) Ltd.
Printed in Singapore

Contents

Editorial Foreword

The aim of this series is to describe and analyse the history of the World since 1945. History, like time, does not stand still. What seemed to many of us only recently to be 'current affairs', or the stuff of political speculation, has now become material for historians. The editors feel that it is time for a series of books which will offer the public judicious and scholarly, but at the same time readable, accounts of the way in which our present-day world was shaped by the years after the end of the Second World War. The period since 1945 has seen political events and socio-economic developments of enormous significance for the human race, as important as anything which happened before Hitler's death or the bombing of Hiroshima. Ideologies have waxed and waned, the industrialised economies have boomed and bust, empires have collapsed, new nations have emerged and sometimes themselves fallen into decline. While we can be thankful that no major armed conflict has occurred between the so-called superpowers, there have been many other wars, and terrorism has become an international plague. Although the position of ethnic minorities has dramatically improved in some countries, it has worsened in others. Nearly everywhere the status of women has become an issue which politicians have been unable to avoid. These are only some of the developments we hope will be illuminated by this series as it unfolds.

The books in the series will not follow any set pattern; they will vary in length according to the needs of the subject. Some will deal with regions, or even single nations, and others with themes. Not all of them will begin in 1945, and the terminal date may similarly vary; once again, the time-span chosen will be appropriate to the question under discussion. All the books, however, will be written by expert historians drawing on the latest fruits of scholarship, as well as their own expertise and judgement. The series should be particularly welcome to students, but is is designed also for the general reader with an interest in contemporary history. We hope that the books will stimulate scholarly discussion and encourage specialists to look beyond their own particular interests to engage in wider controversies. History, and particularly the history of the recent past, is neither 'bunk' nor an intellectual form of stamp-collecting, but an indispensable part of an educated persons's approach to life. If it is not written by historians it will be written by others of a less discriminating and more polemical disposition. The editors are confident that this series will help to ensure the victory of the historical approach, with consequential benefits for its readers.

A.J. Nicholls
Martin S. Alexander

Preface

The work is the product of extensive cooperation and exchanges between the authors. Indeed the Introduction and Conclusion were written jointly. There was, however, a division of responsibilities for the individual chapters. Stephen Padgett was responsible for chapters 1, 4 and 5; William Paterson was responsible for chapters 2, 3 and 6.

The authors wish to thank Longman and Anthony Nicholls as series editor for their patience in awaiting the completion of this volume and for their very helpful comments on the manuscript. Their suggestions on the presentation of material were especially useful, and have been incorporated into the book. Thanks is also due to Dr Richard Gillespie of the University of Warwick for his comments on material relating to the new Mediterranean democracies. Naturally, any errors of fact or infelicities of interpretation remain the responsibility of the authors.

Glossary

APO	Ausserparliamentarische Opposition: extra-parliamentary opposition (West Germany)
CBI	Confederation of British Industry
CDU	Christlich-Demokratische Union: Christian Democratic Union (Germany)
CERES	Centre d'études, de recherches et d'éducation socialiste: Centre for Socialist Studies, Research, and Education, a group on the left wing of the French Socialist Party.
CFDT	Confédération Française et Démocratique du Travail: the French socialist confederation of trade unions
CGIL	Confederazione Generale Italiano del Lavoro: General Confederation of Italian Labour
CGT	Confédération Générale du Travail: the French communist confederation of trade unions
CSU	Christlich-Soziale Union: the Christian Social Union (Germany)
DGB	Deutscher Gewerkschaftsbund, (West) German Trade Union Federation
EC	European Community
EEC	European Economic Community
EFTA	European Free Trade Area
ECSC	European Coal and Steel Community
Euratom	European Atomic Energy Authority
FDP	Freie Demokratische Partei: the Free Democratic Party (Germany)
FLN	Front de Libération Nationale: Algerian National Independence Movement

FRG	Federal Republic of Germany
GDR	German Democratic Republic
LO	Landsorganisationen: the trade union federation in, respectively, Denmark and Sweden
NATO	North Atlantic Treaty Organization
OPEC	Organisation of Petroleum Exporting Countries
OECD	Organisation for Economic Cooperation and Development
ÖGB	Österreichischer Gewerkschaftsbund: Austrian Trade Union Federation.
PASOK	the Pan-Helenic Socialist Movement
PCF	Parti communiste francaise: the French Communist Party
PCI	Partito Comunista Italiano: Italian Communist Party
PS	Parti Socialiste: the Socialist Party in France
PSB/BSP	Parti Socialiste Belge/Belgische Socialistische Partij: the Belgian Socialist Party
PSI	Partita Socialista Italiano: the Italian Socialist Party
PSOE	Partido Socialista Obrero Español: the Spanish Socialist Workers' Party
PSP	Partido Socialista Português: the Portuguese Socialist Party
PvdA	Partij van der Arbeid: the Labour Party of the Netherlands
SAF	Svenska Arbetsgivareföreningen: the Swedish Employers' Confederation
SAP	Socialistisk Arbeiderparti: the Socialist Labour Party (Sweden)
SD	Socialdemokratiet: the Danish Social Democratic Party
SDP	Social Democratic Party (Great Britain)
SDS	Sozialistischer Deutscher Studentenbund: the Socialist German Student Federation: the SPD student organisation expelled from the party in 1960
SED	Sozialistische Einheitspartei Deutschlands: Socialist Unity Party, (German Democratic Republic)
SFIO	Section Francaise de l'Internationale Ouvrière: the French Socialist Party, 1905–69
SPD	Sozialdemokratische Partei Deutschlands: the Social Democratic Party of (West) Germany
SPÖ	Sozialistische Partei Österreichs: the Socialist Party of Austria

TUC   Trades Union Congress (Great Britain)
VÖEST Vereinigte Österreichische Eisen und Stahlweke: United
           Austrian Iron and Steel Company

Introduction

DEFINING SOCIAL DEMOCRACY

Social democracy is a hybrid political tradition composed of social-ism and liberalism. It is the product of a division in the socialist tradition between those who seek to realise socialist ideals within the institutions of liberal capitalist society (social democrats) and those who remain outside those institutions with the objective of superseding them through revolutionary force (communists). In particular, social democrats are fully committed to participation in the electoral process and in parliamentary democracy. Indeed, social democracy is often referred to as 'parliamentary socialism'. Social democracy is inspired by socialist ideals, but is heavily conditioned by its political environment, and it incorporates liberal values. The social democratic project may be defined as the attempt to reconcile socialism with liberal politics and capitalist society.

Once one tries to embellish this very broad definition, a number of problems are encountered. Ideologically social democracy has changed markedly over the course of the hundred years or more of its history. Moreover, the social democratic parties have exhibited quite wide variations of ideology. It is, however, possible to identify some common developments. For a very long period, ideological debate and prescriptions centred on the ownership question. A commitment to nationalisation of the basic means of production was, until the 1950s, a central feature of party programmes in parties such as the British Labour Party as well as those such as the German Social Democratic Party (SPD) which had been more influenced by Marxist ideas. Subsequently, the impact of the Cold War, allied to the pervasive character of postwar prosperity, moved most of the parties

1

to weaken their commitment to nationalisation. This change was most dramatically exemplified by the Bad Godesberg programme of the German party (1959) which served to redefine social democracy.

The Godesberg Programme was anticipated by Anthony Crosland's *The Future of Socialism*. Crosland distinguishes five criteria which have subsequently constituted the core values of social democracy: political liberalism, the mixed economy, the welfare state, Keynesian economics, and a belief in equality. These principles were sometimes embodied in formal programmatic statements, as in the case of the German, Austrian and Scandinavian parties. Elsewhere it was more a matter of practice and convention, as in the case of the British Labour Party. In recent years the Crosland/Bad Godesberg conception of social democracy has proved increasingly difficult to translate into practical terms or to defend at the theoretical level. Attempts to redefine social democracy met with only limited success and the parties entered a period of ideological disarray. The collapse of the social democratic consensus led to an intensification of the ideological fission which is a primary characteristic of the parties.

Until the 1950s it might also have been possible to define social democracy with reference to a distinctive pattern of party organisation and social composition. The social democratic parties could be said to have occupied a position between the socially diverse, loosely organised conservative and liberal parties, and the working-class, highly disciplined communist parties based on the principles of democratic centralism. The social democratic parties were cohesive mass membership parties, characterised by relative social homogeneity (predominantly working class) and combining the principle of internal democracy with the practice of leader autonomy. However, these characteristics have become more blurred in recent years. Social democratic parties have lost their class character as they have become 'people's parties' with a socially diverse membership and electorate. Organisationally the parties have become less cohesive and the principle of internal democracy has given way progressively to a leadership orientation. Moreover, the organisational distinction between social democracy and communism has been weakened as the pursuit of the Euro-communist strategy led the latter to shed their democratic centralist character.

Defining social democracy in relation to a 'family' of social democratic parties is problematical, since there is no common nomenclature. The parties adopted titles incorporating a variety of terms: labour, worker, social democratic and socialist. Generally, the northern European parties have readily accepted the adjective 'social democratic' whilst the southern Europeans have been uneasy or even hostile to the term, preferring to call themselves socialist parties. However, social democratic and socialist parties share a common tradition and common characteristics, although there are differences of emphasis. Moreover, in the last decade there has been a definite convergence of the social democratic and socialist parties, with the 'social democratisation' of the latter.

One of the defining characteristics of northern European social democracy which is absent in Mediterranean Europe and the Iberian peninsula, is the close relationship between the parties and the labour movement. While the northern European parties have strong ties to organised labour, the parties in France, Italy and Spain have remained apart. However, the last few years have seen a tentative loosening of party-union relations in the northern European countries, and there are indications that this distinction is becoming less significant.

These then are the strands in the social democratic tradition which are entwined in the postwar history of social democracy. We shall develop them further in the course of this book. Indeed the chapters revolve around these themes, reflecting our view that they elucidate the character and development of social democracy far more than a chronological account or an approach which breaks down the European social democratic tradition into individual countries. We begin, however, with an account of the formation of that tradition, which should serve to illuminate the foregoing definition.

THE ROOTS OF SOCIAL DEMOCRACY

European social democratic parties arose as parties of a newly created class of industrial workers. These denizens of the political and social order of industrial capitalism, bound together by a common experience of powerlessness and exploitation, saw their only hope of emancipation in mass organisation. A new genus of political party emerged. Unlike the parties of conservatism and liberalism which at the time were little more than coteries of prominent individuals, social democrats formed mass membership parties, disciplined and hierarchical, almost military in

3

organisation. Their strength lay in their capacity for mobilising the working class. Conditions of life and labour in industrial society bred a class solidarity which became the parties' leitmotif. With the emergence of labour organised politically on a mass scale, socialist ideas, hitherto the domain of intellectuals, began to acquire political reality and historical force. Foremost amongst these was Marxism; an exposition of the inner workings of capitalism and the class relations which condemned labour to servility. Marxism outlined the historic rôle of organised labour as the bearer of a new society, and it became the 'official' ideology of the movement. Social democracy grew to become a major political force in the industrial heartlands of northern Europe where the leviathan of capitalism loomed largest. In the south, the slow and uneven march of capitalism permitted the survival of peasant and artisan, inhibiting the advent of working-class socialism on social democratic lines.

Established in 1875, the German Social Democratic Party (SPD) was the cradle of Marxian social democracy. However, the party did not take up Marxism unconditionally. Important sections of the party rejected the road of outright class struggle and confrontation with the state, preferring to work through parliament for gradual social and political reform. However, after German social democracy resurfaced from proscription under the anti-socialist laws (1878–90), Marxism dominated its ideological perspective and permeated its early programmes. Around the turn of the century German social democrats were caught up in a vigorous debate over the relevance of Marxist ideology. There were some who wanted to modify party doctrine, and others who played down the importance of ideology altogether. In practical day-to-day politics a cautious pragmatism had come to dominate the SPD by 1914, but for all this Marxism continued to play at least a formal rôle in the party. It was symbolic of the parties ghetto existence, outside the mainstream of German politics.

In Austria, the Low Countries and Scandinavia social democracy also derived some inspiration from Marxism. Drawing on SPD programmes, statements of party principle often contained references to the classical axioms of Marxism. An 1885 programme of the Swedish social democrats, for example, began with a preamble affirming that 'labour is the true source of all wealth and culture, and the return thereof should accrue to him who performs the task'. Openings in the constitutional order, however, and a limited working-class constituency led the Scandinavians progressively to revise their principles to allow them the flexibility to form alliances with bourgeois parties. For their part too, the Belgians were less doctrinaire than their German counterparts, more inclined to the tangible than to niceties of theory. Like social democrats in the Netherlands they were more concerned with the suffrage issue than with the longer term struggle for socialism.

In Britain labour was slow to organise itself politically. An independent parliamentary group (the Labour Representation Committee) was formed in 1900, adopting the title Labour Party in 1906, but it was not until after the First World War that labour was fully organised on a mass scale. It was significant too that the early party steered clear of the terms 'socialist' or 'social democratic' in its title and constitution. Reflecting the rather apolitical ethos of craft unionism, the new party was oriented towards practical trade union issues like labour law. In the British Labour Party, socialist ideology was overshadowed by a labourist ethos derived from its trade union roots. Outside of its labour wing, the party was strongly influenced by Fabian socialism. Respectable and middle class, many of them civil servants, the members of the Fabian Society were not convinced of the power of the theory, concentrating instead on practical measures of reform, and the 'permeation' of public life. A socialist workers' party emerged in London, the North and Scotland, predating the Labour Party itself, but with its links to non-conformist religion it was inspired more by the Sermon on the Mount than by *Das Kapital.* Marxism made virtually no impression at all on the Labour Party.

The hesitant and uneven growth of industrial capitalism in southern Europe deprived socialism of its driving force. The growth of the industrial working-class was slow, and labour movements correspondingly small. By 1910 the French labour movement still numbered less than one million, as against over one and a half million in Britain and nearly two and a half million in Germany. State repression contributed to the curtailment of labour movement growth in France but it also served to accentuate the revolutionary spirit of labour. Highly politicised trade unions felt that they held their destiny in their own hands; they had little faith in the constitutional order and political parties. The Spanish labour movement was even smaller, and dominated by a form of anarcho-syndicalism even more highly charged and virulent than in France, particularly so in the Catalan region. The inability of Spanish socialism to penetrate the industrial heartlands of Catalonia crippled the movement from its infancy. In Italy too, divisions between socialists and anarchists were endemic. The regimentation of the northern labour movements was alien to the individualistic and spontaneous outlook of labour in these countries, and the merger between socialism and labour, characteristic of northern Europe, failed to take place. Lacking the ballast of organised labour, socialism remained dominated by intellectuals and prone to factionalism and fragmentation.

Among the myriad parties and groups of the French Left, two mass socialist parties emerged: the *Parti Ouvrier Français*, under the Marxist Jules Guesde, and the Independent Socialists of the reformist Jean Jaurès. In 1980 these parties merged to form the *Section Française de l'Internationale Ouvrière* (SFIO), but its membership of 90,000 (1914) was miniscule compared to the SPD's million members. Moreover, lacking a strong base among industrial workers, the party relied heavily on the peasantry. It thus lacked the sense of purpose of an avowedly workers' party, and continued to be plagued by ideological and personal disputation. In Spain, the *Partido Socialista Obrero Español (PSOE)* dated from 1879, its leaders inspired by the Marxist and labourist variants of North European socialism. In 1888 the party took the initiative in forming a trade union, the *Union General des Trabajo (UGT)* in an abortive attempt to subordinate the labour movement to socialist leadership. Alien to the mass of Spanish labour, however, the PSOE remained small and divided. Italian syndicalism was less extreme than in France or Spain, and for a time it was possible to accommodate the tendency within the *Partito Socialista Italiano (PSI)*. In fact the PSI contained a bewildering mosaic of factions and tendencies each striving for hegemony, and the result was a party quite incapable of effective or concerted action.

The parties of northern Europe displayed a much clearer sense of purpose, although it was not entirely the purpose for which they had been founded. They became geared to converting their mass following into electoral majorities. Parties were turned into vote-gathering machines, and progressively less emphasis was placed on the functions of agitation, direct action and mass mobilisation. Increasingly the parties sought support from social classes outside the working-class to augment the ranks of their electorate. As they did so they either divested themselves, by stages, of their Marxist ideology (as in Scandinavia and the Low Countries) or else maintained a symbolic allegiance to Marxist orthodoxy whilst adapting in practice to the dictates of political expediency (as in Germany and Austria). Explanations for the transformation of social democracy in the decade before the First World War are various. Michels (1959) detected an inevitable process of bureaucratisation and élite domination in mass parties. Gay (1952) identified a dilemma facing democratic socialism. Caught between fidelity to ideological roots and the pull of political power the parties ultimately gravitated towards the latter. Others have pointed to the logic following from the entry of the parties into the electoral arena (Przeworski 1980) and the pull of reformist trade unions (Marks 1939).

The growing ascendancy of reformism and 'ballot box socialism' provoked conflict within those parties, like the SPD, which contained both reformist and revolutionary socialists. It was also the source of divisions within international socialism (Joll 1974, 77–186). The First International had been established in 1864 as the International Working Mens' Association to act as the tribune of socialism across Europe. Marx had been closely involved in its foundation, but it had collapsed after only twelve years in a breach between his followers and those of the anarchist Michael Bakunin. Its successor, the Second International, was committed to Marxian socialism and international socialist solidarity, but the decade preceding the outbreak of war revealed signs of the unravelling of both. There were three major issues of contention. Firstly, the willingness of some parties to broaden their class horizons and seek alliances with bourgeois parties clashed with the Marxist principle of class purity. Secondly, the Russian revolution of 1905 underlined the contrast between the insurrectionary fervour and dynamism of social democracy there and the staid reformism of the western European parties. The question 'reform or revolution' which had exercised European socialists greatly in the late 1890s, returned to the International Congress agenda. In the face of differences arising from these issues it was possible to preserve a semblance of inter-national solidarity only by agreeing broad doctrinal principles whilst allowing considerable scope for their interpretation and practical application.

The questions which carried the greatest significance for inter-national socialism, however, were those which touched on the sharpening rivalries and conflicts between the European nations, the attendant clamour of nationalism and the unrelenting build-up of military and naval strength. Patriotism and socialist solidarity met head on, and the ambivalence of the parties' response cast a dark shadow over the International. Ringing declarations of international fraternity and condemnations of 'capitalist wars' served to conceal the indecisiveness and ultimate impotence of the International, and the Basle Congress of 1912 conjured an illusion of confidence and optimism which in hindsight appears pitifully hollow.

> For France and Germany the hour of reconciliation has struck. There is to be no more war between Germany and France...Great Britain and Germany should arm, but not in a race to build warships for a war that will bleed them white, but aim to overcome misery and oppression...The International is strong enough to speak in this tone of command to those in power and if necessary to follow up their words with deeds. War on war, peace for the world, hurrah for the Workers' International.
>
> *(Speech by Belgian delegate, cited Joll 1974, 156.)*

As late as July 1914, socialists were reiterating these sentiments, but the following month socialist parties in all the western European countries endorsed national mobilisation for European war, exploding the myth of socialist internationalism.

The First World War was a watershed for European socialism, bringing to an abrupt close its era of innocence and optimism. It was compounded by the Bolshevik revolution in Russia and the foundation in its aftermath of the Third (communist) International. Barring the door to all but 'simon-pure communists' (Landauer 1976, 797) the new International required member organisations to subscribe to twenty-one conditions, which included an explicit commitment to insurrectionary agitation and revolution, a total disavowal of reformism, and abstention from any kind of bourgeois-democratic institutions. Bolshevik-style discipline and the subordination of parties to the International's Moscow-based directorate were obligatory. Effectively, the conditions created an immutable barrier between communism and social democracy; indeed this was the intended purpose.

The schism gave democratic socialists dominance over the Left in all the countries of western Europe. In Germany, however, its consequences were to be of historic proportions, weakening resistance to the rise of fascism and dictatorship. Having taken on government responsibility in 1918 in a hastily proclaimed republican state, SPD leaders found themselves allying with the remnants of the Imperial regime to suppress a communist-led revolution. The legacy of bitterness from the civil war as well as the *diktat* from Moscow to the KPD subsequently stood in the way of a common front against Hitler.

Disorientation and uncertainty were the principal characteristics of social democracy in the interwar years. Having broken with revolutionary communism the parties now identified with liberal democracy, though this was often veiled by the rhetoric of radicalism. Although they were antagonistic to capitalism they had no clear-cut alternative to offer. Social democrats thus became ensnared in the interwar crisis of the political and economic order of liberal capitalism. It was against this background that the parties entered government. Minority administrations or coalitions, their administrations produced little in the way of socialist reform. Indeed, the most striking feature of social democratic government was the slavish pursuit of economic and financial orthodoxy as the slump deepened. In Britain, the Labour Prime Minister, Ramsay MacDonald, and Chancellor, Philip Snowden, adhered rigidly to the doctrine of the balanced budget, and it was only a Cabinet revolt which prevented the 1929–31 government from cutting financial assistance to the unemployed in a desperate bid for monetary stability. Economic orthodoxy was equally characteristic of Hjalmar Branting's three minority administrations in Sweden and Hermann Müller's SPD-led coalition in Germany. Léon Blum's Popular Front in France attempted to break free of its grip, but like other governments of the Left was confronted with a 'wall of money' – financial interests which held the key to national economic survival, able to exercise a tacit veto over economic policy.

In Italy and Germany the collapse of the liberal order into fascist dictatorship meant the physical liquidation of social democracy. Elsewhere it appeared to have exhausted its political potential. However, the early 1930s marked the beginning of a long and often hesitant process of renewal and redefinition. The earliest evangelist of Keynesian social democracy (see Chapter 1) was Ernst Wigforss, principal theoretician of the Swedish party. Drawing on the pre-Keynesian demand management of the Stockholm school, Wigforss popularised the economics of the deficit budget as a means of stimulating growth. Urging the party to overcome both the vestigial allegiance to neo-Marxism and the pull of liberal orthodoxy, he was largely responsible for the breakthrough of 1932. A programme of public expenditure and employment creation was rewarded by electoral victory and a return to office. A subsequent alliance with the Agrarian Party enabled the SAP to implement its programme and lay the foundations for the postwar hegemony of social democracy in Sweden.

It is notoriously difficult to trace the genealogy of ideas, their assimilation into political currents and translation into action, and it would certainly be wrong to identify the Sweden of the 1930s as the exclusive progenitor of expenditure-led recovery. Roosevelt's New

Deal and the economic mobilisation of Nazi Germany were contemporaneous and indeed, larger in scale. However, the Swedes were responsible for harnessing the new economics to social democratic objectives and creating the Swedish model of the full employment welfare state. They also pioneered what one observer has called the 'historic compromise' of social democracy with capitalism. Addressing the Gothenburg Bourse Society in 1938, Wigforss argued that 'neither the working-class movement nor private capitalists could hope to suppress the other altogether, that they should recognise this fact, and should cooperate to achieve their common interest – increased efficiency in production' (Tilton 1979, 309). The Swedish model of social democracy did not take recognisable shape until well into the postwar era, but the lines of the blueprint were beginning to emerge.

Although only the British, Swedish and Swiss parties survived the anvil of fascism, the Second World War imparted a renewed sense of purpose to social democracy. An anti-fascist war brought none of the conflicts between patriotism and socialism which had torn the European Left apart in 1914. Fascism and dictatorship in Germany, Italy and Spain underlined the consequences of a divided Left, and resistance movements served to unite socialists, communists and progressive liberals, eclipsing the debilitating conflicts of the past. In Britain, Labour had returned from its decade in the political wilderness to take up key posts in the wartime Cabinet. Party intellectuals reflected on the old order and envisaged its transition (Durbin 1940; Cole 1942; Laski 1943), whilst in government white papers and royal commissions the outline of a new social order was emerging. As hostilities neared their conclusion, resistance groups and governments in exile drew up plans for the future. Characteristic of all these initiatives was the conviction that there could be no return to the moribund world of *laissez-faire* capitalism.

CHAPTER ONE

Social Democratic Ideology

Ideological diversity is one of the hallmarks of social democracy, reflecting the diverse political philosophies on which it has drawn and the motley social composition of the parties' membership and electorate. The entry into the parties of new social strata in the postwar era – in particular the new middle class – intensified their cultural and ideological diversity. Accommodating diversity in order to prevent fragmentation often meant cultivating vagueness and ambiguity in party programmes. Fluidity is another of the defining characteristics of social democratic ideology. An acute electoral orientation bred a pragmatic flexibility which frequently subordinated doctrine to electoral strategy. In any case, most social democrats, and almost all of their leaders, were unresponsive to all-encompassing systems of thought or utopian visions of the future. Consequently, social democracy carried much less doctrinal balast than its rival ideology of the Left, communism. Its ideology resembled a kaleidoscopic mosaic of ideas and values, constantly changing in response to new circumstances and in the light of practical experience.

Whilst eschewing doctrine, however, social democrats have taken *programme* writing extraordinarily seriously. Programmes have traditionally begun with a preamble elaborating (albeit in the most broad and general terms) the parties' fundamental principles, going on to identify the objectives towards which party activity was to be geared in the foreseeable future. The apogee of programmatic social democracy was in the immediate postwar years, and it is here we begin this chapter.

11

WORKING-CLASS SOCIALISM AND PROGRAMMATIC SOCIAL DEMOCRACY

In the aftermath of the Second World War, social democracy appeared to hold the key to the future. *Laissez-faire* capitalism had been undermined and discredited by the interwar depression. Unprecedented engagement on the part of the state in the regulation and control of wartime economies could be read as a signpost to planned economic development. Having failed to fulfil its social responsibilities in peacetime, and having in many countries collaborated with the Nazi occupation, capital had lost the right to dominate. The devastation of industrial capacity and the economic infrastructure was, moreover, so great that it was hard to envisage a market-led recovery. European coal production stood at a mere 40 per cent of the previous level, the capacity for power generation was drastically reduced, and in some countries manufacturing industry was at a standstill. Many of the Continent's major cities had suffered wholesale destruction. 20 per cent of the French housing stock had been either destroyed or seriously damaged. Britain had lost four million dwellings, Germany ten million. Railway and road networks were paralysed (Mayne 1970, 29–33). The gigantic tasks of reconstruction appeared to demand the driving force of the state, and it was easy for social democrats to equate the idea of state-led reconstruction with their own belief in a socially regulated economy. Wartime conditions, moreover, had profoundly changed relationships between classes (Middlemas 1979, 272–4), generating pressures from labour for a more just social order. Keynes had given this egalitarian *élan* an economic rationale with his argument that a buoyant economy depended on broadening the base of consumption through a more diffuse distribution of income and wealth (Skidelsky 1979, 57). It was not difficult to reconcile the democracy of consumers which all this implied with social democracy's traditional drive towards equality.

Social democrats had found sympathisers for their principles and programmes in the wartime movements of resistance to Nazism in which they had participated alongside communists and left-liberal christian democrats. For two years after the war, social democracy, communism and christian democracy merged in demands for the economic, social, political and moral reconstruction of Europe. The French Resistance Charter of 1944, for instance, had called for a more just social order, the nationalisation of monopolies, a rational reorganisation of the economy, guarantees on workers' rights and a comprehensive system of social security (Urwin 1981, 23). The early programmes of the christian democrats in Germany echoed some of these demands for socialisation in the economy and a more socially responsible state. In Norway a programme for economic reconstruction on the basis of state planning was concluded with all party support, and in Austria a nationalisation programme was drawn up in 1945 by social democrats and their allies. The British Labour Party's blueprint for the postwar order had been set out in wartime policy documents, reflecting a broad national consensus which had taken shape in a variety of all-party and expert committees during the war. In short, socialism was in the ascendant; for the first time its objectives and programmes dominated the political agenda. The sense of euphoria which socialists felt was expressed by the French socialist leader, Léon Blum:

> Today the phase of polemic is over. Socialism can move from its militant to its triumphant period. The social system which it attacked and by which it was attacked is now falling into ruin, and even where it still carries on it does so without belief in itself and in contradiction to its own laws. Socialist assumptions and axioms have been taken over by men and parties who have waged the most ferocious of wars against socialist organisations. It is on the foundation of socialist principles that societies, whether consciously or not are everywhere being reconstituted.
> *(Cited in Graham 1965, 61.)*

At the dawn of a new era and with socialist principles in the ascendant, social democrats everywhere drew up sweeping programmes for the postwar order. Running through these programmes were three central themes: the socialisation of the means of production; state planning and control in the economy; security and equality in society.

Socialisation

It was not that socialisation represented part of a fully elaborated socialist theory of the economy, for social democracy contained no such theory. Nor did it form an element in a grand strategy for changing the exercise of economic power, since the dominant conception of socialisation was of industry owned by the state but operated along capitalist lines. Rather its impetus usually came from three main sources:

> ...the traditional, matter of course identification of socialism with the removal of the means of production from private ownership; the urge to put the Party's hands on important levers of power, thereby weakening the power position of the traditional anti-socialist forces; and...the need

13

for public direction in the reorganisation of the chaotic, denuded, and
largely ownerless industrial machine.   *(Shell 1962, 201)*

In the principle of socialisation it was still possible to detect the
influence of Marx, who had identified the ownership of the means
of production as the foundation of the social and political
dominance of the bourgeoisie. Some party programmes made
genuflections towards this conception. Thus, in its 1946 *Declaration
of Principles* the French socialist party (SFIO) asserted that its
objective was the 'substitution for the regime of private property a
regime in which the natural wealth, along with the means of
production and exchange, will become collective property, and in
which, as a result, classes will be abolished' (Graham 1965, 150). In
this as in other matters, the SFIO retained a residual commitment to
Marxism, but it was expressed only in their rhetoric, serving as a
symbol of an ideological tradition and a totem of party ritual.
Another overtly Marxist party was the Italian socialist party (PSI), the
most radical of the European socialist parties in the early postwar
years. Here socialisation played virtually no rôle in the party's
thinking. State ownership was tainted by association with Mussolini,
under whom a large and ramshackle public sector had been created
in the 1930s.

For the West German Social Democratic Party (SPD), socialisation
symbolised the traditions of a party which had re-emerged in 1945
on the organisational and ideological foundations of the pre-1933
period (Petry 1973, 78–9). It was also a key demand of the trade
union movement. In the aftermath of the Third Reich the industrial
élites (particularly those in coal, steel and chemicals) had lost their
legitimacy. Collaboration with National Socialism meant that they
had forfeited any claim to ownership rights. Even the Christian
Democratic Party in its Ahlen Programme of 1947 acknowledged
that German capitalism was discredited. Moreover, the western allies'
law against cartels appeared to signal the demise of large-scale
business in the heavy industrial sectors. The early postwar policy
initiatives of the SPD reflected this prevailing anti-capitalist temper.

The German party's thinking on the future of the economy was
expressed by its leading economic spokesman, Viktor Agartz, in
terms of the interrelated concepts of 'economic democracy'
(Wirtschaftsdemokratie), 'democratic planning', and 'socialisation'
(Huster 1978, 35–41). Agartz sought a 'third way' between communism and capitalism which placed economic power in collective
hands whilst avoiding the rigid centralisation of the Soviet model.

He also sought to avoid the state socialism of the nationalised economy. Socialisation meant the restructuring of big industry, within the public realm and under a variety of forms of social ownership. The state's rôle in the overall coordination and planning of the economy was to be complemented by decentralised planning initiatives which at the level of the enterprise meant *Mitbestimming* (co-determination or worker participation). This blueprint for the remaking of the German economic order stemmed from a neo-Marxist analysis of capitalism (and its links to fascism) but it produced a formula for a variant of a mixed economy which was not incompatible with liberal democracy. It was a much more comprehensive and systematically elaborated conception than those prevailing in social democratic parties elsewhere in western Europe.

Agartz's conception was endorsed by party congresses in the immediate postwar years, but it was at odds with the western allies' (particularly American) visions of the future. It lost ground progressively in the political struggle over reconstruction in the western zones of Germany, and with the renaissance of liberal capitalism in 1948 the SPD itself began to retreat from the proposals. Although the party continued to demand the socialisation of key industrial sectors there were those, like Heinrich Deist, who were prepared to come to terms with the market economy. By 1952, when the first comprehensive postwar programme was issued, the German social democrats had 'overtaken the British Labour Party...in the drift of the European Socialism away from public ownership' (Childs 1966, 96).

The British tradition of socialism was less radical than most of its continental counterparts. Except for a brief period in the 1930s Marxism had made no impression on Labour Party ideology. Commentators have stressed the doctrineless character of Labour politics (Miliband 1972), its collectivist (Beer 1965) and populist (Drucker 1979) overtones. Labourism was an empiricist or practical brand of ideology. The 1945 programme, *Let us Face the Future* asserted the party's practical character with some pride: 'The members of the Labour Party, like the British people, are practical-minded men and women' (Labour Party 1945; cited in Bealey 1970, 164). Its proposals for nationalisation were set out in these terms. By 1945 nationalisation and state economic planning had become the centrepiece of Labour's state collectivist conception of socialism. This conception owed much to the Fabian Society – an intellectual circle of middle-class, left-liberal social reformers for whom state ownership meant the exercise of political responsibility over the

15

rational administration of an economy geared to social need. Labour's model for the nationalised industries was Herbert Morrison's 1931 Bill for the reorganisation of London's transport services on the basis of an independent public corporation, accountable to parliament. The justification, set out in the postwar programme and in Labour's defence of its measures in parliament, was couched in terms of the necessity of subordinating private interest to national goals. Thus neither the conception nor the practical form which nationalised industry took was logically dependent on socialist ideology (Jones and Keating 1985, 59).

Planning

The planning philosophy also had a mixed intellectual parentage. Purposeful state intervention in economic life was, of course, neither new nor the exclusive property of socialists. It had been pursued in nineteenth-century Germany, the Soviet Union, fascist Italy, the Third Reich and Vichy France, as well as wartime Britain. Popularised among social democrats in the 1930s as a response to the crisis of the market economy, it became after the war a centrepiece in the conception of 'state socialism' which was dominant in the northern European parties. Social democrats had no more a coherent view of the rôle of economic planning than they had of socialisation. It was little more than a series of unrelated expedients in which the rational ordering of economic activity for the fulfilment of national objectives was combined with an ill-defined desire to transform the economic and social order.

The rational dimension of the planning philosophy was expressed in a policy document of the British Labour Party in 1944. 'Full employment and a high standard of living...can only be secured within a planned economy...and above all by the transfer to the state of power to direct the policy of our main industries, services and financial institutions' (Miliband 1972, 276). In the Socialist Party of Austria (SPÖ) the goal was defined as 'a crisis-free expanding economy, which was to be achieved by the coordination of centrally determined over-all production priorities for individual branches of industry' (Shell 1962, 211). The Socialist Labour Party (SAP) in Sweden underwent a temporary radicalisation at the end of the war, and adopted a more ambitious version of the planning philosophy which emphasised the transformative element. The 1944 *Party Programme* stated that the goal was 'to transform the economic organisation of bourgeois society so that the right of determination over production is placed in the hands of the entire people, the majority is liberated from dependence upon a few owners of capital, and the social order based on classes is replaced by a community of citizens cooperating on the basis of freedom and equality' (Sainsbury 1980, 34). In the election campaigns of 1944 and 1946, however, the SAP conformed to the general tendency of the northern European parties to present planning as a means of attaining material goals.

The practical and political implications of the planning philosophy had not been well considered. In particular, the relationship between government and private economic interests hostile to state control proved problematical. Furthermore, there was a conflict between state control and the economic freedoms enshrined in liberal democracy. As liberal capitalism reasserted itself in the late 1940s, social democrats retreated. The Labour government in Britain, for instance, was quick to acknowledge that 'the people of a democratic country will not give up their freedom of choice to their government. A democratic government must therefore conduct its economic planning in a manner which preserves the maximum possible freedom of choice to the individual citizen' (HMSO 1947, Cmd 7046). Above all though it was inflation and the cold war which stifled planning initiatives. From 1947 onwards the control of inflation and monetary stability took priority over socialist measures for reshaping the economy. Simultaneously, with the onset of East/West confrontation, the west closed ranks behind liberal capitalist values.

Of the Labour government's Economic Survey for 1950, the *Economist* observed that 'there is nothing here of the notions of "democratic planning" as proclaimed in earlier surveys which presented a working pattern for the year's economic effort and left all men of good will to work for it. Indeed, the perplexing thing about the survey for 1950 is its lack of a plan' (*Economist* 1 April 1950, cited in Miliband 1972, 305). In its policy towards nationalisation the Labour leadership had already adopted a consolidationist position, speaking at the 1948 conference of the need to consolidate the newly created public sector before contemplating its extension (Howell 1976, 167). The Austrian party was travelling down a similar road. Its programme of 1952 mentioned neither socialisation or planning. Instead it emphasised economic security 'through far-sighted development of the country's productive resources' and an 'increase of the national income through increased productivity'. In Norway too, after the 'unusually deliberate and ambitious planning and regulation' of the 1940s the Labour Party quickly followed the 'international trend towards liberalisation and reaffirmation of market forces' (Esping-Andersen 1985, 216).

Social citizenship

The third pillar of working-class socialism in the immediate postwar years was the ideology of the welfare or social citizenship state. It represented the extension of the liberal doctrine of political equality into the social and economic spheres. Welfare socialism was closely interwoven with liberal collectivism, and with Christian and ethical variants of socialism. Nowhere was this more apparent than in Britain. The formative influences on the philosophy which inspired Labour's welfare state were R.H. Tawney, a christian socialist, and William Beveridge, a collectivist liberal reformer. Tawney, described by Hugh Gaitskell as '*the* Democratic Socialist *par excellence*' (Greenleaf 1983, 439), took as his central theme equality, which he defined in humanist terms. 'A society is free in so far and only so far as...its institutions and policies are such as to enable all its members to grow to their full stature.' He believed that collective social action through the state had the potential to 'generalise...advantages associated in the past with the ownership of property...it can secure that, in addition to the payments made to them for their labour, its citizens can enjoy a social income which is available on equal terms to all its members' (cited Greenleaf 1983, 460–2). Beveridge believed that 'there are vital things needing to be done in Britain which can only be done by common action' (cited George and Wilding 1976, 86). In his view, the state was the key to the abolition of social evils. Whilst Tawney was idealistic, Beveridge was practical and pragmatic, and both strands were incorporated in Labour's welfare ideology. It was an ideology which reflected also the Fabian belief that 'through gradualism and permeation the capitalist state could be persuaded to reform itself' (George and Wilding 1976, 74).

In Scandinavia the welfare ideology was associated with K.K. Steincke and F. Zeuthan (Denmark) and with Ernst Wigforss and Gustav Molle (Sweden). They built, in the 1930s, on earlier (largely liberal) initiatives in an attempt to find 'a workable socialistic social policy' (Esping-Andersen and Korpi 1984, 46). It was in the first postwar decade that the foundation for the modern Scandinavian welfare state was laid. 'The prevailing emphasis was to universalise coverage and equalise benefits with a comprehensive system of protection and to endow all individuals with a citizen right to basic security and welfare' (Esping-Andersen 1985, 157). The principle of citizenship rights reflected the work of the English social theorist, T.H. Marshall, who had elaborated a blueprint of a 'solidaristic society'. The solidaristic dimension of the social citizenship state stemmed from the universality and equality of benefits. 'Equalisation is not so much between classes as between individuals within a population which is now treated for this purpose as though it were one class' (Marshall 1950, 56). This shift of emphasis away from class was a precursor of the 'peoples' party' posture towards which social democratic parties were to move. The British/Scandinavian ideology of welfare inspired reforms in other countries too. However, its central principles – universality and uniformity of benefits – had to vie with entrenched practice. The Ghent model, by which trade unions and mutualist associations undertook responsibility for administering social security, and decentralised and *ad hoc* systems of social insurance, often proved resistant to the principles of Tawney, Beveridge and Marshall.

Social democracy, Marxism and liberalism

Programmatic social democracy flourished briefly in the immediate postwar years because it was consistent with the goals of economic reconstruction and had a contribution to make to the postwar settlement. It was also the culmination of the reformist ideology of practical, incremental socialism within the confines of capitalist society which had become dominant in the northern European parties before the war. In Mediterranean Europe, however, reformism had still to compete with theoretical Marxism, which inspired aspirations towards a much more fundamental social transformation than the one envisaged by reformist social democracy. Moreover, the French and Italian parties were both electorally weak. The Left vote was divided – unfavourably for the socialists – between themselves and the better-organised communist parties. With no prospect of a clear-cut electoral mandate the socialist parties in France and Italy were occupied by the search for political formulas to sustain coalition governments. Between 1945 and 1947 both parties were involved in tripartite governments with communists and christian democrats, but the increasing incompatibility of these parties, and the consequent government instability, forced the socialists to consider the longer-term future.

Coalition relations raised major questions of the socialists' own ideological orientation and identity, and the process of self examination which ensued revealed deep divisions in both parties. In Italy, the Socialist Party (PSI) split between a left-wing majority faction under Pietro Nenni, which leaned towards the communist, and an anti-communist minority which broke away in 1947 to form the Italian Social Democratic Party. The departure of the latter strengthened the PSI's left wing, further reinforcing the party's powerful Marxist tradition. In opposition after 1947, PSI strategy became geared to a 'democratic defence' against what they saw as a capitalist/catholic restoration of old power relations (Hine 1975, 441). Although there was no formal split in the French Socialist Party (SFIO), it was evident at its thirty-seventh and thirty-eighth congresses in 1945 and 1946, that the party was divided over both strategy and doctrine. The prewar militants retained a deep-seated respect for socialist traditions and saw the SFIO as a working-class, Marxist party with a strong affinity towards the communists. The revisionists, on the other hand, sought to reorientate the party towards ideological pluralism and a humanist form of socialism which they hoped would attract middle-class progressives. Led by Blum, the revisionists succeeded in persuading the 1945 congress to adopt a resolution on basic principles which went some way to meeting their objectives (Cahm 1972, 256). The following year however, they were defeated by the traditionalist Guy Mollet, representing the working-class, doctrinaire socialism of northern France. Blum's resolution was revoked in favour of a *Declaration of Principles* which reaffirmed the character of the SFIO as 'essentially a party of revolution' dedicated to the abolition of capitalism through class struggle (Simmons 1970, 219). This affirmation of the doctrine of working-class socialism could not conceal the fact that in most of France the SFIO was a *petit bourgeois*, small-town provincial party. Its electorate came predominantly from the lower ranks of officialdom. Doctrine, and the rhetoric derived from it had a powerful emotional meaning in the SFIO, but was of little practical significance.

In both the French and Italian parties major questions of ideological principle and a preoccupation with coalition strategy overshadowed programmatic activities. Politics in Mediterranean Europe continued to be construed as a conflict between rival ideologies and cultures (Catholic/Marxist, republican/monarchist). The rational, administrative style of politics characteristic of northern Europe was alien here. Consequently, programmatic social democracy did not make its mark in these parties in the immediate postwar years.

Even in its northern European heartlands, social democracy lost its impetus at the end of the 1940s. Its successes had stemmed from the experience of depression and war which had undermined the ethos of liberal capitalism. The revival of economic life restored the political self confidence of the entrepreneurial middle classes, and the parties which represented them began to reassert their traditional economic and political values more forcefully. The deepening cold war had the effects of reinforcing these values still further. For most social democrats the ideology of socialisation, economic planning and social citizenship, had not represented a frontal attack on capitalism. It had simply postulated a new relationship between the liberal state and the capitalist economy. Carried beyond a certain point, however, state interventionism began to encroach on liberal values such as the economic rights of entrepreneurs, and individual liberty. At this point, social democrats began to retreat from the programmes for working-class socialism which had characterised the immediate postwar years.

THE ROAD TO IDEOLOGICAL REVISION

The 1950s saw a strengthening of a tendency which had been visible in the parties almost from their inception. From an early stage they had sought support from social groups outside the working class (Przeworski 1980, 25–9). However, in spite of gestures towards broader class appeal, they had continued to project an image of themselves as working-class parties. Now they went further in their attempts to expand their social base, styling themselves as catch-all or peoples' parties (Kirchheimer 1966, 187). In many cases they began to leave behind the symbols of their former working-class identity and roots. The axioms of working-class socialism were progressively displaced by a more diffuse ideology of managed, or welfare capitalism. Accepting the mixed economy and the welfare state as the parameters of reform, social democrats adopted an essentially humanist perspective in which the goals of individual fulfilment and personal liberty were uppermost.

Social democracy and Keynesianism

A number of developments had combined to undermine the working-class socialism of the immediate postwar era. Firstly, the relative decline of the manual working-class, and its differentiation along the lines of skill and sector, meant that the parties found themselves with a shrinking and increasingly heterogeneous class base. Consequently, electoral success was dependent on the mobilisation of a wider socio-economic constituency. Secondly, in the 1950s most countries experienced a wave of economic growth which brought with it full employment and an affluence which embraced large sections of the working-class. The sustained growth of a capitalist market economy, rather than its subordination to direct state control, now appeared to be a guarantor of the economic security of the masses and the harbinger of an economic democracy of consumers. Thirdly, social democrats perceived changes in the structure of the economy. The separation of capital ownership from the exercise of control in capitalist enterprises had brought about the disappearance of the autocratic owner-boss and the emergence of a new breed of salaried managers. The 'managerial revolution' (Burnham 1945) had transformed capitalism according to this view, bringing a more relaxed, liberal and technocratic style of control. Fourthly, with the institutionalisation of Keynesianism, governments now exercised broad indirect control of a mixed economy. Economic power had passed in some measure, from private to social control, without a large-scale transfer of ownership or the introduction of a comprehensive planning system of direct controls. Finally, the conflict between capital and labour which had bred social democracy, now became more muted. Rising profits and tight labour markets gave trade unions the bargaining strength to win concessions without the sharp confrontation of earlier times. These developments appeared to herald 'the end of ideology' (Bell 1960), and in this new era, the doctrines of working-class socialism took on an anachronistic appearance.

The ideological transformation of social democracy was not accomplished at a stroke. It was one thing for social democrats in government to adopt Keynesian policies – usually quietly and without fanfare. It was quite a different proposition to adopt an ideology of Keynesian social democracy. Keynes had outlined the political economy of modern, managed capitalism which was attractive to social democrats for a number of reasons. Firstly because it appeared to bring the economy under political control, 'It held out the prospect that the state could reconcile the private ownership of the means of production with democratic management of the economy. Democratic control over the level of unemployment and the distribution of income became the terms of the compromise that made democratic capitalism possible' (Przeworski 1980, 207). Social democrats had found a resolution to the historical conundrum of how to reconcile socialism and the market, opening the door to 'a third way' between communism and capitalism. Secondly, Keynesianism legitimised the doctrine of equality, since it demonstrated that economic expansion depended on broadening the base of consumption through a more diffuse distribution of income and wealth. Thirdly it provided a formula for a high-performance economy in which the claims of capital and labour could be reconciled. Having shunned class confrontation, this formula for accommodation was highly attractive to social democrats. Fourthly, Keynesianism was the economic foundation for 'welfare capitalism'. Without adversely affecting the economic equilibrium, the surplus from a performance economy could be diverted into social security and welfare programmes.

The new conception of Keynesian social democracy became dominant in all the northern European parties, and was set out systematically in Anthony Crosland's seminal work, *The Future of Socialism*, in which he urged socialists to rethink their principles and programmes in the light of postwar circumstances. Crosland's work was first and foremost an expression of total confidence in Keynesian economics and the unbridled power of governments to manipulate the economy in any way, shape or form they thought fit. For him the economy had been conquered and capitalism transformed. To the modern reader it will appear as though Crosland was writing in a different age, and indeed he was.

> Capitalism has been reformed almost out of recognition. Despite occasional minor recessions and balance of payments crises, full employment and at least a tolerable degree of stability are likely to be maintained. *(Crosland 1956, 517)*

> Acting mainly through the Budget, though with the aid of other instruments, *the governments can exert any influence it likes on income distribution*, and can also determine within broad limits, the division of total output between consumption, investment, exports and social expenditure. *(Crosland 1956, 27 authors' italics.)*

For Crosland, twentieth-century capitalism was qualitatively different from its forebears. The modern mode of ownership and control which we have already described, had implanted within it the seeds of economic democracy in the sphere of production, whilst affluence had created a democracy of consumers. Society was now much less aggressively individualistic. Economic class relations had become more equanimous, and whilst inequality still existed, society tended to exhibit 'an egalitarian ambience' on which socialists must now build to extend democracy further into the social sphere. Here a residue of poverty and social distress remained to be eliminated. Status hierarchies and class resentments, remnants of the old class structure, had to be wiped out through a democratisation of the education system. Inequalities of wealth, the accretion of bygone excesses of income inequality, were to be evened out through inheritance taxes. And finally, socialists had to turn their attention to the creation of a cultural democracy. Having satisfied quantitative demands in a society of mass consumption, it was time to address questions of the quality of life.

There was almost complete accord between Crosland and the contemporary liberal view of modern capitalism expressed by writers such as J.K Galbraith (Galbraith 1958) and Joseph Schumpeter (Schumpeter 1954). It was a view which accepted capitalism as the most rational system for the organisation of economic life, the maximisation of national wealth and the promotion of general welfare. Equally, this view was an endorsement of liberal pluralist democracy as a political system in which no particular class or interest exercised unwarranted dominance. To be sure, certain aspects of modern society had proved resistant to change. It was the task of social democracy to enact modernising reforms, streamlining the economic and social order where the archaic had persisted.

The politics of ideological change

The readiness of the European parties to embrace the liberalised doctrines of democratic socialism varied quite widely from country to country. In Scandinavia, West Germany and Holland, the transition was relatively smooth, culminating in a watershed around 1958–60. By this time, all these parties had adopted programmes from which the axioms of working-class socialism had been largely expunged. In Austria, the process was less thoroughgoing, and residual traces of old doctrines remained. In Britain and Belgium the Left of the parties proved resistant to change, and in the British case ideological revision was attenuated in the 1960s in an uneasy compromise between revisionists and fundamentalists. In France and Italy, socialist parties were even more reluctant to cast off their traditional ideological mantle. Here the road to ideological revision was long and faltering.

Sweden The road from socialist orthodoxy to Keynesianism had been taken in Scandinavia in the 1930s (Tingsten 1973), and after a brief period of postwar radicalism these parties quickly reverted to a Keynesian model of social democracy. The Swedish social democrats developed a particularly sophisticated version of the model. They did not subscribe to the assumption which capitalism shared with the liberal theorists that economic power had shifted decisively away from capital towards the managerial class. For the Swedes it remained one of the central purposes of social democracy to enforce social control over the traditional powers and prerogatives of capital. However, public ownership had little or no part to play in the Swedish party's model of functional socialism. The core of this strategy, expressed by a prominent party theorist in the 1960s, was 'to divest our present capitalists of one after another of their ownership functions... they will then remain, perhaps formally, as kings, but in reality as naked symbols of a passed and inferior stage of development' (Esping-Andersen 1985, 23). This was an exercise upon which the Swedish party embarked with a series of creative policy initiatives like Gosta Rehn's 'active labour market policy', and the establishment of state investment funds and public boards of administration to oversee economic life.

Those economic initiatives were set in the context of a political programme which emphasised their democratic character.

> The aim of the social democratic Party is to let the ideal of democracy leave its mark on the whole order of society...so as to give each individual the opportunity of a rich and meaningful life. The social democratic Party aims at extending the peoples' freedom to ever wider spheres. In order that the majority may enjoy more freedom, it may be necessary, in many cases to decrease the power of the minority. This extended freedom also presupposes greater equality, if freedom is not in actual fact to be the preserve of a small number. There is no conflict between freedom and equality. On the contrary, they are interdependent. *(Cited in Sainsbury 1980, 179)*

Economic ownership and equality of income and wealth were marginal in the party's 1960 programme. Democratic control of the economy occupied the central position. The programme took a qualitative rather than a quantitative approach to equality, emphasising cultural and educational opportunity as the basis of individual fulfilment. This was at the heart of the humanist socialism which Swedish social democracy now represented, and in which class politics had little part to play.

Ideological revision was smooth and rapid in Sweden for four main reasons. Firstly, the prewar precedent for Keynesianism gave it legitimacy, both in the party and in the country. Secondly, the presence in key party posts of creative reformist theorists like Ernst Wigforss was a spur to ideological revision. He was the inspiration behind an ideology which combined immediately attainable reforms with a longer-term vision of a socialist future, in a synthesis with which all sections of the party could identify (Tilton 1979, 505–20). Thirdly, the exceptionally strong links between the Swedish social democrats and organised labour also played a part in promoting ideological change. At the apex of the labour movement was the powerful trade union confederation the *Landsorganisationen* (LO), which was an equal partner in policy initiation and gave its full backing to the new ideological formulas. Fourthly, the political strength of the Swedish trade unions in relation to organised capital enabled the social democrats to implement reform initiatives which served to vindicate the new ideology.

The Netherlands By the early postwar years, the Dutch party had travelled a considerable distance from its Marxist beginnings. In 1946, the title Social Democratic Workers Party had been amended to the Dutch Labour Party (PvdA) in an attempt to broaden the party's constituency beyond the working-class (Wolinetz 1977, 348). The new party's first programme still bore the stamp of Marxist theory, containing a statement of Marx's dictum that labour was the principal element in the productive process and acknowledging the continued existence of class struggle. The programme also contained the axioms of working-class socialism – equality, state regulation of the economy and nationalisation. However, at the same time it explicitly recognised the value of a strong private sector of the economy, where that sector served the public interest. Moreover, it also expressed humanist principles which could be attributed to the contemporary Flemish socialist, Hendryk de Man. By 1958, the Dutch Labour Party had spent more than a decade in government, during which time the economy had been reconstructed and the welfare state built. In spite of being ousted from government in that year the party retained a marked orientation towards pragmatism and the exercise of power. The following year, the party issued a new programme in which the residue of its Marxist past was purged and the programmatic socialism of the immediate postwar years was submerged in diffuse principles which mirrored the general trend of northern European social democracy.

Austria The Marxist tradition had been more deeply engrained in the Austrian Socialist Party (SPÖ). However, prewar theorists such as Otto Bauer and Max Adler had created 'Austro-Marxism', more flexible and reformist than the orthodox doctrine. The party's postwar leader, Karl Renner, gave an even greater emphasis to moderate, democratic reform within the confines of a capitalist economy. Nevertheless, the postwar party held to the 1926 Linz Programme, with its Marxist overtones, until 1958 when the New Programme was adopted. The 1958 programme stressed that the SPÖ was a party of 'all working people', rather than the more narrowly defined working-class. Its trinity of guiding principles, Liberty, Justice and Security, mirrored those of the unconditionally revisionist Bad Godesberg programme of the German social democrats. Like the Swedish party's 1960 programme, the New Programme emphasised the democratic character of social democracy, calling for 'unrestricted political, economic and social democracy' and adding that 'socialism is democracy fulfilled' (Sully 1981, 61).

However, the Austrian party's Marxist heritage and the presence of a Left wing faction, led by Josef Hindels inhibited it from a full renunciation of the tenets of working-class socialism. The 1958 programme made explicit mention of economic planning and socialisation alongside a commitment to Keynesianism. The ambiguity of this position was institutionalised in the New Programme: 'as long as the ups and downs in the economy have not been eliminated through socialist planning, full employment will have to be assured through (Keynesian) anti-cyclical measures' (Shell 1962, 193). On the one hand, the programme referred to a struggle against capitalism and exploitation. On the other it indicated an acceptance of the mixed economy as it stood at the end of the 1950s, and in which there would remain scope for entrepreneurial initiative. In practice, the party was an acquiescent partner in a coalition devoted to capitalist reconstruction in the early postwar years. Yet the core values of working-class socialism were sufficiently strong to prevent it from expunging them from its 1958 programme. An earlier draft had stated that nationalisation had largely fulfilled its purpose in Austria. However, after some controversy this statement was deleted, and the final draft had left the door ajar to an extension of public ownership. There was further ambiguity in the Austrian party's rather vague concept of 'the third way'. The 1958 programme stated that 'democratic socialism stands between capitalism and dictatorship. It must achieve its aims while fighting them both: for it can come to terms with neither capitalism or communism' (Sully 1981, 62).

Austrian politics in the 1950s, tended towards polarisation with continued conflict between the SPÖ and its main rival, the right-wing Austrian People's Party, over the future of existing nationalised industries. Thus the nationalisation issue remained alive. Full-scale ideological revision was further discouraged by the continued existence, until 1969, of a small but significant communist electorate. Fearful of losing working-class support to the Communist Party (KPÖ), the social democrats were reluctant to break decisively with their past or to distance themselves too far from the communists. It was not until Bruno Kreisky's succession to the SPÖ leadership in 1967 that the party embarked wholeheartedly upon ideological revision.

West Germany The apogee of ideological revisionism occurred in the West German SPD. The party had been reconstituted in 1945 on the basis of the 1925 Heidelberg Programme, which abounded in Marxist rhetoric, although its substance was not incompatible with liberal democracy. The SPD had long since ceased to be a Marxist party of the working-class, but it remained bound by the socialist traditions of the pre-1933 era. Its iconoclastic leader, Kurt Schumacher, made some gestures towards ideological change but was not prepared to countenance full-scale programmatic revision (Paterson 1977, 184). His death in 1952 cleared the way for a programme review, and the crushing election defeat of the following year lent urgency to the exercise. However, the debate which followed was rather unfocused and was confined to the reform groups from a new generation of Parliamentarians and from the party's Bürgermeisterflügel (mayoral wing) made up of pragmatists whose occupancy of public office at state and city level had given them an open ideological outlook. In 1955 a Programme Commission was formed to begin the drafting process.

The banning of the German Communist Party (KPD) in 1956 removed an obstacle to ideological revision and a third successive electoral defeat the following year intensified the pressure. Debate was now much more widespread than before, more comprehensive in its scope and more concrete in the proposals which emerged. 'Criticism concerned the entire spectrum of party affairs, embracing...the main lines of economic and foreign policy, as well as organisation and the composition of the top leadership' (Klotzbach 1982, 402–3). Debate centred on the conflict between two conceptions of the SPD as *Arbeiter-oder Volkspartei*, (workers' party or peoples' party). One of the principal reformers, Carlo Schmid, expressed the issue as one of the party's openness. For him, reform meant transforming the party into one, which was not only attractive to those who believed in its programme *in toto*, but also to those who were broadly supportive, even though there might be a few ideas to which they could not subscribe (Klotzbach 1982, 417–18). Schmid had in mind the new middle class, to which the workers' party image was unattractive.

The Stuttgart Congress of 1958 was a milestone in the history of German social democracy. In addition to accepting the draft programme, the Congress approved a streamlining of the party's organisational structure. Elections to the Executive confirmed the forward march of the reformers. Working groups were established to give an impetus to policy generation, especially in the new issue areas of cultural policy and technology. The programme which was presented to the Bad Godesberg Congress of 1959 went even further than the draft approved at Stuttgart in distancing the party from its past. It omitted the draft's introductory preamble which had contained a critique of capitalism and the class-divided society it engendered, alongside a catalogue of the achievements of organised labour (Klotzbach 1982, 437). In the final version, the programme began instead with a short appeal for mastery over human problems and the fulfilment of man's potential in a new and better order of society (Klotzbach 1982, 445). This humanist ethos permeated the programme, exemplified in the basic principles of *freedom, justice and solidarity* on which it was based.

Disavowing the party's Marxist heritage, the programme emphasised the eclectic philosophical sources of democratic socialism in the Christian ethic, classical philosophy and the humanist tradition. It went on to endorse the liberal pluralism of the West German state and the market economy, calling for an extension of democratic principles into the social and economic sphere. Thus the Godesberg Programme combined an acceptance of the postwar order with an appeal for reform in a formula which was to typify European social democracy in the 1960s and early 1970s. The overhaul of ideology and tradition on which the SPD embarked at Bad Godesberg was the initial step in a far-reaching exercise in renewal in which the symbols and protocol of the party's past were abandoned, the party apparatus refined and a modern technology of image projection and election campaigning adopted. A dynamic new Chancellor candidate, Willy Brandt, replaced the worthy but staid figure of Ollenhauer, who increasingly resembled a relic of a bygone political age.

Britain   If Bad Godesberg represented the apotheosis of ideological revisionism, the experience of the British Labour Party represented its nadir, at least as far as northern Europe was concerned. In the Labour Party there was no Marxist heritage to be erased. However there was in some sections of the party, a deeply engrained emotional attachment to the principles of working-class socialism as expressed in the constitution which Labour had adopted in 1918. Clause IV represented an explicit commitment to socialism, defined in terms of 'the common ownership of the means of production and the best obtainable system of popular administration and control of each industry or service'. In the absence of a clear-cut doctrine on the one hand, and a well-defined policy programme on the other, the principle of public ownership served in lieu of both. It was a sanctified symbol of the party's past and its socialist commitment. The attempt to amend the public ownership clause in the constitution aroused great passions, not merely on the Left, but amongst those traditionalists, who on other matters were in line with revisionist thinking.

Public ownership had been under discussion in policy groups in the party throughout the 1950s (Howell 1976, 209–14). Generally speaking, policy papers and programmes embodied a calculated ambiguity on the issue. The centre-right majority in the Parliamentary Party and the National Executive Committee were satisfied with the mixed economy as it had been established by the 1945–51 governments. However, they were prepared to make some limited conciliatory gestures to the Left minority which wanted to see the public sector extended. A third successive defeat in 1959 raised the stakes of the discussion, and in the party conference of that year the issue was brought to a head by the party leader, Hugh Gaitskell. According to Gaitskell's analysis, electoral stagnation and decline was a result of labour's failure to adapt to social and economy changes which had rendered the party's working-class image obsolete, (Howell 1976, 222).

A majority of the party, and its influential union wing, shared Gaitskell's belief that the identification in the public's perception of Labour with nationalisation had contributed to electoral decline. They wanted to see the party developing a broader range of policies with a more diffuse appeal. However, support for proposals to take policy revision to its ultimate conclusion in constitutional amendments was restricted to a relatively small circle of committed revisionists on the Right. Gaitskell was publicly identified with them, but he did not himself publicly voice their demand for the deletion of Clause IV. Instead he called for a new declaration of aims to stand alongside and supplement it. Accordingly, a constitutional addendum, 'An Amplification of Labour's Aims', was drawn up and adopted by a majority on the National Executive Committee in March 1960. A compromise in the time-honoured Labour Party fashion, the statement reaffirmed the commitment to selective public ownership whilst endorsing the mixed economy and explicitly acknowledging the vital rôle of the private sector. Despite broad satisfaction with the terms of this outcome within the party, and the fact that it had been supported by trade union representatives on the National Executive Committee, it was thwarted by the labour movement at large. Four of the big six trade unions rejected the statement at their congresses, and in the face of this opposition and with the prospect of certain conference defeat, Gaitskell backed down (Haseler 1969, 170–1).

It has been suggested that Gaitskell made the mistake of underestimating the strength of sentimental attachment to Clause IV as a symbol of party tradition (Haseler 1969, 172), or indeed that he failed to recognise the function of symbols as a focus of party unity (Howell 1976, 206). His successor had an acute awareness of the significance of Clause IV: 'We were being asked to take Genesis out of the Bible. You don't have to be a fundamentalist to say that Genesis is part of the Bible' (Wilson, cited in Sked and Cook 1979, 207). In his bid for reconciliation, the pragmatist Harold Wilson adopted a subtler though less thorough going approach to ideological revision. His ill-defined concept of the 'technological revolution' was a sufficiently malleable formula for modernising the party's image without a decisive break with constitutional principle or the party's past.

The Labour Party's loose confederal structure, in which trade unions exercised preponderant weight, helps to explain why the party bucked the European trend towards ideological revision. The parliamentary leadership had less control over decision-making organs than their continental counterparts with more rigidly centralised party structures. Control depended on an alliance of party and trade union leaders, and the ability of the latter to exercise authority over their own unions. For most of the party's history, union bosses had been able to sustain the alliance, but over this issue, and that of disarmament, they were unable to deliver the necessary support. However, notwithstanding the abortive outcome of the constitutional question, the revisionist perspective dominated the party by the end of the 1950s. The personality of the Left's figurehead, Aneurin Bevan, and the victory of the Left on the question of unilateral nuclear disarmament at the 1960 Conference (reversed a year later) should not be allowed to obscure the fact that the Right wing was successful in implementing a progressive revision of policy. Nevertheless, the very existence of a Left wing opposition faction at the end of the 1950s marked the Labour Party out from most other northern European parties.

France In France, the mythology and symbolism of socialist doctrine was even more resistant to change. The Socialist Party's 1946 Declaration of Principles had defined its ideology in Marxist terms, but the actions of the party in parliament and government in the Fourth Republic (1946–58) had borne little relation to doctrine. Indeed, the French socialists had been seriously compromised by the responsibility of socialist ministers for a harsh colonial policy in Algeria, and for the Suez debacle. The party's integrity and identity had been badly weakened. Moreover, with the consolidation of the Gaullist right after 1958, the SFIO was squeezed between parties to its right and left. The response was a reassertion of the fundamentalist, Marxist strand in the French socialist tradition and a renewed emphasis on the 'essentially revolutionary character of the party' (Simmons 1970, 112). This reflex reaction to the threat of marginalisation in the party system was expressed in the Fundamental Programme of 1962. The programme toned down the vocabulary of the Declaration of Principles, and took some account of developments in the economy and society since the war. However there was no new policy programme to accommodate these developments, nor was there any serious re-evaluation of doctrine. As party leader, Guy Mollet, put it 'some people, and I was among them, feared that our Party was moving towards revisionism. But our Party has realised a synthesis and it is necessary to preserve it' (Simmons 1970, 218). In fact party doctrine had ossified, and Mollet's 'synthesis' served merely as a formula for maintaining unity between Marxist and reformist wings of the party. Restating its traditional, but largely rhetorical commitment to revolution, the SFIO also left the door open to a limited rapport with the Communist Party (PCF), the strength of which was an important factor inhibiting ideological revision.

The traditional conceptions of French socialism as expressed in the Fundamental Programme were challenged, however, by Gaston Defferre in his bid for the socialist ticket in the 1965 Presidential election. Defferre's intention was to create a broad alliance out of the disparate independent parties and groups which surrounded the SFIO on the centre-left of French politics. The idea, part of a strategy to challenge the growing power of Gaullism, was not new, but it was highly controversial in two main respects. Firstly, Defferre's plan to include Catholic groups in a 'catch all' electoral alliance was in defiance of the Socialist Party's anti-clerical traditions. Secondly, it involved opening the membership of the new alliance to 'sympathisers' who were not committed socialists in the traditional sense. Thus it meant adopting a flexible, pluralist brand of northern European social democracy hitherto alien to France. Defferre himself was in this mould. Unusually for the SFIO, he had a personal appeal to the broader public beyond the ranks of the party faithful. As Mayor of Marseilles he had developed a reputation as a pragmatic reformer. His quest for the Left's Presidential candidacy was also, therefore, an exercise in modernising the party, and changing the tone and contents of its ideology. Deffere failed on all counts because he mounted too direct an attack on the symbols and myths of party life. The party had remained what it was in the Fourth Republic, essentially a '12 per cent party' with a small membership (barely 70,000 in the early 1960s) dominated by minor civil servants and municipal councillors. Faced with competition from the communists, the SFIO had been unable to establish a strong presence in the working-class electorate. Its predominantly small-town, rurally based constituency was rooted in the more backward strata of French society where a romantic revolutionary radicalism still flourished. The character of the party's electorate made the socialists resistant to the modernising effects of social and economy change (Wilson 1971, 33-5).

Italy A pronounced Marxist tradition and the presence of a well-organised communist party also made the Italian Socialist Party (PSI) resistant to 'social democratisation' or ideological revision. Nevertheless, the party did undertake a significant new strategy during the late 1950s and early 1960s. Adopting a more autonomous stance from its erstwhile communist ally, the PCI, the socialists began to build bridges with the ruling christian democrats, culminating in the formation of the Centre-Left coalition between the two in 1963. The following year, the PSI distanced itself still further from the communists, withdrawing from reciprocal arrangements in municipal elections. At the same time, the socialists reunited with the Social Democratic Party (PSDI) which had broken away in 1947.

Coinciding with their entry into the Centre-Left coalition, the Italian socialists adopted a programme which was similar to the north European model in some important respects. It included a commitment to full employment and a reallocation of resources from private consumption into public investment in housing, welfare, education, transport and technology. At the heart of the programme was a blueprint for planned structural reform in the economy. This project was evolved by the PSI Budget Minister, Antonio Giolitti, along with Riccardo Lombardini, the leading figures of a group of technical policy experts in economics, urban planning and law which became influential in the 1960s. The new emphasis on policy expertise to the party mirrored the general trend in European social democracy. However, in contrast to the German social democrats, for example, the PSI's policy experts remained within the ideological tradition of Marxian socialism. Their conception of a planned system of economic development on socialist lines was markedly different from the northern European variant of 'economic steering'. The difference was immediately apparent from their 1963 Manifesto which stressed the system transformative aspect of economic planning. 'As it is conceived by the socialists it is objectively in contrast with the outdated structures of the existing system ... planning policy does not correspond to the needs of rationalisation and regulation of the process of economic development but to the political will to strike at capitalism in both the short and long term' (Hine 1978, 239).

The new alignment of the socialists towards the centre of Italian politics, its reform programme and its reliance on technical experts did not amount to an ideological revolution in the party. Realignment was rather a strategy designed to challenge the dominance of the communists and christian democrats in the party system. The reform programme was part of this strategy, and party leaders were quite explicit in distinguishing it from reformist social democracy (Hine 1978, 32). The new strategic and political departures were not accompanied by any dramatic deviation from the party's ideological tradition. Yet like the French party, the PSI had taken the first tentative steps down the road to ideological change.

THE ERA OF 'MANAGED GROWTH' AND THE CHALLENGE OF THE NEW LEFT

Ideological convergence

Social democracy in the immediate postwar years had been a hybrid political philosophy embracing both socialism and liberalism, but it was one in which the traditional principles of socialism were still clearly recognisable. By the 1960s, however, the various parties' socialist profiles had been reduced to mere shadows. Revisionist social democracy had come to terms with reformed liberal capitalism. A compromise was now reached in which a market economy was made responsive to certain social ends – general affluence and economic security, full employment, individual fulfilment within an open society. The traditional goals of social democracy had, in large part, been met and its ideology was progressively assimilated into the politics of consensus. Old political battlefields were deserted as conservative and christian democratic parties came to accept the terms of the compromise.

There was, in short, a convergence between the parties of Right and Left. Ideology continued to play a rôle in internal party life, since many party activists were still inclined towards it. It served, moreover, as a focal point for their loyalties, a cement binding the party together. In election campaigns and manifestos, however, it was increasingly marginalised. Political competition increasingly revolved around competence and efficiency. 'Labour government works' was the slogan employed by the British Labour Party in the general election of 1966. In the West German Bundestag election of 1969, the social democrats used the record of its Economics Ministry in the Grand Coalition to convey a similar message. Ideology was indelibly identified with class politics. As such it was inimical to the 'peoples party' image which social democrats sought to create in their attempt to forge broad electoral alliances cutting across the boundaries of class.

Social trends encouraged social democrats in this project. The 1960s saw a further erosion in the cohesion of social groups. The working-class, increasingly differentiated along the lines of skill and sector was now much less responsive than previously to rallying calls based on the ideology of class. Equally, the traditional middle class was breaking up, with the emergence of the new middle class. An important element in its emergence was the decline of organised religion and the progressive secularisation of society in western Europe. A middle-class electorate oriented towards traditional, religious values had been impermeable to social democracy. The growth of a new, secular, middle class opened up new avenues of electoral recruitment. Social democratic parties set themselves to tap this new resource by muting their earlier anti-clericalism and emphasising their ideological openness and diversity. Modernity and social progress became their leitmotif, further weakening class ideology.

Revisionism in practice

The underlying assumption behind the new conception of social democracy was that in an age of affluence and with the instruments of Keynesian economics at the disposal of governments, the fundamental problems of industrial society had been solved. Distributional conflict, which had characterised industrial society in previous eras, and which had laid at the root of class politics, was now well on the way to resolution. Economic growth was the key to this new conception. In most western European countries growth was vigorous in the 1960s, but it was often rather uneven. Structural defects began to appear in the economy and stability was disturbed by periodic bouts of inflation. Moreover, growth and prosperity had bypassed certain socio-economic groups, leaving a residue of social want and deprivation. For social democrats the elimination of poverty was inextricably bound up with economic growth. As Labour Party policy documents put it, 'economic growth is the key to Labour's social programme…[it] sets the pace at which Labour can build the fair and just society we want to see…higher living standards and a fair chance in life for everyone can only be achieved with a strong efficient and expanding economy' (cited Beckerman 1972, 44). In short, growth was vital, not simply for its own sake, but for the completion of the social citizenship state which was a central element in the new conception of social democracy.

In response to structural defects and uneven development in the economy, social democrats now advocated a more interventionist form of Keynesianism than had previously been practised. They took care, however, to differentiate their model of 'fine tuning' from those forms of economic control and planning which they had advocated earlier. Indicative planning, or global steering as it was termed in West Germany, meant government bodies gathering and assessing data on the economy, making forecasts of future trends and intervening to steer those trends in predetermined directions. It also meant coordinating the different sectors of economic activity and harmonising the goals of competing economic interests within the framework of an overall national plan. The British Labour Party included a commitment to indicative economic planning in its 1964 manifesto. It stated Labour's intention of creating a new Department of Economic Affairs with 'the duty of formulating, with both sides of industry, a national economic plan'. The new government apparatus signified 'the New Thinking that will end the chaos and sterility'. Labour was poised to 'swing its plans into instant operation...restless with positive remedies for the problems the Tories have criminally neglected' (Miliband 1972, 358).

The general enthusiasm for indicative economic planning amongst social democrats concealed an underlying ambiguity, since 'planning can have a dual nature, either reforming or rationalising' (Hayward and Watson 1975, 447). Whilst left-wing social democrats concentrated on its reforming potential, those on the centre-right of the parties saw planning simply as a means of managing a capitalist economy on technological and rational lines. This was an era in which technological expertise played a more important rôle in social democratic politics than did reform ideology in its traditional sense. Labour's programme Signposts for the Sixties, promised 'a new status for scientists in government and a new rôle for government-sponsored science in industrial development' (Sked and Cooke 1979, 215). In order to accommodate the Left wing of his party Harold Wilson conjured up a vision of socialism and science in a partnership for progress. Generally though, the parties adopted a 'neutral' problem-solving approach to politics. As the Danish party's 1961 programme put it, social democracy contained 'the answers to the problems of modern society, not by offering a rigid theory, but by tackling without prejudice the problems of the future' (Miller 1968, 64). Policy experts came to the fore in an orgy of policy generation and output. In Germany specialist party conferences were convened in which experts coined a new jargon of political economy (Heimann 1984, 2069). The Austrian party, under the new leadership of Bruno Kreisky was feverishly engaged in formulating policy documents, with over one thousand experts participating in the exercise.

In the face of this emphasis on social and economic engineering conducted by experts, the traditional ideological concerns of social democracy were eclipsed. Just as public ownership played little part in the new political economy of social democracy, the principle of equality suffered a similar obscurity in the sphere of social policy. It was widely believed, especially in the welfare state countries of Scandinavia and Britain, that the advent of mass consumption, together with progressive taxation schedules and welfare programmes, had eliminated the grosser excesses of economic inequality. Equality was now redefined in liberal humanist terms. The parties' basic programme generally omitted any explicit reference to economic inequality. The Danish party's 1961 programme was based on a triad of principles which included equality alongside liberty and fraternity, but it was expressed in a rather diffuse form as 'the democratisation of society as a whole so that the possibilities of free choice economically and culturally are brought within the grasp of each individual' (Fitzmaurice 1981, 104). Social democrats often conceived of the welfare state in terms of a broad egalitarian philosophy, but it has been observed that the precise meaning of equality in this context was rarely specified (Esping-Andersen 1985, 170). The pursuit of equality would have meant challenging the allocative or distributive mechanisms of the market across a wide area of social policy, and would have required a level of state penetration into the economic and social order which most social democrats were unprepared to countenance. Their efforts were therefore directed at the concept of equality of opportunity which it was possible to reconcile with market capitalism.

Social democracy enjoyed a period of intellectual and political dominance in northern Europe in the 1960s. It appeared to contain a magic formula for successful 'growth management', economic and social well being in an open and liberal society. However, behind the image of modernity and dynamism there was an ideological vacuum. In an age of consensus politics, social democracy exhibited a somewhat bland appearance. Moreover, in government, the parties and often their trade union allies were seen by many as part of the established order, and were identified with the perceived shortcomings of that order. They were therefore vulnerable to the challenge of the New Left.

The New Left

The movements which comprised this resurgence of radical socialism mobilised discontent with the ideological sterility of consensus politics and impatience with the slow pace of economic and social change. Predominantly young, educated and middle class in social composition, the New Left took various organisational forms in different countries. In the Netherlands the movement arose within the Labour Party itself, penetrating deep into the leadership corps and effectively capturing the party (Wolinetz 1977, 354-9). The Danish social democrats faced the challenge of a new Leftist Socialist Peoples' Party (SF) which had arisen out of protest at Denmark's membership of NATO. The Extra Parliamentary opposition (APO) in West Germany explicitly rejected the party format, and was in any case little more than a loose assembly of diverse Left groups based in the universities. Ultimately, German social democrats were able to absorb APO members into their own ranks. In France and Italy, the New Left was similarly incoherent, but was much more dynamic, making common cause with young factory workers. The movements culminated in the explosive 'events' of 1968 in France and the 'hot autumn' of 1969 in Italy. Here the Left was less susceptible to assimilation into the socialist parties, which suffered considerable disorientation in the face of the challenge. In Britain, the challenge from the Left took the form of a rising tide of militancy in the labour movement, which undermined the internal equilibrium of the Labour Party, and its capacity to govern.

The immediate result of the New Left challenge in the late 1960s, combined in some countries with a marked rise in worker militancy, was to force social democratic parties to undertake an exercise in ideological reappraisal. One of the principle themes of the continental New Left had been *autogestion* – popular participation in decision-making in the workplace and in public administration. *Autogestionaire* socialists were strong in the newly formed French Socialist Party (PS), and its 1972 programme *Changer la vie* was built on this principle of libertarian socialism. It was also useful to the Italian party in its attempt to profile itself against the 'authoritarian' communists. In the Scandinavian countries, the Left's critique of the existing social order was directed against the rigid and narrow bureaucratisation of decision-making in the corporatist state.

The Swedish and Danish parties both issued new programmes in response to the Left's challenge, promising a more aggressive pursuit of reform and opening up the issue of economic democracy. The SAP's ambitious Meidener Plan was conceived during this period of policy reappraisal and innovation. In Sweden, as in France, economic democracy (or *autogestion*) gave the party a new sense of ideological purpose and dynamism. The Danish party, on the other

39

hand, in spite of its new programme, was unable to break free of the ideological and political stagnation of the 1960s (Esping-Andersen 1985, 213).

Having broken with the Grand Coalition in 1969, the German party was able to respond to the challenge posed by the Extra Parliamentary Opposition movement by emphasising its reform programme and by engaging in a dialogue with the Left. As leading party in the new Social Liberal coalition, it presented itself as the harbinger of a more democratic society (Heimann, 1984 2038–9), and the government's dynamic *Ostpolitik* programme lent force to this claim. The SPD also set in motion a review of its 1959 Godesberg Programme. However, these reform initiatives soon burned themselves out. The lasting impact of the leftist challenge was the entry of the 'New Left generation' into the party. It had the effect of changing both the socio-economic profile and ideological tone of the SPD, resulting in the destabilisation of internal party life.

The problems which social democrats faced in West Germany were replicated in other north European parties. The legacy of the Left's challenge was an ideological renaissance which placed a new emphasis on the reforming aspects of social democracy. New demands were being made on the parties to look beyond the horizons of modernity and managed growth, towards a more radical redistribution of economic power and rewards. At the same time, however, it was becoming clear that the limits of growth management, state intervention, the welfare state and the politics of accommodation had been reached. Indeed, the critics of the New Left had argued this themselves. Even before the onset of the international recession in 1973–74 social democratic politics had shown signs of disorientation, decay and stagnation.The recession precipitated the incipient crisis in the northern European parties. Ironically, their crisis coincided with the social democratisation of the southern European socialist parties.

THE TRANSFORMATION OF SOCIALISM IN FRANCE AND ITALY

As we have seen, the French and Italian parties resisted the moves towards ideological revision which the northern European parties undertook in the 1950s and 1960s. Political cultures which encouraged ideological polarisation, and communist rivals which dominated the landscape of Left politics inhibited them from taking the revisionist road. In the 1970s, however, both the newly created French Socialist Party (PS) and the Italian Socialist Party (PSI) took decisive turns by which they broke with their respective pasts. In both parties, electoral defeat and stagnation was the midwife to change. The debacle of Gaston Defferre's humiliating defeat in the French presidential election of 1969, the disappointed hopes of the PSI in 1976 and 1979 provoked in both parties a far-reaching reappraisal of old political and strategic formulas. Moreover, signs of modernisation and secularisation in both societies suggested that there were opportunities for parties of reform and social progress to exploit. Social change was reflected in electorates in which observers detected a latent flux, encouraging the parties to look for new political openings. Responding to these openings, both parties embarked on organisational overhauls and ideological initiatives which were to bring them closer to the mainstream of European social democracy.

However, neither party fitted altogether comfortably into the existing tradition of European social democracy. The PS retained the penchant of the French Left for abstract theoretical debate, often conducted in the rhetoric of radical Marxism which contrasted sharply with the empiricism of the north European parties. In Italy, the signs of flux in the party system proved to be an illusion. Unlike the French party, the PSI was unable to break the dominance of its Communist rival over left-wing politics, remaining weak both organisationally and electorally. Yet a stalemate in Italian party politics allowed the party to play a rôle in coalition government out of all proportion to its meagre strength. In these circumstances, the party engaged in a game of tactical manoeuvre in which ideology became all but irrelevant. The PSI embraced social democracy cosmetically, but in reality it became a 'wheeler dealer party' in which the exercise of government power became an end in itself. So whilst the PS exhibited a leftist appearance in relation to the north European parties, the PSI was to their right.

Social democratic parties everywhere have developed an increasing tendency towards a leader orientation, (see Chapter 2) but in both the French and Italian parties this tendency has been unusually pronounced. Adopting a presidential style, their leaders have either stood somewhat aloof from party and party ideology, as in the French case, or have simply dictated policy and programme to a pliant party, (in the case of the PSI). This pronounced leader orientation is something which the two parties had in common with the social democratic parties of the new Mediterranean democracies

(Hine 1986, 238–5). It stemmed from the central rôle which leaders played in the rebirth or renewal of these parties. The transformation of French and Italian socialism was inextricably connected to the meteoric political careers of two men – François Mitterrand and Bettino Craxi. Both were responsible for reshaping their respective parties organisationally, freeing themselves in so doing from the shackles which bound their predecessors.

The emergence of the French Socialist Party

Mitterrand's rise in the labyrinth of the French Left preceded Craxi's by almost a decade, and his was the more formidable achievement. His strategy was to bring the disparate elements of the non-communist Left together, first in a federation then into a single party. In so doing he had to bring about the liquidation of the existing party (the SFIO), in order to create a new one (the Socialist Party). The project was undertaken by stages, between 1965 when Mitterrand fought the presidential election as candidate of the non-communist left, and 1971 when at the Épinay Congress he was installed as leader of a Socialist Party which had been formed two years previously. Mitterrand's design was to enter into partnership with, whilst at the same time wresting political ascendancy from the communists. Accordingly, in 1972, the new party concluded the *Common Programme of the Left* with the PCF, and in 1974 the two parties fought the presidential election in harness. Coming within a hairsbreadth of winning, Mitterrand amply demonstrated the potential of his new alignment of the French Left and confirmed his own position as Socialist Party leader.

For a number of reasons, the integration of the non-communist Left in a single party was not at first accompanied by any dramatic departure from the radical traditions of French Socialism. Firstly, Mitterrand had succeeded in uniting the Left (where Defferre had failed earlier), precisely because he had not striven to 'social democratise' French socialism. Secondly, left-wing radicalism was an essential element in the heterogeneous coalition of groups which had brought him the leadership at Épinay. The cultivation of this support required that he should demonstrate at least a rhetorical allegiance to the principles of radical socialism. Thirdly, the strategy of 'competitive cooperation' with the PCF, and the success of the Union of the Left formula depended on the Socialist Party adopting a position compatible with PCF.

The Byzantine politics of the Socialist Party in the 1970s revolved around the quasi-institutionalised factionalism which the party inherited from its forerunner, the SFIO. A constantly shifting constellation of factions arose out of the interplay between the party federations in the regions, personality centred coteries, and groups representing the ideological currents of French socialism. The centre of gravity of the party was the Mitterrand bloc, 'a heterogeneous collection of social democrats, Marxists, technocrats and *arrivistes*' (Bell and Criddle 1988, 229–30) and an inner core of Mitterrand's closest confidantes. The ideological profile of this convocation of currents reflected that of its leader. 'Mitterrand's writings, although voluminous, are unrevealing... His collected political speeches do not show a consistent political philosophy'. However, Mitterrand's enigmatic quality had been an enormous asset to him in bringing the non-communist Left under one political roof, and it served him equally well in his management of the new party. The key to his political ideology is revealed in an extract from his book *Un socialisme du possible* (1970); 'reformism seems to me the only possible way, but it has such a bad reputation that one hesitates to say so' (Bell and Criddle 1988, 234–5). Still more emphatic were his 'confidential' remarks to a journalist in 1972: 'I am amazed by the Swedish achievements, and I cannot relate them in public without shocking my own friends and a good part of the militants, not to mention the problem I would have with the Communists. And if I dared to say that the National Health Service in Great Britain is a great achievement of socialism. What an uproar this would produce with militants and voters.' (Cited in Lauber 1983, 34).

A second, clearly recognisable faction at the heart of the new party was the Centre d'études de reserches et d'éducation socialistes (CERES). Self-appointed guardians of the radical and Marxist traditions of socialism in France, CERES saw its rôle as bulwark against the social democratic tendencies within the Socialist Party (Hanley 1986, 69–78). Other defining characteristics of the group were its radical critique of the existing social and economic order, its doctrine of the 'break with capitalism', and a decidedly pro-communist stand (which led its adversaries to characterise its adherents as 'communist wolves in the clothing of socialist sheep') (Hanley 1986, 78). This was a standpoint deriving from a belief in the unity of the Left and a calculation that ties to the PCF would inhibit the PS from moving towards reformism. The focal point of CERES' ideology in the early 1970s was *autogestion*. A narrow rendering of this term would be 'workers' self-management', but its implications went beyond the confines of industrial democracy. It was a codeword for a form of socialism firmly rooted in a mass movement, an economic order based on the widest possible dispersal of power and rank-and-file participation at every level of society.

The other major factions in the 1970s were the Mauroy current and the Rocardians (Bell and Criddle 1988, 222–6, 243–8). Neither had a well-defined ideology, but both were categorically non-Marxist. Rocard stood for 'modernization and efficiency with a humanist face'. Behind his challenge for the presidential nomination in 1979 lay the view that in the aftermath of defeat in the previous year's parliamentary elections, the Union of the Left was defunct and that the future lay in an appeal to the middle ground, with a moderate, reformist programme. Pierre Mauroy was associated with the large PS federation in northern France which had been the stronghold of traditional working-class socialism in the SFIO years. His current was identified by its moderation and concern for practical politics. It was mobilised in 1979 as a force for unity and stability in the party. Both the Rocardian and Mauroy groups attracted the (not inappropriate) sobriquet 'social democratic'. In the Assembly elected in 1981, ninety-eight deputies were identified with these two groups, against 134 for the Mitterrand bloc and thirty-six for CERES (Bell and Criddle 1988, 247).

Commentators who portray the PS as a radical socialist party outside the social democratic tradition tend to stress the weight which CERES carried in the party in the 1970s. 'At all key points in the party's development...CERES had a key rôle. It was a constant catalyst or *primus movens*' (Hanley 1986, 2). This view receives *prima facie* support from the inclusion of CERES in the majority which brought Mitterrand to power at Épinay in 1971, and its subsequent representation in the party's leadership body, the secretariat. It is also given sustenance by the fact that CERES and its figurehead, Jean-Pierre Chevènement, took a leading rôle in drafting the party's 1972 programme *Changer la Vie* along the lines of group's concepts and slogans – notably autogestion and the 'break with capitalism'. In addition, a large part of the influx of members into the PS in the 1970s identified with CERES. For all their plausibility, however, these arguments need heavy qualification. The inclusion of CERES into Mitterrand's majority and its concomitant entry into the secretariat was a practical necessity for Mitterrand. Its importance in the PS in early 1970s, and its ability to draft *Changer la Vie* in its own image, reflected also CERES's usefulness as a bridge to the PCF in the halcyon days of the Union of the Left. When relations between the PS and PCF cooled, and when Mitterrand felt that he could dispense with CERES' support, he did so, at the Pau Congress in 1975. He took up the group again in 1979, but only to defeat the Rocardian challenge for the party's presidential nomination. Measured by congress support for the group and the resolutions which it sponsored, CERES' strength rose from 8.5 per cent in 1971 to 24.5 per cent in 1977, then fell to 15 per cent in 1979. The mid-1970s constituted the high point of its influence, then, but even this level of support would not seem to sustain the view that it constituted the soul of the Socialist Party.

The rhetorical radicalism of the 1970s carried over into the 1980 *Projet Socialiste*, which was once again drafted largely by Chevènement and CERES. It was an echo of the radical tradition of the French Left and a response to the demands of the alliance with the communists. Much of the rhetoric was empty of substance, and significantly Mitterrand did not fight his campaign on the programme but on his own document, *110 Propositions*. The main appeal of the PS to the French electorate was not the *Projet Socialiste* but its identification with *changement* after a quarter of a century of government by parties of the right. The continued prominence of CERES masked a 'presidentialisation' of the party in which factions were submerged or simply bypassed. It would be an exaggeration to say that the PS had espoused a French variant of social democracy by 1981, but the obstacles to such a transformation were being progressively dismantled. Five years of socialist government were to accelerate this process.

The Italian socialists and the pursuit of power

The assimilation of the Italian party into the social democratic tradition was much more transparent than that of the French socialists. Far from hiding behind a veil of rhetorical radicalism, the PSI proclaimed its social democratisation with considerable gusto. The *Theses* approved by the 42nd Congress at Palermo in 1981, and which formalised the party's new identity, were quite explicit in defining the new philosophy as one of 'pragmatism, gradualism and reform' and in disavowing the 'all encompassing philosophies' of the past (La Palombara 1981–82, 923–3). Such a complete break with the past was made possible by an organisational coup in which Bettino Craxi succeeded in wresting control of the party machine from the power brokers who had dominated the PSI from their redoubts in the provinces. In the process the factions, which had previously enjoyed a semi-autonomous existence in the party, were dissolved, and the Left were routed. Craxiani – loyal to their leader – were installed in key posts, and the party took on the characteristics of wax in the hands of its leader.

Typically, the Italian party's ideological 'road to Damascus' had begun as a tactical manoeuvre. In the 1970s, the PSI had veered between the christian democrats and the communists in an attempt to find a solution to the problem of their isolation and impotence in the middle of a polarised party system. The objective had been to exercise a 'pivotal' rôle as an essential component in coalition government. By the mid-1970s, however, hostility between the christian democrats and the communists had abated. The communists had adopted the liberal, pluralist tenets of Euro-communism, and proclaimed their readiness to make 'the Historic Compromise' by entering government alongside socialists and christian democrats. This development carried a threat to the PSI. There was a danger that the socialists would become a marginal accessory to the two larger parties. Consequently they proposed a different scenario – the alternative of a government of the left, with themselves in harness with the Communist Party.

The strategy was set out in the 1978 programme, *A Project for a Socialist Alternative*. The document was unstinting in its admiration for the European tradition of social democracy, and the party subsequently became a vigorous evangelist for social democratic values (Hine 1979, 136). It made it clear that a government of the Left would only be acceptable if it was based on the values of democratic socialism. Behind the programme was a long-term design to realign the Italian Left on 'European' lines – that meant on the basis of socialist hegemony over the communists. To this end Craxi launched an explosive attack on 'totalitarian communism' urging Italy to adopt a form of 'socialism with a human face', which in many of its characteristics resembled the *'autogestionaire'* socialism of the French party.

This was a period of volatility in Italian politics, and circum-stances soon changed. The terrorist killing of christian democrats leader, Aldo Morro, the collapse of the Grand Coalition gov-ernment and the reversion to 'hard-line' Leninism by the communists changed the political landscape (Kogan 1981, 113–44). The 'Left alternative government' formula was no longer on the political agenda, and in order to restore stable government the PSI returned in 1980 to a coalition with the christian democrats.

However, the party maintained and even stepped up its social democratic profile. Social democratisation had not simply been a response to circumstances. It had been the product also of an analysis of Italian society which had taken root in socialist circles. According to this analysis, the 'subcultural blocs' of catholicism and communism, on which postwar Italian politics had been based, were being eroded by a process of secularisation and modernisation (Hine 1979, 142; Pasquino 1986, 122; Farnetti 1985, 123–80). The corollary of this social change would be the weakening of the ideological and political hold of the christian democrats and communists over the electorate. A renewed and 'social democratised' PSI would be able to exploit the ideological space which would open up in the political centre. Working from these premises, the Italian Socialist Party quickened its step down the social democratic road.

The *Theses*, adopted by the Palermo Congress of 1981, confirmed the developments of the previous three years, proclaiming that the PSI was an open and undoctrinaire party, committed to gradual change, but mindful and respectful of the 'principle of continuity' which governed society (La Palombara 1981–82, 932). The Congress also emphasised the new balance of power in the PSI, its reformed organisational format and its new leadership orientation. Craxi's opponents on the Left were defeated, and he was convincingly re-elected as General Secretary by a direct vote of the delegates. Previously the Central Committee had elected the General Secretary, reflecting a collegiate style of leadership. Craxi exercised a much more personalised, almost presidential form of leadership, which was amply demonstrated at the Verona Congress, three years later. Here he highlighted his pre-eminence in the party by appearing only to deliver his opening speech, and later to receive his acclamation (not re-election) as leader (Pasquino 1986, 121–4).

By 1981 the PSI had expunged the symbols and traditions of Italian socialism for a brand of social democracy somewhat to the right of most of the European parties. In economic policy it was unequivocally a free-market party, not only opposed to nationalisation but prepared to return certain nationalised industries to the private sector. In economic management the PSI was torn by the ambivalence not uncharacteristic of social democratic parties between inflation control along 'monetarist' lines and Keynesian packages for reflation and job creation. However, the party contained within its economic bureau those who were prepared to identify themselves as 'hard-line' monetarists and advocated welfare cuts as an answer to Italy's financial crisis. In foreign and security policy the party was unambiguous in its commitment to NATO and the United States. It combined these rather conservative positions with the rhetoric of reform and modernity.

Modernity was seen as the key to winning over the new sectors of Italian society which could no longer identify with either christian democracy or communism. The northern Italian, 'technological' middle class was a principal target in a strategy designed to exploit the supposed disintegration of the old ideological subcultures. The reform theme was expressed in slogans heralding a 'new morality' in place of the corruption and patronage of Italian public life. A 'Grand Reform' was proposed, a package of constitutional changes aimed at streamlining and stabilising government (La Palombara 1981–82, 934). Governability became a central issue of PSI strategy. The party blamed the endemic instability of Italian government on the polarisation of political life and presented itself as an essential anchor of stability. This was part of an overall strategy oriented towards power and the ultimate goal – socialist occupancy of the premiership. Although the PSI made the break with its Marxist past and applied the cosmetics of European social democracy, it is doubtful whether the party properly belongs to the family of European parties. In a number of respects it remained further from that family than the Communist Party, especially with the resumption by the latter of the Eurocommunist road and the dialogue which it opened with the European left. Firstly, the PSI lacked close ties with any section of the Italian labour movement. Secondly, it did not develop a mass organisation of any vitality or influence. Thirdly, it had no firm base or core clientele in the electorate. In the absence of these its ideological development resembled the course of a rudderless vessel. It is a characteristic of modern social democracy that ideology and programme are flexible and often downgraded in relation to the goal of exercising government power. In the PSI they have been subordinated to opportunistic manoeuvre to an unusually high degree. Hence, after Craxi came to power, not only were constitutional and institutional reforms shelved, but previous reforms were actually dismantled (Pasquino 1986, 137). In playing the rôle of 'political entrepreneurs' behind Craxi as 'managing director' the PSI relegated ideology to a position of almost total irrelevance.

SOCIAL DEMOCRACY IN THE RECESSION

The collapse of Keynesianism

The model of social democracy which had taken shape in the postwar period began to show signs of stagnation in the late 1960s. With the international economic recession which followed the oil price rises of 1973–74 its decomposition accelerated. The model had rested on basic assumptions that the economy had been brought under political control through an interventionist state. Capital accumulation was now compatible with full employment and a comprehensive welfare state. General affluence had reduced conflict over the distribution of economic rewards to a point where competing economic interests could be reconciled. Vigorous and sustained economic growth was a precondition of these assumptions. In low or no-growth economies the assumptions simply collapsed. Capitalism now faced a crisis of accumulation, and the liberal welfare state was confronted by a crisis of legitimacy. Social democracy had no ready answers to these crises. Its value system appeared outdated and irrelevant to the problems confronting modern industrial society. Reformist social democracy appeared now to belong to a forgotten and in many ways discredited era. An ethos of aggressive and egotistical individualism had overtaken the principles of collectivism and social solidarity which represented the ethical foundations of social democracy. The politics of accommodation and consensus, in which reformist social democracy had taken root, disintegrated into polarisation and periodic eruptions of conflict. Capital and labour now made demands on each other, and on the state, which governments were unable to reconcile or accommodate. Social democratic parties had become ensnared in the general crisis of the liberal democratic state. The solutions which their rivals proffered and which met a popular resonance, were inimical to their traditions and unacceptable both within the parties and with their trade union allies. Economic discipline and restraint were not their strong suits; here the bourgeois parties held all the aces. Moreover, social democratic parties were often further debilitated through internal conflict over new issues like environmental protection, or newly salient issues such as disarmament, NATO and the defence of the West, and decade-old questions concerning membership of the European Community.

The northern European parties, in which the ideology of managed growth and social reformism was most developed and engrained, experienced the most difficulty in adjusting to the new circumstances and resolving the conflicts. The social democratic parties of southern Europe – Italy, Spain, Greece, Portugal – were less encumbered with the 'ideological baggage' of reformism. The leaders of these newly formed or reformed parties enjoyed considerably more autonomy – because of the weak development of the mass party apparatus – than their northern counterparts. Moreover, in the new Mediterranean democracies, the parties were able to project a sense of purpose – the consolidation and extension of democracy – which the northern parties lacked.

With the collapse of Keynesianism, social democracy lost the political and intellectual coherence which it had appeared to possess in the 1960s. Ideological disorientation and political polarisation followed, as Left and Right entered a conflict arising out of divergent and irreconcilable responses to the crisis. On the Right there was a categorical rejection of 'ideological' solutions in favour of a hard-headed, pragmatic 'realism'. Where the parties were in government this meant 'crisis management' – a moderate version of monetarism in which monetary stability became the unconditional objective of an economic policy characterised by restraint and discipline. There was a sense in which this represented a natural evolution of revisionist social democracy in a period of recession – the ideology of growth management became one of crisis management. The Left's response was a radical rejection of revisionist social democracy. Drawing on a neo-Marxist analysis of monopoly capitalism and focusing on the power of multinational companies and international finance, its adherents advocated an 'alternative economic strategy' based on public ownership, intervention and trade control. It was a philosophy which had been gathering momentum in the British and French parties since the early 1970s, embodied in Labour's Programme (1973) and the PS programme of 1972, *Changer la Vie*.

Britain In Britain, the new economic and political climate was 'officially' recognised in an epoch-making speech by the Labour Prime Minister James Callaghan, to the 1976 Party Conference: 'We used to think you could spend your way out of a recession and increase employment by cutting taxes and boosting spending. I tell you in all candour that this option no longer exists, and in so far as it ever did exist it only worked by injecting a bigger dose of inflation into the system.' (Cited in Holmes 1985, 92). This formal acknowledgement of the break up of Keynesianism was followed some weeks later by a Cabinet meeting at which Anthony Crosland, the evangelist of Keynesian socialism, capitulated to pressure to back Chancellor Dennis Healey's public expenditure cuts. As he did so he pronounced the epitaph on his own vision of the future. For the next three years the government scarcely deviated from a programme of crisis management in which Crosland's conception of social democracy was obliterated. Entering opposition in 1979, the party's right wing, returned to the Keynesian formula of 'reflation plus the classical social democratic policies of income redistribution and social welfare within the mixed economy' (Byrd 1986, 72). However, in view of the recent experience of government this was a far from inspirational formula with which to unite the party and head off the challenge from the Left. For its part, the Left also called for a reflation, but in combination with a more radical approach to economic policy than that implied by the Keynesian paradigm. The alternative economic strategy now became part of the Left's offensive to change the face of the Labour Party.

Labour's shift to the Left was the product of four factors. One was the general tendency of the party to move Left upon entering opposition, exacerbated by acute dissatisfaction in the party and trade unions with the performance of the Wilson/Callaghan governments. A second factor was the changed social composition of the party. The decline of the traditional, relatively passive working-class bedrock and the rise of the ideologically oriented, activist middle-class membership had moved Labour's centre of gravity to the Left (Whitely 1983, 53–79). Thirdly the economic recession had made the centre ground of politics untenable, and finally, Labour's inclination to the left mirrored the rightward drift of the Conservative Party under Margaret Thatcher.

The Left's domination of party conferences from 1979 to 1982, and the National Executive Committee until 1980, along with its steady advance in the Parliamentary Party enabled it to win policy changes including EEC withdrawal and unilateral nuclear disar-mament. In a series of conference decisions, the constitution was amended to open the party up to rank-and-file (and therefore left-wing) influence. In the midst of the internecine warfare which accompanied all this there was an acrimonious and unedifying deputy leadership election in which Tony Benn narrowly failed to defeat Dennis Healey – then the party's elder statesman in terms of experience and *gravitas*. Heightening Labour's discomfort, the issue of the Trotskyite entrist organisation, Militant, became the subject of a bitter feud between Right and Left with the leadership backing off from full confrontation. Shortly before the general election of 1983 a semblance of unity returned, but attempts to bridge gulfs in policy and outlook meant that Labour's Manifesto, though of unprecedented length was vacuous and unconvincing. It also contained a commitment to unilateral nuclear disarmament – which was unacceptable to Labour's traditional electorate. Michael Foot, elected to succeed Callaghan largely because he was the only major figure in the party capable of bridging Left and Right, proved an uninspiring leader. Labour's devastating defeat in 1983 provoked a realignment in the party, with the opening up of divisions between the 'hard' and 'soft' Left factions, which the new leadership team of Neil Kinnock and Roy Hattersley were able to exploit. Indeed the pairing of the Centre-Left and Centre-Right which this 'dream ticket' represented was in itself a move towards ideological reconciliation. However, Labour's remaining internal divisions (rekindled by the bitter miners' strike of 1984) and the manifest lack of any clear and common purpose, were evidence of the party's ideological disintegration.

West Germany   As in the Labour Party, strains in the German social democratic Party were due in large part to its changing social composition. An influx of members between 1969 and 1972 (see chapter 2) had brought with it a new generation of ideologically motivated middle-class activists, which gradually permeated the party's functionary corps. Initially, their criticism of the SPD's lack of ideological purpose had been easily fended off by the Right, who had simply reaffirmed the principles set out at Bad Godesberg. In a counter-offensive to their advance, the Right had taken steps to strengthen the traditional labour movement orientation of the SPD (Heimann 1984, 2192–5; Kastendiek 1984, 407–22). In the last years of the Social Liberal Coalition, however, conflicts intensified, as broad sections of the party challenged the policy of the Schmidt government over nuclear energy, defence and economic management. In government, Schmidt and his backers on the Right were able to deflect or suppress criticism. However, with the collapse of the Social Liberal Coalition policy change was inevitable.

A powerful catalyst to policy change was the rise of the new social movements for ecology and peace, consolidated in 1980 in the formation of the Green Party. A tribune of the postmaterialist Left, the new party rapidly made inroads into the social democratic electorate, provoking the question of the appropriate response. The strategic dilemma which the Greens posed was interwoven with the question of the SPD's character and identity. Favouring a strict demarcation of the party from the Greens, the Right argued for a categorical rejection of the 'new politics' of postmaterialism, reaffirming the SPD's character as a broadly based, moderate *Volkspartei*, firmly anchored in the values of industrial society. The Left, including Brandt, associated themselves and the party with certain aspects of the 'new politics'. Their strategy was to win back the SPD's 'lost children' through a greening of the party. After the election of 1983, with the Greens now in the Bundestag and the SPD apparently confined in an electoral ghetto, the strategic dilemma intensified.

Between 1983 and 1988 party congresses took policy decisions which, while they did not represent a total break from the past, nevertheless indicated the advance of the New Left. These included the renunciation of some elements of NATO strategy and proposals for restructuring the Alliance on more overtly defensive lines (see chapter 4), the phasing out of nuclear energy within ten years, and the 'ecological modernisation of the economy'. Addressing the gender question, quotas were established for the representation of women within the party. Parallel to this process of policy change, the party began drafting a new Basic Programme with the objective of superseding the Bad Godesberg Programme and leading the way towards a redefinition of social democracy. Dominated by the party élite, programme drafting took place relatively smoothly – an exercise in controlled change. Ideological fragmentation was less pronounced in the SPD than in the Labour Party, partly because of the party's élite-centred structure (Meng 1985, 401; Müller-Rommel 1982, 267), partly because the radical challenge was externalised in the Green Party. However, the emergence of this rival on the postmaterialist Left faced the SPD with a series of programmatic and strategic dilemmas, and revealed a gulf between the Old and the New Left within German social democracy.

France In contrast to the British labour party and the SPD, the French Socialist Party escaped the worst effects of ideological fragmentation. Indeed it might be argued that this party underwent a process of ideological concentration, as the factionalism customary in French socialism was overcome by the *presidentialism* inherent in the French political system (Bell and Criddle 1988,

252–60). The militancy and radicalism of the early PS was submerged in the republican ethos of *La France Unie*, Mitterrand's slogan in the 1988 presidential election. At the same time the party was brought by stages close to the mainstream of social democracy which it had hitherto resisted. Assimilation with the mainstream, however, had its price as the PS found itself facing the same ideological stagnation and lack of purpose as the parties we have just discussed.

The radicalism of the programme with which the French socialists came to power and the rhetoric of party leaders in 1981, fostered a belief in some quarters in the novelty and daring of the socialist experiment which set the PS apart from northern European social democracy. For a year, this view was lent substance by widespread nationalisations and selective intervention in the economy, a massive reflation, changes in the structure of income distribution and liberalising reforms in society. Even in these heady months, an undercurrent of nationalism and a drive for national renewal permeated the thinking of the party alongside more socialist aspirations. Mitterrand made rhetorical flourishes in the direction of a bold, new (and explicitly French) socialist future, speaking of 'the renewed hopes of socialism – our socialism – emerging from the depths of our history, born over a century and a half ago. This socialism was able...to renew its strength and regain its full meaning, to the point where it is now the only new idea in Europe.' He was moved to add, however, that 'it extends beyond itself as an inspiration to the nation and requires of us the utmost devotion'. This rhetoric was evocative of a Gaullist past, laced with references to a great *'élan national'* (Lauber 1983, 161), conjuring up a legacy of republicanism with which all sections of the party sought to identify. The Republic was, in this conception, synonymous with the national interest which only the Left, with its policies of social justice and economic renewal through independence, was capable of fulfilling (Hanley 1986, 241).

The failure of the socialist experiment in economic crisis saw a strengthening of republican thinking at the expense of radical socialism. 'The illusion that reflation in one country was possible had been shattered, and with the PCF down in the polls...and unavailable as an ally, the party had no choice but to bid for the centre ground, to which end the abandonment of Marxist rhetoric and the embracing of a *rassemblement républicain*' (Bell and Criddle 1988, 257). The Rocardians in particular expressed the view that the socialist's electoral triumph had owed more to a traditional republican impulse than it had to the socialist radicalism, of the

Projet socialiste. Increasingly 'the Republic' became a symbol of discipline and loyalty for the mobilisation of the French behind the new policy of *rigeur.*

The U-turn in policy was negotiated with remarkably little internal party opposition (Bell and Criddle 1988, 238, 242). The ideological divisions within the Mitterrand camp were briefly exposed, but the pragmatic loyalty of the President's men soon prevailed. The CERES faction might have been expected to act as a citadel of radical socialist ideology, and indeed the group made attempts to rally opposition to the government's new course, but its protests sat ill with its continued presence in government. Chevènement, the CERES leader, left his post as Industry and Research Minister in 1983 (through personal frustration rather than ideological protest), but returned the following year to head the Education Ministry just as the PCF was quitting the government. The extent of CERES accommodation with the new realities of the 1980s can be judged from its acknowledgement in 1983 that socialism was not on the agenda. Chevènement, his radicalism considerably tamed, became an exponent of *La République moderne,* and in 1986 CERES changed its title to *Socialisme et République,* illustrating its integration into the party mainstream. Socialist Party congresses in 1983 and 1985 showed that the retreat from the socialist alternative had been uniform with no major faction resisting ideological retrenchment.

Most of the authors who portray the French Socialist Party as outside the social democratic tradition have stressed the tradition of ideological radicalism in the party, or the distinctive character of aspects of party policy such as *autogestion.* The years 1981–86 exposed the ephemeral quality of this brand of 'socialism of a different kind', enabling the present authors to echo Bell and Criddle (1988) in their judgement of the French socialists and their relationship to social democracy.

> The Socialist Party in the 1980s underwent a transformation: by October 1985, when it met in congress at Toulouse, it had developed a taste for power in place of the opposition mentality more evident in the 1970s. To acknowledge this was not to claim that it had undergone a 'Bad Godesberg' process, and had been transformed from a socialist into a social democratic party; such a transformation did not occur because in essence it was not required, the Socialists' programme having been drawn in the first place from the mainstream of western European social democracy. *(Bell and Criddle 1988, 250–1).*

The failure of the French experiment fatally undermined the credibility of the 'socialist alternative' here and in other countries. It coincided with a disastrous period of electoral decline and government collapse for almost all the north European parties. Between 1981 and 1983 social democrats were displaced from coalition governments in Belgium and the Netherlands, minority social democratic governments fell in Norway and Denmark, and the Austrian party lost its government majority. The status of the British Labour Party as the principal *opposition* party came under serious threat and in West Germany, the break up of the Social-Liberal Coalition was followed by an election in which social democratic support slumped to its lowest level for two decades. In municipal elections in France, the socialists suffered dramatic losses. Following these setbacks, many of the parties embarked upon a programmatic reappraisal designed to find purposeful political formulas for social democracy in a post-Keynesian age. A number of common themes can be identified. Generally, the parties sought a 'middle way' between the 'socialist alternative' and deflationary crisis management as practised by conservative and christian democratic governments. New programmes contained a residue of Keynesianism, being geared to interventionist strategies for state-led economic recovery, with an urgent priority on reducing unemployment. It was, however, recognised that there were financial constraints on state expenditure, and that its impact on unemployment levels would be limited. Other common themes were industrial and economic democracy, the safeguarding of acquired social citizenship rights and the even distribution of the burdens imposed by economic recovery programmes. Programmatic reappraisal also took account of new issues – environment and personal fulfilment, nuclear energy and disarmament – oriented around concern for the quality of life rather than purely quantitative considerations of economic growth.

Sweden It was the Swedish party (SAP) which pioneered the 'middle way' solution of a socially symmetrical crisis package, presented in a programme entitled *A Future for Sweden.* Central to the strategy was the selective rationalisation of the welfare state, the key to which was the 'just and equitable distribution of limited resources'. Moreover, the economic burdens of the recovery programme would be evenly distributed between social groups, with wage restraint balanced by taxes on wealth and share profits. Presenting austerity in the collectivist social democratic idiom of distribution policy, Prime Minister Olaf Palme was able to go into the 1985 election on an aggressive platform of opposition to the bourgeois parties. Social solidarity, he emphasised, was not simply an ethical imperative, it was a prerequisite of and foundation for economic recovery (Walters 1985, 356–69). Similar formulas were subsequently employed by the West German party with its slogan of *'Versohnen statt Spaltung'*, (reconciliation instead of division) and by the British Labour Party in its 'Freedom and Fairness' campaign. The success of such campaigns depended on the national context and cultural environment. In Sweden, a solidaristic political culture (Esping-Andersen 1985, 251–79; Sainsbury 1980, 92–3) fostered support for the SAP's programme as did the popular credibility of the party on the unemployment issue (Webber 1986, 42).

The most innovative departure in European social democracy was the Swedish party's proposal, (mirroring a similar but unsuccessful programme in Denmark) for wage-earner funds (see chapter 6). Brilliantly conceived by the trade union economist Rudolf Meidener, the funds combined multiple purposes. The promotion of collective employee stockholding, and participation in decision-making within the firm, was combined with the encouragement of profitability and investment. An economic recovery programme was combined with an apparatus to extend government control over private-sector investment, broaden the base of economic ownership and redistribute economic rewards. It was also hoped that the trade unions would regard the plan as a *quid pro quo* for wage restraint. In short, the SAP believed that here was a formula for crisis management on social democratic lines. It also represented a further stage in the party's longstanding commitment to reconciling political control over the economy with the operation of the free market.

The introduction in 1983 of the Meidener Plan (see p.161) in 1983 aroused considerable opposition and polarised Swedish politics to an unprecedentedly high degree. The progressive erosion of the social democratic consensus undermined one of the preconditions for the success of the Swedish model. Moreover, the poor performance of the national economy at the end of the 1980s cast further discredit on social democracy in what had hitherto been its heartland. The response of the SAP was to signal a retreat from the old orthodoxies, including the distinguishing feature of Swedish social democracy, full employment in a regulated labour market. The model which had served as a beacon of hope to European social democrats throughout this barren decade began to lose its gloss at the start of the 1990s.

Ideological reappraisal

As has often been the case in the postwar history of social democracy, developments in Sweden had attracted the attention of the other European parties. In the British Labour Party, deputy leader Roy Hattersley and Bryan Gould, the rising star of the Centre-Right in the mid-eighties, identified themselves with the 'market socialism' concept. It was elaborated by the party's adjunct, the Fabian Society (Beecham et al, 1987; Leadbeater 1987; Forbes 1986) in an attempt to modernise the nationalisation formula in recognition of the fact that the scope for public sector monopolies had been irrevocably reduced by a decade of Conservative government privatisation. In a wider sense it was perceived as a step towards the revitalisation of the party and its reorientation on a centrist axis, a manoeuvre which the Right saw as the key to the electoral breakthrough which had eluded Labour in 1983. The market socialism formula (Gould used the term 'social ownership', slightly more acceptable to the traditionalist Left) emerged also out of a recognition that the market could not be suppressed without the deployment of a juggernaut state which was politically unacceptable to large sections of society. Instead, the new concept entailed the diversification of the market and the encouragement of new forms of economic ownership.

The promotion of cooperatives, employee share options, worker buy-outs and new forms of public–private partnerships, was at the heart of market socialism, within 'a framework of laws and institutions that enables different forms of economic organisation...to evolve' (Forbes 1986). The intention was to mitigate the inherently inegalitarian tendencies of the market and to disperse economic power more diffusely. To the Labour Left, however, all this amounted to a retreat in the face of the radical Right, and *de facto*, an admission that the restoration to public ownership of newly privatised industries was not on the political agenda. Fundamentally opposed to this 'trojan horse' of revisionism, the Left mobilised in defence of the high ground of Clause IV, resisting the 1987–88 initiative on policy review.

The approval of the policy review at the 1989 party conference signalled the restoration of the traditional hegemony of the Centre-Right in the Labour Party. Labour was now committed to a multilateral position *vis-à-vis* nuclear disarmament, and a positive appraisal of the market economy in which nationalised industry had a very much reduced rôle. It was clear that the major innovations of a decade of Conservative government – privatisation and the legal circumscription of trade union rights – would be left in place by any future Labour administration. The policy review had rid the party of its electoral millstones – policies in defence, public ownership and labour law which had been identified as the root of electoral failure in 1983 and 1987. Labour's ideological profile no longer rendered the party 'unelectable'. However, in terms of innovation and ideological regeneration it could not be said that the review had made major strides. Broad areas of party policy remained vague and ill-defined. Although Labour's electoral fortunes appeared to be in the ascendant, the impression persisted that the up-turn reflected the unpopularity of the party of government at the end of the 1980s.

Outside Scandinavia, the most active party in terms of ideological reappraisal was the German party, the SPD. Reviewing the principles of the Godesberg Programme, the Basic Values Commission explicitly recognised the demise of the growth ideology which had been a basic assumption of party programmes for more than two decades. The commission concluded that 'few responsible persons still expect that unemployment can be overcome through economic growth, the durability and beneficial effects of which were taken for granted in 1959' (SPD 1985). In the 1980s there were not only economic limits to growth, but also environmental limits. To meet these new constraints, the SPD developed the concept of 'qualitative growth' in which humanist and ecological concerns counterbalanced a purely quantitative appraisal of economic performance. The conception involved the stimulation of research and the direction of investment into a new technology of environmental protection. The 'ecological modernisation of the economy' would simultaneously create a dynamic growth sector with a job-creating potential, and serve social and environmental needs. The attraction of the concept for the German social democrats lay in the fact that it was entirely compatible with the party's belief in state intervention in the market economy for the attainment of social goals. However, although the economy and ecology formula went some way towards meeting the challenge which the environmentalist Green Party posed to the SPD, it did not represent the 'new economic concept' for which social democratic parties sought.

Superseding Keynesian social democracy proved highly problematical. Most of the parties retained a residual commitment to the idea of state-led economic recovery through measured reflation, although their assessment of the employment potential of such intervention was considerably more restrained than it had been. Attacking the 'new individualism' of conservative and christian democratic parties, social democrats re-emphasised their traditional values of collectivism and social solidarity. Their defence of the social or welfare state was based on these principles, but it was combined with a recognition of the limits of welfare finance in low-growth economies. Characteristically, social democrats have amended the old orthodoxies of their political philosophy in piecemeal fashion. The basic value system expressed in the liberal socialist trinity of principles – freedom, justice, equality – has remained intact. However, in the new circumstances of the 1980s, the parties have experienced some difficulty in giving programmatic form to these principles.

With the erosion of the bedrock conceptions of social democracy, the parties have suffered from ideological disorientation. Doctrinal flexibility and an acute sense of pragmatism enabled social democrats to respond relatively quickly to the new circumstances of the 1980s. However, emphasising pragmatism and discipline at the expense of reform, the parties often took on a rather grey appearance, uninspirational and with no distinct vision of the future. Redefining social democratic ideology and attempting to establish a new synthesis between basic values and *Realpolitik* over a wide range of issues, the parties often adopted compromise positions in which ambiguity was not far beneath the surface. To be sure, compromise and ambiguity is endemic to parties which seek to pursue principles and power simultaneously. However, in the attempt to evade apparently irreconcilable policy conflicts, the parties have tended to cloak ambiguous compromises in their programmes with a certain vagueness and generality, detracting from their credibility. In order to compensate they have placed more emphasis on 'image' and on the personal appeal of leaders, reinforcing the long-term weakening of ideology.

SOCIAL DEMOCRATIC IDEOLOGY ON THE SOUTHERN EUROPEAN PERIPHERY

The rise of socialism in the Iberian countries and in Greece was synonymous with the collapse of dictatorship and the transition to democracy. In this euphoric climate of social and political change, the newly created parties in Greece and Portugal, and the re-emergent party in Spain were initially drawn to an ideology of radical socialism. As they were granted legality, however, and meeting almost immediate electoral success, they quickly became institutionalised in the political system. The tasks of nation-building and economic modernisation eclipsed the goals of socialist transformation contained in party ideology. For these parties ideological moderation was a condition of national reconciliation and the concentration of democratic forces (Arango 1985, 150–1).

Ideological change

The pace of ideological revision and the ease with which it was negotiated depended on national circumstances. Lacking a socialist tradition, the Portuguese party travelled most readily down the road, quickly accepting assimilation into the social democratic tradition. The Spanish Socialist Party (PSOE), on the other hand, had a long Marxist tradition which had been kept alive during the Franco years. At its restoration, the radical wing of the party in exile had fought off a challenge from an overtly social democratic faction to establish the PSOE on Marxist lines. Nevertheless, it had strong links with the northern European social democratic parties, receiving financial assistance from the Germans (Carr and Fusi 1979, 224–5). Under the tutelage of González, though with some resistance from within the party, the PSOE edged progressively closer to the western European family of social democratic parties. Of the socialist parties on Europe's southern periphery, the Greek party (PASOK) has remained most distant from the mainstream of social democracy, retaining its distinctive character as a party of national liberation.

Spain As the PSOE reconstituted itself in the last years of the Franco dictatorship it made 'a positive attempt to produce a specifically socialist programme and to identify the political space of socialism in Spain' (Maravall 1985, 134–6). The *Declaration of Principles* which it adopted at its 27th Congress, held in Madrid in December 1976 defined the PSOE as 'a class party...Marxist and democratic', rejecting any accommodation with capitalism and seeking instead 'the suppression of the capitalist mode of production through the conquest of political and economic power' (Maravall 1985, 136). However, PSOE leaders were closely involved in inter-party negotiations over the terms of Spain's new constitutional settlement, and their flexibility and willingness to compromise belied the militancy displayed at the Madrid Congress. González had expressed the view that 'at times it is most revolutionary to be moderate' (Carr and Fusi 1979, 224). His strategy was to address the questions of Spain's constitutional and economic future with consensual solutions commanding support amongst a broad cross section of the electorate. Confrontation was inevitable as the Left perceived González' intention of weakening party ideology. It reached a climax at the 28th Congress of the party in 1979 with the resignation of González in protest at a resolution reaffirming the PSOE's Marxist commitments. With this tactical ploy, the leadership succeeded in subordinating the party to its will. The 28th Congress had approved a reform of the party's statutes, weakening the representation of the rank and file in congresses and facilitating the manipulation of delegate selection by the party bureaucracy. A second congress in 1979 reinstated González and approved a programme which for all its convolution, went some way towards establishing the party's ideological pluralism. 'The PSOE considers Marxism to be a critical, theoretical, undogmatic instrument for the analysis and transformation of society, gathering the various Marxist and non-Marxist contributions that come together to make socialism the great liberalising alternative of our time...completely respectful of peoples' individual beliefs' (Arango 1985, 152–3). Thereafter the PSOE consolidated its identity as a left-of-centre party of democratic and modernising reform. Fighting the election of 1982 on the populist slogan of *cambio* (change) – as PASOK had done before it – it was elected to government with a programme designed to modernise Spain on the lines of capitalist democracies elsewhere in western Europe.

Portugal The Portuguese Socialist Party (PSP) journeyed equally quickly down the social democratic road in its formative years. The revolutionary rhetoric of 1973 and 1974 gave way to militant anti-communism, and indeed, the party played a not insignificant part in the downfall of the leftist military government which had led Portugal out of dictatorship. Adopting a rôle as 'the party of balance and dialogue' (Kohler 1982, 198–9) in a country where politics was sharply polarised, the PSP presented itself as a force for stability and order. Mário Soares consistently styled his party along the lines of its north European counterparts, defining socialism in terms of the familiar triad of social democratic principles, as 'social justice and freedom, the participation of the citizens in the life of the state and society and in the enterprises: [it] means decentralisation and industrial co-determination, it is a regime that must deepen democracy as well as increase solidarity' (cited in Giner 1984, 155). The PSP 'Programme for the 80s', moreover, is built with the bricks and mortar of social democracy. Recognising that Portugal resembled a Third World country in its backwardness, it contained a blueprint for 'Europeanisation'. The programme also contained prescriptions for state-led economic development, a mixed economy, reconciliation between competing economic interests and welfare reforms. It accepted without question Portugal's integration into western Europe and membership of NATO (Kohler 1982, 200–1). Elected to lead a coalition government in 1983, Soares found himself confronted by an acute economic crisis which was only resolved with the aid of the International Monetary Fund. In accordance with the terms of the loan, his government was forced to introduce a package of fierce austerity measures, postponing the reforms to which he was committed.

Greece The Panhellenic Socialist Movement (PASOK) differed from the Spanish and Portuguese parties in several important respects. Unlike the Iberian parties, PASOK retained its character as a national liberation movement well after the transition to democracy. Formed in 1974 out of a movement of resistance to the infamous Colonels' regime it defined itself as 'a movement of the working and underprivileged people of Greece'. Its objectives revolved around the attainment of 'national independence, the sovereignty of the people, social liberation and democratic progress' (Featherstone 1987, 123). Intensely populist in style, it derived its ideology from an analysis of the relationship between the peripheral Greek economy and the centres of international economic power. Like the Portuguese socialists, PASOK regarded Greece as a Third World country, but the conclusions which the Greek party drew were quite different from those of the Portuguese. According to PASOK's analysis, the subordination of the national economy to foreign capital had been responsible for perpetuating backwardness. Progress depended not on the integration of Greece into the western European economy, but on its independent development on socialist lines (Lyrintzis 1984, 111; Kohler 1982, 128–30).

This reasoning bore an affinity to neo-Marxist theories of imperialism and monopoly capitalism, and indeed PASOK associated itself with Marxism in its early years (Featherstone 1987, 126–7). Whilst the Iberian parties unreservedly associated themselves with western European social democracy, PASOK explicitly rejected this tradition, preferring to identify with regimes as diverse as Yugoslavia, Hungary and the one-party socialist countries of the Arab World (Clogg 1987, 136). However, advocating the socialisation of production, decentralisation and self-management in economic decision-making, democratisation of the state machine and the creation of a welfare state, party programmes bore some resemblance to the social democratic model. Eclectic and diffuse, PASOK ideology was not easy to pin down. Its populist character and its overriding concern for national sovereignty and independence were its strongest features. The former was expressed in the charismatic leadership and overpowering dominance of its leader and founder Andreas Papandreou (Clogg 1987, 142–4). The latter reflects the aspirations of the party's predominantly petty bourgeois constituency. However, notwithstanding the uniquely Greek appearance of PASOK it was possible to identify a tendency towards convergence with mainstream European socialism, particularly, as we shall see, after the party took power.

From the mid-1970s, the socialist parties of the new Mediterranean democracies were significantly more successful than the older, better-established parties further north. Their success reflected the contribution which they had made to the transition to democracy. They became symbols of the new regimes, focal points of integration in what had until recently been polarised societies. As such, all three parties developed a broad social base in the electorate, adopting a populist or catch-all profile to which a sharply defined ideology was alien. Although their programmes sometimes made a rhetorical commitment to radical socialism, socialist rhetoric was toned down in varying degrees by leaders who steered the parties towards an ideology of modernity and progressive reform. With the transformation of opposition parties into parties of government this tendency was accentuated. Faced with the onerous tasks of democratic and economic consolidation, González, Soares and Papandreou responded by instilling into their parties a well-developed sense of pragmatism. Thus the social democratic parties of Europe's southern periphery underwent an accelerated process of ideological transformation in the first decade of their existence. It might be said that the protracted changes which we have already observed in the older parties of northern Europe were compressed here into this single decade.

CHAPTER TWO

The Internal Life of Social Democratic Parties

THE SOLIDARITY COMMUNITY

Peter Lösche has tellingly described the classic features of a social democratic party as a 'solidarity community' based on a unity of party programme, organisational form and social base (Losche, 1988). Organisationally the distinctiveness of social democratic parties lay along two dimensions. Externally, the party was part of a wider labour movement which included the trade unions and the cooperative movements, and party members would invariably belong to the other two pillars of the labour movement and in most cases the trade unions and the cooperative societies were able to participate directly in the decision-making bodies of the party. Internally, the parties were distinctive in two ways; a dense organisational network existed to cater for every conceivable interest of the individual party member and to channel it into a party-affiliated organisation. These bodies covered a very wide spectrum, but favourite activities included chess, stamp-collecting and hiking. This stress on the capacity of the party to satisfy the needs of members reflected a desire to have a broad membership base and a recognition that their potential adherents were excluded from many of the social institutions of existing societies. Social democratic parties were interested then not only or even primarily in winning voters, but in creating and maintaining 'solidarity communities'. The ratio of members to voters was thus much higher than in bourgeois parties.

The party was also seen as a 'democratic community' and its organisational structure represented an attempt to realise inner-party democracy; a goal which distinguished it both from bourgeois and communist parties. This commitment to internal democracy has been well summarised by Kurt Shell.

> ...decisions are to be reached democratically, i.e. through participation and free discussion by its members; these decisions are to be binding on the elected Party leadership; and those who are delegated by the Party to represent it in legislature or government shall consider themselves entirely as the agents of the Party and subject to its continuous guidance.
> *(Shell 1962, 95–6)*

Socially, the classic social democratic party was based on the working class. Its roots lay in the factory and its central aspiration was to give voice to the working class. The overwhelming bulk of members and voters were workers, but they were also overwhelmingly skilled industrial workers. When social democracy spoke politically, it was as the voice of the skilled European worker. There were, of course, intellectuals in the party, but nearly all of them had their origins in the skilled working class and had acquired their intellectual formation through party channels, For example, the German SPD had a Party High School in Berlin where the future cadres of the party were taught by Rosa Luxemburg before 1914.

Pre-1914

The classic social democratic 'solidarity community' had begun to undergo changes even before the advent of the First World War. The most obvious feature was the inability of the parties to realise the principles of the democratic community. The running of the very complex organisational networks demanded a vast increase in the party bureaucracies, which developed a growing importance. The parliamentary leaderships became more autonomous and in many cases succeeded in expanding their electoral base. Their autonomy was further heightened once they started to participate in government. The doctrine of party democracy remained intact but the parties increasingly operated in a top down manner; a tendency which was reinforced by the predisposition of the still largely working-class membership not to defy the leadership since they still clung to the wider values of the labour movement derived from industrial struggle. Such values emphasised unity as a primary virtue. These developments tended to reduce the need for active commitment and participation by the individual member and to replace it by permanent and formal organisation, better adapted to the electoral battle.

The interwar period

The organisational network still remained largely intact in the interwar period. Social life was still largely carried on within the party and party members still relied on the party press for political information. This dense organisational network was much less developed in the British Labour Party, however, since membership in the Labour Party was largely indirect through membership of a trade union and the incentive to participate in the party was correspondingly reduced.

The largely homogeneous social base of the parties was also changing as attempts were made to broaden the base of electoral appeal. The Scandinavian parties responded to the Great Depression by forming coalitions of workers and farmers around a programme of wage restraint, full employment and agricultural subsidies. Elsewhere in Europe the situation was also changing. In Germany many working-class members, especially in the large industrial centres, had joined the Communist Party. By 1930 about one-quarter of the party membership possessed non-proletarian origins. This compared with about 10 per cent in 1905–06. Even more striking was the percentage of parliamentary party leaders (35 per cent) whose social origins were middle- or upper-class.

The bourgeois origins of this significant proportion of the parliamentary leadership is often held to be associated with an embourgeoisment of the SPD since it is argued further that social democrats in parliament redefined themselves in terms of the rôle they had come to play and thus, even those whose origins were not bourgeois, were likely to become 'embourgeoised' simply by becoming parliamentarians.This argument ignores two factors. Firstly, the close links with the trade unions and their leadership which prevailed in the latter half of the Weimar Republic. These close links were expressed in the high proportion of trade unionists in parliament and in the SPD-led Cabinets. More crucially, the authors who argue the embourgeoisement thesis overestimate the rôle of parliament as a socialising agency. These parliamentarians were also still heavily involved in the life of the party – a party in which although the proportion of bourgeois had increased, it still remained a minority. Both party and society had altered from imperial times, but the party was by no means a mirror image of German society. It was still profoundly different both in its preponderance of working-class members and its non-hierarchical mode of social and personal interaction.

The transition to peace

Outside Britain and Scandinavia the end of the Nazi regime meant the re-establishment of social democratic parties after a period of banning and exile. The most striking feature of the re-establishment of social democratic parties is the preservation of continuity – the party as solidarity community emerged relatively unscathed from the caesura of Nazi domination of Europe. There was very little rewriting of programmes: the party programme was still seen as a key guide to political action. The British Labour government of 1945 regarded its central task as carrying out the Labour Programme of 1945. While party programmes remained intact there was some change in the party's social base. Social democratic parties began to attract some supporters of bourgeois parties who had been disillusioned by the dismal performance of these parties in the face of the Nazi challenge. There was also some loosening of the bonds between the unions and the party in a number of countries, in particular West Germany and Holland.

Germany Continuity was especially marked in the case of the SPD. The SPD after 1945 was in many respects the recreation of the Weimar SPD. When Kurt Schumacher was confirmed as chairman in 1946, about two-thirds of the members had belonged to the SPD in the Weimar Republic. On this basis the SPD recruited a mass membership extraordinarily quickly, until a high point of 875,479 was reached in December 1947. In these very early years, the mass membership was attracted back again, as much by the feeling of belonging that the movement provided as by the prospect of the party being given immediate access to political power. What strikes one is the potency of the old symbols and associations connected with the SPD. Accounts of these years often refer to digging up the party flags which had been buried during the Nazi years. They also tell of the desire of the party members, often including ex-concentration camp inmates, to have their party books brought up to date for the Nazi period. The Nazi period had in fact strengthened that feeling of emotional community we normally associate more with a movement than a political party. This point is well made by Lewis Edinger:

> More than any other major political group in West Germany, the SPD was rooted in the past. It was not a new party in either name or membership, but was explicitly re-established on hallowed principles that had sustained loyal adherents through twelve years of Nazi oppression. Whether they

69

had been imprisoned or exiled, or had simply quietly survived the Hitler era, post war members were generally united by a strong in-group feeling that was rooted in the traditional goals and sentiments of socialist solidarity, as well as in memories of shared experiences in the highly integrated party of Weimar days. It was a feeling based less on specific common aspirations than on an emotional sense of community, a feeling that the party united in camaraderie the best and the most decent Germans, a feeling that was reaffirmed daily by the symbolic use of the familiar Du and the appelation [Comrade] amongst most party members.   *(Edinger 1965,409)*

It was this continuity in emotional attitudes and party membership that frustrated Schumacher's early attempts at party reform. Schumacher had often fallen foul of the party bureaucracy in the Weimar period and he was initially at least convinced of the need for more participation by younger and more radical grass-roots elements. There were some indications that this might be possible. Formerly, the key functionary in the party, the district Secretary, had been a salaried official of the Executive Committee. Now he was to be selected and paid by the district organisations. Control of the nomination process for elections, which had been in the dead hands of the national party leadership in Weimar, was now in the hands of district leaders. Lastly, the national leadership was almost entirely dependent upon dues collected by the districts. Indeed, until 1950, it was the districts which set the level of subscription.

However, these factors did not prevail and within a fairly short time the SPD had begun to display the bureaucratisation and ageing process that was so marked in Weimar. There were three main reasons for this. First, the attitudes and composition of the party membership. Not unnaturally, they treated newcomers with suspicion since, if they were young and had been politically active, they were likely to have been members of the Nazi party. Radical left-wingers were equally cold-shouldered because of the virulent distrust of the German Communist Party (KPD) among older members, given the policy of the communists in the closing stages of Weimar and the conclusion of the Nazi–Soviet Pact in 1939.

Second, these latent suspicions of the communists were reactivated by SPD perceptions of Soviet conduct in East Germany. Very quickly the SPD became concerned with opposing communist influence everywhere, including the factories and trade unions. As the Cold War deepened, the notion that it would be possible to hold to a middle way between communism and capitalism quickly became discredited and all debate and innovation of a leftward direction was looked on with disfavour.

Lastly, there was Schumacher himself. Schumacher had a genuine wish for more participation at the grass roots. However, he had an even stronger conviction that, just as the SPD was the only force morally and intellectually qualified to lead postwar Germany, so only he could lead the SPD. This inevitably meant that control of the party became for him the main priority. This necessitated relying on the established party leaders at the local level. At the centre, Schumacher was supported by the ex-London *emigrés* Erich Ollenhauer, Fritze Heine, Willi Eichler and Herta Gotthelf, together with three associates from Hanover: Alfried Nau, Herbert Kreidemann and Egon Franke. Gradually they became indispensable aides to Schumacher, and when the Party Executive Committee was formally re-established in 1946 they became its inner nucleus of salaried members. This meant that the Executive was dominated by people who relied totally for their eminence on Schumacher. Any innovation in policy or organisation could only come from Schumacher as was dramatically demonstrated during his illnesses when the Executive was powerless to act.

Austria The re-establishment of social democracy in Austria constituted a more decisive rupture with the past than in the case of the SPD. The recreation of mass membership base was to prove much more difficult. The old Austrian Party, the SDAPDÖ, had reached a peak of 708,839 members in 1929, and it took until 1955 until the postwar SPÖ again reached the comparable figure of 691,150. Many of these members, in marked contrast to the SPD, were new members. Kurt Shell, writing in 1962, observed:

> Two-thirds of the present membership are postwar recruits, and two-thirds of this present membership are over forty years of age. This seems to indicate that the Party today is to a considerable extent composed of men and women who, out of indifference or hostility, refused to join the Party before 1934. Attracted to the postwar Party by the changed situation in which it operates, these new members in turn contribute to the further detachment of the party from its ideological roots. *(Shell 1962, 86)*

There are two further important interconnected features of the change in party membership in Austria. The first and most obvious was the changed position of Vienna. In 1929 Viennese members made up 58 per cent of the total party membership. This had declined to 42 per cent in 1955 and at some points after 1945, it was even smaller. This decline was a result of large-scale demographic shifts. Approximately 200,000 Viennese had moved to western

Austria and they were replaced by 100,000 *Volksdeutschen* (ethnic Germans) from areas traditionally antipathetic to social democracy. Perhaps even more important was the virtual elimination of Vienna's sizeable Jewish community (176,034 in 1934). This community was very largely identified with social democracy, and up until 1934 had usually made up half the membership for the Executive Committee of the party. It was above all the Viennese Jewish community which had made the Austrian party the most intellectually lively of all European parties.

> The disappearance of Jews from prominent Party positions has gone hand in hand with the elimination of the Socialist 'intellectuals'... compared to the sixteen Socialist members of parliament in 1919 who were listed as writers and editors, the Socialist parliamentary representation since 1945 has contained only one... The tension between theoreticians and activists, which was one of the characteristics of the old Social Democracy, has thus disappeared through the elimination of the species 'socialist intellectual' *(Shell 1962, 79–80)*

THE VICTORY OF THE CATCH-ALL PARTY?

The 1950s

The re-establishment of social democratic parties on the traditional pattern had taken place in the immediate postwar climate in which the electoral future of the parties looked bright and the links between party programme, organisational form and social base were still intact. These links began to fray in the 1950s as the effects of the economic boom, which began with the decade, diffused through western European society. The pattern of occupations began to change with the expansion in the service sector and the relative decline in the number of skilled workers. Consumption patterns and leisure pursuits were also radically altered by the sustained prosperity. Perhaps more crucially the parties were, with the exception of the Scandinavian parties, in an electoral trough. The apparent strength of the social democratic parties' organisation, the uncompromising nature of the party programme and an electoral appeal that was still largely based on the working-class, were now seen to be electoral disadvantages. Outside Scandinavia, bourgeois parties had either regrouped, as was the case with the christian democrats in Germany, or revised their policies. In Britain the Conservative Party had rethought its policies under the influence of Ian McLeod and Rab Butler.

The social democratic parties responded by a wave of programmatic rewriting, best exemplified by the Bad Godesberg Programme of the SPD in 1959 (see chapter 1). In a number of cases the rewriting of party programmes was not seen to be enough and the broadening of the electoral appeal was also seen to require a dismantling of some of the elements of party organisation that set the social democratic parties apart from their bourgeois adversaries. This process was most marked in the Federal Republic. The Bad Godesberg Conference not only ratified a new party programme, it also accepted the dropping of many of the old symbols associated with the party – the symbols which were associated in the minds of party members with the notion of the party as a solidarity community. The colour of party membership books was changed from red to blue and party members were expected to stop addressing each other as Comrade and to use the term 'party friend'. The flag of the Federal Republic was now flown alongside the traditional red flag above the party headquarters. However, this transition encountered some resistance. The Hanover Party Conference of November 1960 had been designed as a showcase for the new SPD. Willy Brandt was adopted as Chancellor Candidate for the 1961 election and the conference broke with tradition by singing the national anthem. The smoothness of the transition was marred, however, by the spontaneous decision of the party chairman, Erich Ollenhauer's wife to strike up the old party anthem on her guitar and to sweep the conference in a rousing rendition of it, to the obvious discomfiture of the new team.

In the 1950s Otto Kirchheimer argued that west European party systems were being transformed by the success of the catch-all party which forced other parties to emulate it if they were to have any chance of success (Kirchheimer, 1966). The catch-all party seeks to represent all social groups and to operate primarily as an electoral party, i.e. to be seen to make appeals to all groups in the electorate and to give priority to electoral success rather than ideological purity. Emphasis is laid not on agitation or extra-parliamentary activity, but rather on governing, research and expertise and a pragmatic – some would say technocratic – approach to the problems of the day.

Kirchheimer's claim that the catch-all or people's party, was triumphing throughout western Europe, was much overstated except in relation to the Federal Republic, where the extraordinary electoral success of the christian democrats, culminating in the unique electoral majority of 1957, did put the SPD under great pressure, but even here there were limits. Given the historical strength of the organisation of the SPD, the class background of the members and the formal procedures for participation by the party membership, it was never possible for the party leadership to operate totally as a catch-all or people's party without reference to the party membership, but in general terms this view of the party remained the accepted one in the SPD throughout the 1960s.

The priority was now on electoral success rather than maintaining the party as a *Gesinnungsgemeinschaft*, as a community of the faithful. 'That the party exists not to sustain the organisation, but that the organisation is there to attain and determine governmental power – to have made this clear is what is historically correct about the series of reforms associated with Bad Godesberg' (Narr et al 1976, 91).

The changes in other party organisations were much less dramatic. Anthony Crosland argued strongly that the Labour Party in Britain needed to shed its cloth-cap image and adopt a clear people's party identity. The attempts of the party leadership to move in that direction were however frustrated by the party's structure and the privileged access it gave to the trade unions who were wholly opposed to any changes that would detract from their special rôle.

In Scandinavia there was very little change in the internal organisation of the parties in the 1950s. They continued to poll very well, and their network of educational centres and cooperatives, together with affiliated associations of pensioners, tenants and housing cooperative members, still allowed the parties, especially in Sweden and Denmark, to maintain a social democratic hegemony. Party organisations continued to function very successfully as agents of electoral mobilisation.

The challenge to the catch-all party

The wave of programmatic rewriting and the dropping of some of the special features of social democratic party organisation exhausted the social democratic response to the consumption explosion of the 1950s, and for a period relative calm descended on the internal life of the parties. This calm was to some extent deceptive. The invasion of Hungary in 1956 had led to a large-scale exodus from west European communist parties. This did not mean that those who had left orthodox communist parties had abandoned their Marxist analyses. Freed from the constraints of the party line, many of these ex-communists were extremely active in 'the New Left' in or on the fringes of European social democratic parties. This New Left had a major influence on student opinion, especially in the burgeoning social science faculties of European universities, and were to play a major rôle in the student protest movement which culminated in 'the events' of 1968 in France.

Germany The radicalisation of the student movement had a profound impact on a number of parties, notably the SPD. The 'New Left' position inside the SPD had been identified in the late 1950s with the *Sozialistischer Deutscher Studentenbund* (German Socialist Students' Federation). It was soundly defeated at the Bad Godesberg conference and, in July 1960, the SPD executive withdrew financial support from the SDS and founded the SHB, the *Sozialdemokratischer Hochschulbund*, which it envisaged as an organisation to help recruit academics into the SPD rather than an organisation primarily concerned with developing alternatives to official party policy.

In November 1961 the leaders of the SDS and some of their prominent supporters were expelled from the SPD. Cast out of the mainstream of West German politics, the SDS nevertheless remained influential in student politics. In the years between 1961 and 1965, this was largely a matter of providing an audience for, and disseminating the ideas of the Frankfurt School of social theorists and the young Marx.

Things began to change from 1966 onward – '1968' in Germany began in 1966. The decision of the SPD leadership to enter the Grand Coalition in November 1966 with its christian democratic rivals served to delegitimise it in the eyes of many of its younger and more active supporters and potential supporters. Leading figures in the SDS had been associated with critiques of representative democracy, but the formation of the Grand Coalition brought them support from some of the most avid supporters of representative democracy inside the SPD who were outraged by what they perceived as its manipulation and betrayal in the decision to enter a Grand Coalition. An emerging alliance between the SDS and disaffected members of the SPD was strengthened by what was perceived as a climate of growing authoritarianism in the FRG. In the view of those on the Left this authoritarianism had been evident in Ludwig Erhard's concept of a 'formed society', but it was the events surrounding the visit of the Shah of Iran to West Berlin in early June

1967 and the intention of the Grand Coalition to introduce emergency laws that made these perceptions the basis of a mass movement of protest, the APO (*Ausserparlamentarische Opposition*).

This mass movement of protest incorporated at least four kinds of left-wing dissenters, which have been very well categorised by Kurt Shell:

(1)   Radical socialist democrats who wished to preserve and defend the achievements of the 'Rechtsstaat' and who saw no alternative to working for reform in and through the SPD. APO clearly meant to them extraparliamentary action, a means to arouse and pressure the parties, parliament, and government. Though highly critical of German foreign policy toward the East (and generally favouring the recognition of the DDR), they opposed cooperation with the SED or any groups tainted with Stalinism.

(2)   Socialists, hostile to, or despairing of the SPD, moderately critical or friendly toward the SED and the DDR, eager to form broad alliances for purposes of extraparliamentary or electoral action. The constitutional framework remained imperative, either out of conviction or because of fear of legal prosecution.

(3)   Revolutionary Marxists, Trotskyites, and Maoists hostile to the 'bureaucratic' socialist regimes of the Soviet Union and Eastern Europe, but affirming the need for organisational centralisation and discipline. A socialist party was seen as useful only if it were determinedly revolutionary, 'the way the KPD (Communist Party of Germany) was till the middle of the twenties'. They rejected all forms of 'hippie' politics and 'political happenings' lacking the necessary revolutionary seriousness.

(4)   The 'Anti-Authoritarian' Marxist–anarchist Left, anti–parliamentary on ideological grounds, emphasizing direct action, cultivating spontaneity and libidinal liberation, aiming at a mass base not through formal organisation but through joint commitment to action and revolutionary work 'at the base'. It was hostile to established Communist parties and to all organisational tendencies with bureaucratic implications.   (Shell 1970, 635–50)

For the leadership of the SPD parliamentary party the gulf between the extra-parliamentary opposition and the policy of the SPD in the Bundestag was greater than that between the SPD and CDU/CSU parliamentary parties. The strategy of the parliamentary party was to come to power through acceptance of the orthodoxies of the politics of the Bonn Republic whilst the extra-parliamentary opposition represented the German face of the generational politics of a transnational New Left.

There were six main areas of disagreement between the Extra-Parliamentary Opposition and the SPD leadership. Firstly, there was a profound gulf in their attitudes towards US foreign policy and their views of American policy in Vietnam. Public trust in the United States remained high in the Federal Republic and had been reinforced, especially for many younger West Germans, by the Kennedy presidency. Willy Brandt was the Foreign Minister of the Grand Coalition and the SPD strategy of demonstrating its fitness to govern necessarily entailed being seen to be regarded as reliable by the United States. It was also important for Brandt not to alienate the United States as he undertook his first cautious steps in 'Ostpolitik'. These considerations meant that the SPD leadership refused to condemn American policy in Vietnam and were concerned to keep the topic off the SPD's agenda. The APO were morally outraged both by American policy and the SPD's failure to condemn it.

Secondly, there were new major differences in attitudes towards the emergency laws. A precondition of the formation of the Grand Coalition was an undertaking by the SPD to accept a set of emergency laws after having opposed all previous drafts. The APO was opposed in principle to emergency laws which they took to be a symptom of a growing authoritarianism. The laws were also opposed by the German Trade Union Federation. This opposition was led by IG Metall, the Metal Workers' Union, and its charismatic leader, Otto Brenner, who were most concerned by the impact of emergency laws on the right to strike.

There were continuous demonstrations against the proposed emergency laws, culminating in the 'Sternmarsch' of 11 May 1968. A major weakness of the APO, however, was its inability to mount joint demonstrations with the trade unions who objected to some of the groups who were involved in the organisation of demonstrations like the 'Sternmarsch'.

The struggle against the emergency laws was a central theme of extra-parliamentary opposition in 1968. It was seen as a way of rejecting an authoritarian future as well as throwing off an authoritarian past. The laws were passed on the 30 May 1968 against the opposition of fifty-three members of the SPD parliamentary party.

Thirdly, the APO was bitterly opposed to the SPD's entry into the Grand Coalition. The decision to enter the Coalition in November 1966 was a severe shock to many party members. It was also a source of provocation to those further to the left of the SPD who would nevertheless normally vote for the SPD. The party leadership attempted to deflect opposition by calling two special conferences in

December 1966 and November 1967 to discuss the issue. This strategy proved inadequate as neither of these conferences had any powers of decision and the party leadership was put under considerable pressure to bring forward the date of the biennial conference and to have a retrospective vote on the question as to whether or not it had been right to enter the Grand Coalition. At the subsequent conference in Nürnberg in March 1968, a resolution critical of the decision to enter the Grand Coalition was only rejected by 147–143, and the subsequent party executive resolution in favour was only adopted by 173–129.

Such a narrow majority, especially in the year before a federal election, is almost unknown in the SPD and indicates the strength of feeling in the SPD against the entry into the Grand Coalition. This antagonism was very much stronger amongst ordinary party members and was universal in groups and individuals to the left of the SPD. The decision to enter into the Grand Coalition did pay off electorally for the SPD in 1969 but it did present the Federal Republic with its first test of legitimacy for a significant section of educated young West Germans.

Fourthly, there was widespread scepticism in the APO towards the concept of representative government, to which the SPD leadership and the bulk of SPD supporters were completely committed. This loyalty to representative government was a product of the failure of the more participatory Weimar Republic and the horrors of the Third Reich. It had been strengthened by the failure of the *Paulskirche* movement and the anti-nuclear movement *Kamfpf dem Atomtod* (see chapter 6).

Scepticism in the APO about the primacy of representative government was hardly surprising, given the creation of the Grand Coalition. There was far more enthusiasm in APO for strategies of confrontation and direct action. As the movement developed, disagreements surfaced about the utility of direct action, and its limits were stressed by Germany's leading social theorist, Jürgen Habermas, hitherto sympathetic to the APO, in a famous lecture in June 1968.

Fifthly there were sharp differences of perspectives towards political violence and the rules of the game. Although there were internal disagreements within the APO, they were prepared to envisage 'limited rule violation' and violence to property, if not to persons. The disagreement here with the main body of the SPD on acceptable means was a very profound one. The SPD had been badly scarred by the Weimar experience and the Third Reich. They were therefore totally opposed to the politics of violence and fiercely committed to the rules of the democratic game. They were thus particularly appalled by the revival in the context of the APO of '*Sprechchöre*' (slogan choirs) which reminded them sharply of the communists and Nazis of their traumatic past. Often what was seen as anti-authoritarian by the APO looked extremely authoritarian to SPD members with historical memories of the Weimar tragedy.

Willy Brandt, in general the most sympathetic of the SPD leadership to the goals of 1968, was appalled by a confrontation with young demonstrators at the 1968 Nürnberg Party Conference. 'I do not believe that quietness is the citizen's first duty: but it is the case that some people misuse freedom of opinion to establish intolerance and terror. One must see that and one must not accept it. The mob remains the mob even when it is composed of young faces.' (Cited in Schonauer 1982, 120.)

These disagreements were very obvious in relation to the Springer Press. Although the SPD disliked the policies of the Springer Press, which were markedly anti-socialist, it did not feel able to endorse the violent blockades of the Springer publishing houses initiated as a reaction to the attempted assassination of the student leader, Rudi Dutschke. There was also a difference of view in how to respond to the neo-Nazi party, the National Democratic Party. The SPD wanted to ignore it as much as possible and defeat it electorally. The APO wanted to defeat it on the streets.

Finally, the SPD's insistence on demarcation on the Left created insurmountable barriers against the APO. Patrolling the border with groups to its left both organisationally and ideologically has been a continual preoccupation of the postwar SPD. It was for instance one of the grounds for the Executive's decision to expel the SDS in 1960. This issue raised continual problems in this period. It led to the expulsion of the prominent SPD left-wingers, Ristock and Beck, from the SPD in Berlin in February 1968 for taking part in an anti-Vietnam demonstration in which non-SPD left-wing groups played a leading rôle. The participation of many SPD members in the so-called '*Sternmarsch*' on Bonn in May 1968 took place against the advice of the party leadership because of the involvement in its organisation of extra-SPD groups. SPD members who did participate carried placards around their necks pro-claiming 'Ich bin SPD-Mitglied' (I am an SPD member) to under-line the fact that they were breaking a taboo. This was one of the aspects of unorthodox Left politics that most disturbed the leadership of the SPD and the promulgation of the so-called

'*Radikalenerlass*' (radicals' decree) in January 1972 can reasonably be seen as their reaction.

The emergence and development of the Extra-Parliamentary Opposition had an immediate impact on the SPD, though it will be argued that it was its long-term significance that is the more important. Its immediate impact in 1968 was to harm the SPD electorally. The party leadership had expected the economic recovery from 1966 identified with Karl Schiller to benefit the SPD electorally and were particularly disappointed by the unexpectedly poor result of the *Land* election in Baden-Württemberg in April 1968 when the SPD vote declined from 37.3 per cent to 29 per cent. Baden-Württemberg is a state with a markedly high percentage of students and one lesson the party leadership drew from the result was that the SPD should attempt to absorb as many APO members as possible. This policy was identified with Willy Brandt. This preference of Brandt's conformed to his general long-term rôle of integrator and reconciler in the SPD. In this particular case it was also a product of reflection on his own experiences at the end of the Weimar Republic and of dialogue with his radical sons. Brandt signalled his policy of opening the party to the APO during the debate on the emergency laws. It was a policy which had fairly wide support in the Party Executive and even Karl Schiller was moved to declare: 'Come in – mit allen Euren Methoden' (with all your tactics).

In pursuit of this policy, the SPD held a special conference for youth in January 1969. The conference revealed a fair degree of misunderstanding and suspicion between the representatives of youth and the party leadership. The policy of attracting APO members into the SPD began to be very successful as APO itself had clearly run out of steam and in 1969 most APO adherents voted for SPD.

The generational character of APO meant that it had its greatest impact on the Young Socialist (JUSOs). The JUSOs have the status of a Working Group within the SPD and all SPD members under thirty-nine can participate, though many choose not to. The reconstruction of the party after 1945, largely on the basis of an ageing prewar membership, meant that there was a permanent need to recruit future younger and more active cadres. This task was largely entrusted to the JUSOs and they were outstandingly successful. All members of the Federal Executive of the Young Socialists between 1946 and 1967 later became Members of the Bundestag.

In line with their rôle as a recruiting agency for party cadres, the JUSOs had traditionally been fairly quiescent. Börnsen provides an illuminating insight into the general atmosphere in his quotation from the yearbook of the JUSO sub-district of Obertaunus, near Frankfurt: 'In 1965 representatives of the branch went to Bonn with the victorious pair from our last dancing competition. We were shown around the Bundestag by Comrade Kurt Gscheidle. We took part in a Bundestag debate as listeners. The day drew to a harmonious close over Kaffee and Kuchen.' Other activities during the year included an extended study of Moliere's 'La Malade Imaginaire' (with a theatre visit), a discussion about water supplies to the Obertaunus and a visit to the building site of the new Frankfurt metro (cited Börnsen 1969, 68).

This picture began to change with the decision to join the Grand Coalition. A number of JUSO branches took part in spontaneous demonstrations against this decision. The general climate inside the JUSOs altered quite rapidly in 1967/8. Feelings against the emergency laws ran very high among the JUSOs and, at their Congress in Frankfurt in May 1968, which coincided with the last stages of the legislative progress of the laws, they put Helmut Schmidt, as the representative of the Party Executive, under considerable pressure.

The Young Socialists also began to change at the local level. In terms of membership many supporters of APO who were not themselves SPD members, took part in JUSO activities. A survey carried out by the JUSO themselves at the end of 1968 indicated that in two-thirds of the branches a quarter of the JUSOs were not themselves members of the SPD. The change in JUSO activity was particularly visible in Frankfurt and Berlin. In Frankfurt local MDBs were visited in the middle of the night in the weeks before the decision on the emergency laws and asked to explain how they intended to vote. JUSOs started to contest the candidacies of sitting MDBs, for example, Karsten Voigt stood against Georg Leber, a well-known member of the SPD parliamentary party and a trade union leader.

The impact of the APO on the SPD was both profound and complex. The entry of the bulk of the APO into the SPD completed the radicalisation of the Young Socialists (JUSOs). In the early 1970s the JUSOs were to be the vehicle for the new issues that the former APO members brought with them. They were concerned above all with the issue of participation, with trying to infuse some life into the ostensibly participatory structures of the party, and with going beyond them by advocating the imperative mandate whereby representatives would be tied to the views of the ordinary members (the Basis).

The Netherlands The student movement had, arguably, an even greater impact on the PVDA, the Dutch Labour Party. Initially there was relatively little contact. The Dutch Labour Party, like its Belgian neighbour, was one of the most revisionist in western Europe and the leadership prided itself on its skill in practising the politics of accommodation. By contrast, Amsterdam in the 1960s was one of the leading centres of the student movement and the students formed a political grouping, the PROVOs, which was successful in gaining representation on the Amsterdam City Council. Their ideas on participatory democracy and self-realisation were even more important than those of the SDS and exerted a powerful pressure both on existing Dutch parties and Left opinion in Europe generally. The Dutch New Left emerged in this milieu rather than as a reaction to the invasion of Hungary. Almost all had a university education and worked in universities, research institutes, the media, social work or governmental bureaucracies. New Left was formed in 1966 but never constituted itself as a formally organised group within the PVDA, which was, in any case, forbidden by party statutes.

The party leadership came under intense pressure from the right wing which by 1968 had founded its own faction-Democratic Appeal, to expel the New Left. The PVDA was in a weak position, however, and losing votes to a number of anti-establishment parties, especially Democrats '66, which won 4.7 per cent of the vote in 1967. This weak electoral position of the PVDA and the danger that New Left might leave the party and compete electorally forced PVDA leaders to adopt a conciliatory stance towards New Left. The New Left could credibly contemplate leaving the PVDA given the very low threshold of electoral representation in Holland. New Left positions rapidly gained support within the PVDA and by 1969 nine out of the twenty-four members of the Party Executive were elected on the New Left ticket. The right-wing members of the party left to form a new party, Democratic Socialists '70 and the victory of the New Left was complete by the following year when it secured a majority on the Party Executive and its candidate became Party Chairman. New Left members by now constituted an increasing proportion of the parliamentary party.

The impact of the New Left victory on the PVDA has been well described by Stephen Wolinetz:

> The formal structure of the Party remains the same, yet the relations among leaders and followers are different. Party leaders are anything but authoritative. Imbued with a participatory ethos and suspicious of authority, PvdA members display an 'organised mistrust' of Party leaders,

and engage in persistent attempts to control and influence them. Party activists demand extensive programmatic commitments and insist that elected representatives render account of their actions and explain any deviations from previous commitments. Meetings at all levels are now open to all Party members, and the Party Council – formally an administrative body elected by regional federations, now serves as interim Party Congress in which ministers, parliamentary leaders and the Party Executive are called to account. Both the Party Council and the Party Congress have turned into participatory events in which delegates vent their feelings and leaders attempt to explain themselves.

(Wolinetz 1977, 361)

France The intellectual ferment associated with the student movement also had a crucial impact on developments in France. The transition to the Fifth Republic had a strongly adverse effect on the S.F.I.O. A group of SFIO militants left to form a new party, the PSA (later the PSU) when the veteran SFIO party leader, Guy Mollet, appeared to support de Gaulle's advent to power. The focus of the new regime was on the president. This posed particular problems for the Left which was factionalised and divided, and the SFIO set about building alliances. Its candidate, François Mitterrand, had the support of communists, socialists and radicals in the 1965 presidential election.

The Left was still highly factionalised, however. A great deal of energy was invested in political clubs. Former members of the PSU regrouped in the UCRG, founded by Alain Savary in 1964, and more orthodox Marxists constituted the core membership of Jean Popperen's UCGS. Most of the clubs participated in the Convention of Republican Institutions, founded by François Mitterrand in 1965 to underpin his presidential campaign.

Within the SFIO itself a group of left-wing intellectuals had constituted the CERES group. The founding members included Jean-Pierre Chevènement, Georges Sanne and Didier Motchane. François Mitterrand attempted to tie the whole ramshackle structure together by forming the FGDS after the presidential election of 1965.

The events of May 1968 had a major impact on these groups and rendered them extremely hostile to the SFIO which one activist described as the party of 'Suez, CRS [French para-military police and the anti-heroes of 1968] and centrism'.

The decision of the SFIO to nominate the strongly anti-communist, Gaston Defferre, as presidential candidate at its party conference in May 1969, without consulting other groups, further undermined its credibility and at the conference in Issy-Les-

Moulineaux in July 1969 most of the groups, now including Jean Popperen, combined to vote out Guy Mollet as Party Secretary and replace him by Alain Savary. At the ensuing Epinay conference in 1971 François Mitterrand became leader of the newly formed *Parti Socialiste.*

The student unrest in Paris in May 1968 had a catalytic effect on the Left. Its early success had demonstrated the vulnerability of the Gaullist regime, but de Gaulle's subsequent electoral triumph demonstrated the limits of a movement when confronted with an election. The old party machine of the SFIO was seen to be part of the problem and most of its prominent members played little part in the *Parti Socialiste.* It also had a galvanising effect on intellectuals whose contribution to the debate on the future of the Left in France was greatly influenced by their experience of 'the events'. In particular 'autogestion', the most significant French ideological contribution to democratic socialist theory, was transformed from an idea about the organisation and control of the productive process into a new theory of political democracy, stressing the autonomy of the individual and of society regulated by contractual relations rather than by the state.

THE REVIVAL OF FACTIONS

Max Weber drew a distinction between parties based on ideology and those based on patronage. Factionalism, he argued, is far more persistent and pervasive in ideological parties as groups struggle for control of the party programme. In patronage-based parties tendencies form around particular personalities, but they rarely have the durability of factions based on ideological division. The programmatic basis of social democratic parties has meant that factionalism has therefore always been a major problem for social democratic parties. Contrary to Weber's view, patronage has also often been associated with factionalism in social democratic parties. Social democracy invokes the exercise of patronage in the form of selective intervention in favour of particular groups, e.g. trade unions, council house tenants and welfare claimants and, unlike traditional individually based patronage, this group based patronage interacts with and reinforces factional struggles based on ideological differences. Not only then are social democratic parties more prone to faction, but they have felt themselves more disadvantaged by lack of unity. Bourgeois parties have often had strong support in the most important centres of power in the economy and society in general; they have also often been rich in financial resources. Lacking the resources of bourgeois parties, social democratic parties have, as we have seen, traditionally relied on the commitment of a mass membership, a commitment which is endangered by any threat to unity. This has resulted in social democratic parties traditionally devoting a great deal of attention to the problems posed by factions. When the leadership has been strong they have sometimes been able, as in Holland, to have factions banned by party statute, and all social democratic party statutes set out to discourage them, e.g. Article 4 of the Statutes of the French *Parti Socialiste* opposes the existence of 'organised tendencies'. Where factions have been too strong to be banned, as in the case of the British Labour Party and the SFIO in France, party leaders have had to devote an enormous amount of policy attention to the management of factions.

Factionalism in social democratic parties reached an early peak in the years leading up to the First World War, when the struggle in the SPD between the revisionists, headed by Eduard Bernstein, who wanted to bring the SPD's revolutionary programme in line with its reformist practice, and the Left, led by Karl Liebknecht and Rosa Luxemburg, who wished to change the reformist practice, absorbed the energies of the party leadership.

The division of European socialism into communist and social democratic parties after 1918 greatly reduced the intensity of the factional struggle inside social democratic parties and transferred it to the plane of inter-party rivalry with the communists. Factions did not die out, however, and they assumed an increasing importance as opinions diverged about how to respond to the challenge of Nazism. It was to prove a major weakness in the case of the Austrian Party. Factional struggle also persisted in the British case, where the Communist Party had failed to exert much attraction for the bulk of the Left who preferred to operate in either the Independent-Labour Party (ILP) or the Labour Party.

In the postwar period factions declined further in importance. They were still a notable feature in the French SFIO and the British Labour Party, but elsewhere they had declined in importance. In Austria, the Revolutionary Socialists were noticeable by their absence in the postwar party, and the two main lessons drawn from the 1930s were the desirability of avoiding intra-party conflict with the bourgeois forces and the necessity of party unity. More generally, the division of Europe into two camps and the unequivocal identification of social democratic parties with anti-communism greatly reduced the importance of the Left. Moreover, the Marxist tradition appeared to have lost much of its intellectual vitality and capacity to illuminate social developments.

These developments culminated in the wave of programmatic renewal at the end of the 1950s, of which the Bad Godesberg Programme (1959) of the SPD is the best example. The de-programming of most social democratic parties highlighted the weakness of the Left, who were unable either to mobilise support or to present a convincing alternative analysis. Britain is a partial exception here, but the failure of Britain to follow the Bad Godesberg route owed much more to the indirect structure of the party and the privileged position of the trade unions than to the strength of the left-wing faction, Tribune.

Contrary to expectations these changes did not mean the end of factionalism. The revival of the Marxist intellectual tradition in west European universities, together with the growth of a New Left and the experience of the student movement, was to transform the social democratic parties in the 1970s.

Germany – The Challenge of the Young Socialists

The main catalyst for change inside the SPD was the changing party membership after 1969. The failure of the Extra-Parliamentary Opposition and the break-up of the SDS, combined with SPD victory and the promises of reform identified with Willy Brandt, led to a vast influx of new members in the period after 1969. The demands of these new members were articulated by the Young Socialists.

The response of the party leadership to the challenge from the JUSOs was not to expel them, as they had done with the SDS, the SPD student organisation in 1960, but to attempt to integrate the JUSO into the party. This was done in two ways. Firstly, many JUSO activists were encouraged to become party functionaries, since the postwar veterans were nearing retirement. This often led them to align their views more closely to the mainstream of party opinion. More ambitiously, an attempt was made to involve the whole party in programmatic endeavour and to project the discussion about the Godesberg Programme into the future. At the Saarbrücken Conference of the party in 1970, a long-term programme commission was established to draw up a draft orientation programme for the years 1973–85. Although this commission was safely under the chairmanship of Helmut Schmidt, several JUSOs and left-wingers were given places on the commission.

Willy Brandt resigned as Chancellor in May 1974, but remained chairman of the SPD (Paterson, 1975). Helmut Schmidt had become Federal Chancellor, while Herbert Wehner remained leader of the *Bundestagsfraktion*. Initially this arrangement worked well and the late 1970s saw a marked diminution in the factional conflict which had plagued the Brandt years, and there was some revival of SPD fortunes after the trough of 1974.

The Young Socialists were unsuccessful in the goal of taking over the party at federal level. They were, however, very successful in displacing the established leadership of a large number of local parties, for example Munich and Frankfurt. (See Braunthal 1984). Thus local parties were deeply divided for a number of years as the right-wing members fought back.

Factionalism also emerged at a parliamentary level. The SPD parliamentary party has been dominated traditionally by a group of right-wing trade-unionist members, known as the *Kanalarbeiter*, an expression which corresponds to their self-image as 'the parliamentary navvies' who do all the necessary dull but unglamorous work. The Left in the parliamentary party organised initially in 1969 in the 16th Floor Group (of the then new parliamentary building) and then in the *Leverküsen circle* in 1972, which took its name from the town in which they met. There was no possibility of the Left taking over the parliamentary party, and the main objectives of the Left faction are to offer support to each other when defying the parliamentary whip, to try to move the parliamentary party some distance to the Left and to support left-wing candidates for parliamentary party posts. The organisation of a left-wing faction in the parliamentary party led the *Kanalarbeiter* to regroup themselves somewhat more tightly in the *H.J. Vogel circle*. The secure dominance of the Right, which was never seriously imperilled, has meant that, although factions have been active in the parliamentary party, there has been little or none of the very bitter factional strife which characterised relations inside local SPD organisations.

Factional strife within the party as a whole receded during the period after 1973. For a time the Left was, with some exceptions at the local level, on the defensive. It faced a West German electoral law which made secession apparently an unpromising alternative, since they would have to clear a 5 per cent threshold for representation. There was no evidence at that time that such a potential electorate existed in a country where suspicion of socialism remained rife. The slavish adherence of the DKP, the newly legalised

German Communist Party (1968), to the GDR rendered it an unattractive alternative. The narrow middle-class social basis and the overwhelmingly academic orientation of the Young Socialists had tended to cut them off from other members of the party. In contrast to the situation in Holland, the trade unionists in the party had taken an explicitly hostile line and the JUSOs never established a successful industrial base. Lastly, and perhaps most importantly, the onset of the world economic recession in 1973 deprived them of much of their potential support in the left-centre of the party and rendered much less attractive their pleas for zero growth.

Although West Germany was less affected directly by the 1973 recession, its psychological impact was threefold: it undermined the position of Willy Brandt's government, unable now to carry through the reforms which it had promised. Brandt was then replaced by Helmut Schmidt, who was preoccupied with the problems of the domestic economy rather than reform, and who was therefore unwilling to accord any priority to left-wing views. Secondly, with the change in the economy the job prospects of young people diminished and their radicalism, at least initially, tended to evaporate. Thirdly, the impact of economic recession correlated with a swing to the Right in the political system as a whole and a period of waning support for left-wing ideas in the party.

Factionalism in the British Labour Party

Factionalism has accompanied the British Labour Party throughout its history and this pattern has continued unabated throughout the postwar period. As in other social democratic parties factionalism has been most identified with the Left of the party. The Left was fairly well represented in the Attlee government of 1945–50 and the Left faction which emerged in 1947 'the Keep Left' group had only twenty members in the Parliamentary Labour Party (PLP) and posed few real problems for the Labour leadership.

However, resignation of the Minister of Health, Aneurin Bevan, in April 1951 ushered in a period of serious conflict. Bevan had resigned when the Chancellor of the Exchequer, Hugh Gaitskell, proposed that charges be introduced for false teeth and spectacles. Bevan's resignation was followed by those of Harold Wilson and John Freeman. Out of government, Bevan became the leader of a formidable faction which was much helped by its control of the weekly *Tribune*. The Bevanites, as they quickly came to be called, were numerically well represented in parliament and commanded the allegiance of the majority of constituency activists. They were strongly opposed to west German rearmament, an issue on which even many NATO supporters in the Labour Party had ambivalent views, and the issue was only finally resolved in favour of the leadership at the Scarborough Party Conference in 1954.

This victory for the party leadership reflected a decline in the influence of the Bevanites since the heady days of 1951/2. As in other social democratic parties, factionalism coexisted with a strong desire for party unity and many in the centre of the Parliamentary Labour Party, often referred to as 'the Keep Calmers', were alienated by the Bevanites' habit of not voting in accordance with PLP decisions after they had been defeated in internal PLP votes. Bevan was, in any case, a mercurial and contradictory figure who had some difficulty in keeping the Bevanites together. By 1956 he had begun to move closer to Hugh Gaitskell, who had defeated him to become leader of the Labour Party in 1955. In 1958 at the Party Conference, Bevan alienated most of his supporters by supporting the British independent nuclear deterrent, and a new faction, 'Victory For Socialism', was formed. Bevan died in 1960.

After Bevan's death the main Left faction in the Parliamentary Labour Party has been known as the Tribune Group. Its influence rose after the loss of the 1970 election and it provided an influential platform for the propagation of the Alternative Economic Strategy. This strategy was designed to address what the Left perceived as the two major problems of the British economy: a declining rate of investment and the dominance of multinational firms. The plan envisaged selective import controls and planning agreements with the hundred leading companies.

The Tribunites have remained an important force in the Parliamentary Labour Party, but since 1982 the Left has been divided in parliament. Neil Kinnock and a number of other prominent members of the Tribune Group failed to support Tony Benn, the Left's candidate for the Deputy Leadership in 1981, and since then a distinction has been made between the hard and the soft Left, with the Tribune Group being counted as the soft Left and the Campaign Group as the hard Left.

The Right in the Labour Party had rarely felt the need to organise since the party was normally run by an alliance of right-wing trade union leaders and the leadership of the Parliamentary Labour Party. One exception to this was the Campaign for Democratic Socialism formed in 1960 to support Gaitskell's views. It was, however, an extra-parliamentary organisation and never enjoyed his official endorsement. This relationship began to fray in the 1970s as the trade unions became increasingly difficult to manage from the centre and a new generation of left-wing trade union leaders took over the major unions. In 1974 the Right in the Parliamentary Labour Party formed the Manifesto Group to contain what they saw as pressure from the left in the party. The Manifesto Group was extremely successful as an electoral machine for posts in the Parliamentary Labour Party and government, but the gradual exhaustion of the classic reformist position à la Crosland ensured that they had relatively little impact on wider arguments. The Manifesto Group was flanked from 1977 by the extra-parliamentary group, Campaign for a Labour Victory. In practice, CLV was dominated by its parliamentary members and never really succeeded in establishing a mass basis. It was disbanded in 1981 when a majority of its committee supported the Limehouse Declaration of the nascent Social Democratic Party, which was led by four of the best-known figures on Labour's Right: Roy Jenkins, Shirley Williams, David Owen and Bill Rodgers. The Manifesto Group was finally wound up in 1982. Those on the right of the Labour Party who remained loyal formed a new grouping, Labour Solidarity, which campaigned for Denis Healey as Deputy Leader of the Labour Party. Later it petered out.

The changing social composition of social democratic parties and the problem of identity

The social democratic party in its classic form as a 'solidarity community' had a clearly identifiable social profile. It was a party based on the skilled and unionised working class, with the ideal typical member being a metalworker. This profile had always been subject to change but in the last twenty years the pace of change has accelerated markedly as the service sector has expanded rapidly in all the advanced industrial societies of western Europe. In a party model where the mass membership plays a key rôle in electoral mobilisation, changes in the size and social composition of the social democratic parties have important implications for the direction and effectiveness of the parties.

Scandinavia In the early postwar years the Scandinavian parties enjoyed a member/voter ratio which was only rivalled in Austria. In the intervening period the membership for the Danish Party

declined sharply after 1960, with a slight recovery after 1973. There
was also a decline in party membership in Finland from 1948 until
1962, when it started to rise again. The decline in Norway began in
1945, but is not as steep as in Denmark, and the Swedish social
democrats actually increased membership significantly from 1960.
The Swedish and, to a much lesser extent, the Norwegian party are
still in a position to exercise a social democratic hegemony.

Table 2.1 Party Membership: Scandinavia.

Country	Party	Year	Membership
Denmark	Social Democrats	1960	259,459
		1970	177,507
		1974	122,822
		1975	122,394
		1976	123,140
		1980	c. 125,000
Finland	Social Democrats	1976	101,727
Norway	The Norwegian	1960	165,096
	Labour Party	1970	155,254
		1974	130,489 (lowest)
		1979	158,724
		1980	153,507
Sweden	Social Democratic	1960	801,000
	Labour Party	1970	890,000
		1973	967,000
		1975–6	1,100,000

Source Paterson and Thomas 1986, p.87

There is a great deal of data on the changing nature of the
electoral support for the Scandinavian social democratic parties but
little on the changing character of the party membership. The
provisions for trade union affiliation in the Swedish and Norwegian
cases would suggest that the trend away from a working-class base is
less marked than in many other European parties.

Britain The member/voter ratio has always been much lower in
Britain, unless one counts as members those who are affiliated
through the affiliation of their trade union. Individual membership
of the Labour Party increased from 191,045 in 1945 to 1,013,022 in
1952. It then declined steadily until it reached 277,000 in 1981. The

steady erosion of union membership after 1979 has also adversely affected the number of affiliated members. This declining membership of the Labour Party was evidence of a weakening penetration of British society, and mirrored the party's ineffective response to the challenges of the Thatcher government.

The social composition of the party has also changed. A study conducted in Sheffield in the early eighties (Chandler et al; 1982) indicated that party members are drawn disproportionately from the middle class and specifically from the public sector concentrated in education and social work.

France The old French Socialist Party, the SFIO, was always something of an exception. Membership was always low. It fell from a post-liberation high point of 355,000 in 1964 to 70,000 by 1965. The membership of the PS was 170,000 in 1979. The social composition of the French Socialist Party has always been much less clearly based on the working class than its northern sister parties, and the changes, although marked, have been correspondingly less dramatic.

In 1951 working-class members accounted for only two-fifths of the total membership, a proportion which had halved by 1973. Two-thirds of the members in that year were from a lower-middle-class background and 20 per cent were in various professional and managerial categories. In the following year, out of 4,700 new members of the Paris Federation, only seventy were working-class.

Table 2.2 Social Composition of Membership of the French Socialist Party 1951–73

	1951 (%)	1970 (%)	1973 (%)
Business, managerial and professional	3	15	20
Farming, shop-keeping,lower managerial and clerical	53	61	61
Workers	44	23	19

Source M. Kesselman, 'The Recruitment of Rival Party Activists', *Journal of Politics*, February 1973 (cited in Bell and Criddle 1988, 200).

Germany While data on the membership of other social democratic parties is fragmentary and impressionistic, the SPD has always kept very detailed membership records, including details of occupational background. SPD membership reached a peak of 875,000 in 1947. It then declined steadily till the end of the 1960s. Between 1968 and 1976 party membership expanded from 732,000 to a postwar peak of 1,020,000. It has now stabilised at approximately one million members. There was marked change during this period in the social background of new members. In 1958 over one half of new members had a working-class occupation, by 1982 scarcely one-fifth of new members were manual workers.

Table 2.3 New SPD party members by occupation 1958–82

	1958	1966	1972	1982
White-collar employees and civil servants	21.0	27.5	34.0	33.1
Manual workers	55.0	49.4	27.6	21.5
Housewives	11.2	9.0	9.0	13.7
Pensioners	5.4	4.1	3.7	9.2
Students	n/a	n/a	15.9	12.8

Source Susanne Miller, *Die SPD vor und nach Godesberg* (Neue Gesellschaft, Bonn, 1974) and *SPD Jahrbuch 1981–1983* (SPD, Bonn, 1984).

The new members of the SPD were much better educated than their predecessors. Of new members in the 1970s, 22 per cent had the ABITUR (A-level equivalent) as compared with the mid-1950s, when over 91 per cent had received only the most basic school education (Kolinsky 1984, 79). The social composition of these new entrants indicated changes in West German society. Although a very clear majority were in middle-class occupations, an equally clear majority came from working-class backgrounds and had risen socially (Kolinsky 1984, 77). Not surprisingly these new entrants were, as has already been noted (see The challenge of the Young Socialists), to cause considerable problems for the party leadership. However, despite a period of turbulence and the almost complete failure of the generation of '68 (as we shall call them for convenience) to change the policy priorities of the SPD leadership, they were very successful in gaining office in the SPD itself. Of the party office-holders in 1977, 58 per cent had joined the party within the preceding decade and only one in ten office-holders had been a member of the party since 1950 (Kolinsky 1984, 81). Party office-holders were much more clearly middle-class than the membership of the party and an even larger gulf separated them from those who normally vote for the party.

Traditionally an important function of the SPD organisation was to provide an avenue for working-class participation in politics. The markedly middle-class character of party office-holders implies that this is much less the case than formerly. Office-holders with working-class occupations now typically occupy the less important positions such as *Beisitzer* (alternates),(Kolinsky 1984, 82).

A recent investigation of two neighbouring party branches in the Ruhr town of Mülheim sheds some interesting light on this. One branch was located near the Mannesmann steel plant. It was dominated by the Right and had a high proportion of members with a working-class background. In this branch, office-holders were typically trade union functionaries, an aristocracy of labour, rather than ordinary shop-floor workers. The city-centre branch was dominated by civil servants, students and people not working in manufacturing industries. In both branches advancement for ordinary working people was blocked.

The Netherlands　The change in the social composition of the Dutch party was very close to that of the SPD with an even more marked change towards public sector caring occupations. At the 1978 party conference of the PVDA 90 per cent of the delegates were of middle or upper-class background and 47 per cent worked in the public sector. Fifty-eight per cent of the delegates had undergone some form of higher education or professional training as compared with only 10 per cent of PVDA voters (Middel and Van Schurr 1981, 244).

Southern Europe　The southern European socialist parties have always been more middle class, reflecting a divided Left and the much smaller concentration of heavy industry. The Spanish party differs from the others in having a higher proportion of blue-collar members, but even here the delegates and office-holders are overwhelmingly white-collar and professional (Hine 1986, 95). They are also increasingly from the public sector as the southern European parties in government place their own nominees in the administration.

THE PASSING OF THE SOLIDARITY COMMUNITY

The concept of the 'solidarity community' of the social democratic party is now more or less extinct. It comes closest to surviving in Sweden but elsewhere it is alive only in the sense that amputees can experience pain in limbs that they no longer have. In Denmark the party organisation is dying, both figuratively and literally.'Today party clubs cater primarily to old-age pensioners (bingo games and coffee) and, once the old-generation members die, so will the clubs'(Esping-Andersen 1985, 118). Knut Heidar's analysis of the Norwegian Labour Party is almost universally true.

> Today there is very little left of the 'special character' of the Labour Party. The vitality previously found at its grass roots is no longer impressive. Its declining membership – as in other parties – prefer television at home to party education in the town hall. At the same time the party culture is still marked by old traditions. The prime minister remembers her days in the children groups organised by the movement. The old labour songs are sung at meetings. Every party Congress still – to some embarrassment of the delegates – ends with the first verse of the International, although to their relief they then immediately change to the first verse of the national anthem   *(Heidar 1989)*

The erosion of the social identity of the social democratic parties has led to the loss of that remarkable fit between structures and members' aspirations. The newer academically educated members feel frustrated by what they see as the too limited opportunities for participation and by the social functions performed by party meetings. Working-class members on the other hand feel alienated by an academic and abstract discourse which they can no longer relate to their immediate experience at the work place.

The consequences of the decay of social democratic party organisational networks has been starkly summarised by Esping-Andersen:

> The importance of party organisation for electoral mobilization and party vitality cannot be ignored. It works two ways. On the one hand, it promotes political mobilization. It may also help avert splits, cleavages, and fragmentation. Powerful organisation affects broad solidarity, which in turn will be decisive when the party's politics are under strain – as in the EEC debate in Norway and Denmark. Where the party's organisational apparatus has collapsed, issue differences and ideological splits will more readily translate into zero-sum confrontations, precisely because the party will have no framework within which controversies can be debated and differences reconciled. Instead, splits are more likely to produce defections and alienation or, alternatively, a more authoritarian leadership style.   *(Esping-Andersen 1985,–120)*

The struggle for inner-party democracy

The internal structure and the party statutes of all west European social democratic parties represent an aspiration to realise inner-party democracy. A developing tension between the formal commitment to participatory democracy and actual practice had become apparent before 1914 and was brilliantly characterised by Robert Michels as 'the Iron Law of Oligarchy', i.e. whatever the formal structure, power and influence accrue to the leadership group.

The participation of social democratic parties on government and the high value accorded to unity and solidarity in the labour movement strengthened the position of the party leadership *vis-à-vis* the members in the decades after the First World War. Inner-party democracy did not die out completely. The need for legitimation by party conferences did constrain the party leadership, and occasionally party conference would, on particularly controversial issues, overturn leadership policy, but this was relatively unusual and there was no guarantee that party conference decisions would be binding on the party in government. Policy decisions were made by a small leadership group. The situation is very well described by Knut Heidar in relation to the Norwegian Labour Party:

> In the memoirs of key figures within Labour during the 1950s and 1960s, there emerges a pattern of highly centralized decision-making. 'Some of us have been talking together' was the expression most often used by the Prime Minister and Party Leader, Einar Gerhardsen, when important issues were introduced e.g. in the Central Committee – a sure sign there was no need for further discussion. The 'some of us' were generally the prime minister's most trusted ministers, the party secretary, the leader of the trade union movement and the editor of the central Labour paper.
>
> *(Heidar 1989, 5)*

The Netherlands   This situation began to change in the late 1960s. The change came first and most completely to the Dutch party. 'Prior to 1966, the PVDA in Holland was a democratically constituted organization, but one in which leaders led and followers followed...' (Wolinetz 1977, 361).

The triumph of the New Left made a dramatic difference to the way in which the party conference operated. Until 1967 the conference agenda was very largely determined by the party leaders, who invariably prevailed in debate. The time available for the leadership has been dramatically curtailed and the number of resolutions has greatly increased.

Germany   As the social composition of party members altered and those who had experienced the student movement joined the social democratic parties, demands for more open and participatory structures spread. The entry of former members of the APO into the SPD after 1969 greatly increased the pressures for inner-party democracy. They pressed for the operation of 'the imperative mandate'. This would have meant that delegates to any of the higher party bodies and to parliament would be controlled by those who elected them. If they wanted to diverge from a position that they had been mandated to represent, they would have to secure a new mandate from 'the basis'. Such a notion, while clearly close to the ideas of participation implicit in the organisational structure of the SPD was unwelcome to the party leadership and was held to conflict with the constitution in relation to parliamentary deputies.

Although the idea of the imperative mandate was defeated, many more critical resolutions are put forward at party conferences and newer members of the parliamentary party are much less ready to adopt the convention that, once defeated at an internal parliamentary party meeting, the defeated faction votes together with the victorious group in the ensuing parliamentary vote.

Britain   The attempt to realise inner-party democracy in the British Labour Party was shaped by the nature of the special relationship with the trade unions. The parliamentary leadership of the Labour Party had been insulated from the pressure of the party activists by the trade union bloc vote. An alliance between the parliamentary leadership and the largest unions would guarantee victory at the party conference. This arrangement began to break down in the 1970s. The unions themselves became much less amenable to leadership control and the union leadership were often unable to deliver their part of the bargain. The leadership of the large unions, most notably the TGWU (Transport and General Workers' Union), was also noticeably to the left of previous positions, and to the left of the parliamentary leadership. The erosion of the party leadership/trade union axis greatly strengthened the chorus for party democracy by making it much more difficult for the party leadership to prevail at conference. Those who wanted to reduce the autonomy of the parliamentary leadership concentrated on three issues: a mandatory reselection of MPs, the election of the party leader and the formation of the manifesto.

Mandatory reselection challenged a practice that, once adopted, a British Labour MP enjoyed complete security of tenure. This had long been a source of concern to the Left in the party since security of tenure was seen to have the effect of insulating the sitting MP from party pressure; in the absence of which his devotion to realising party goals tended to be sacrificed in the interest of making a wider electoral appeal.

In the 1950s the National Executive Committee, dominated by an alliance of the parliamentary leadership and a number of right-wing union leaders, regularly intervened to protect right-wing MPs in difficulties with Bevanite-dominated constituency parties. In the 1970s the NEC changed its policy and restricted its intervention in selection matters to safeguarding the party's procedures rather than protecting the security of tenure of sitting MPs.

The campaign for Labour Party democracy was launched in 1973. It was originally a movement of the traditional Left outraged by the refusal of Harold Wilson to accept a conference resolution in favour of the nationalisation of Britain's twenty-five largest companies. It quickly took up the theme of reselection of sitting MPs by local parties to ensure that MPs were accountable to local party activists, with a clear threat of deselection for those who lost activist support.

The issue of reselection at first divided the parliamentary-based Tribune Left from the extra-parliamentary Left, who were unsympathetic to the concept of the rights of the sitting MP. It failed to gain conference support in 1974, but there were some well-publicised cases in 1976, when sitting MPs were deselected by their constituency parties. There was a notable battle in Newham North-East when a Trotskyite-dominated local party attempted to deselect Reg Prentice, a Labour Cabinet Minister. The attempt failed, but the general case for mandatory reselection was strengthened by Prentice's action in resigning from the Cabinet and crossing the floor to join the Conservatives in October 1977. After a series of conference battles, reselection was adopted at the 1979 Brighton conference. Contrary to expectations, the change did not lead to a wholesale war of attrition against the Right in the PLP, and the Shadow Cabinet at the beginning of the 1990s was in fact dominated by figures on the centre and right of the party.

Between 1979 and 1981 there was a series of conference battles over control of the election manifesto. Election manifestos are agreed at a joint meeting of the NEC and the parliamentary leadership. The Labour Party Constitution lays down that party conference resolutions which have been passed by a two-thirds majority should form part of the manifesto subject to a veto by the party leader (Clause V, Section 2). In 1974 Harold Wilson made extensive use of the veto, and control of the manifesto became part of the party democracy debate. The debate was further exacerbated by Prime Minister James Callaghan's use of Clause V, Section 2 to exclude a whole range of policies, one of which was the abolition of the House of Lords.

Ultimately Michael Foot was able to defeat the challenge in 1981, though only after a last-minute change of vote by one large union (USDAW, the shop-workers' union).

A third of the conflict issues concerned control over the selection of the party leadership. The Campaign for Labour Party Democracy failed in its first effort in 1978 to have the party leader selected by an electoral college of MPs, trade unions and constituency parties, rather than simply by the Parliamentary Labour Party. However, a National Executive Committee proposal to alter the constitutional position of the leader, from leader of the parliamentary party to party leader, was adopted; a change which logically implied participation by the whole party in the choice of the leader. The next three years were dominated by argument over the terms on which this would be based. The 1979 conference decisively rejected the idea of an electoral college. In 1980 the electoral college concept was adopted but there was no agreement on the weightings to be accorded MPs, unions and constituency parties.

The way in which the party was to participate in the election of the party leader was decided at a special conference at Wembley in January 1981. The National Executive Committee had endorsed the idea of a 33/33/33 split before the conference. Most MPs favoured 50 per cent (MPs), 25 per cent (unions), 25 per cent (constituency parties). David Owen, Bill Rodgers and Shirley Williams argued in favour of one member, one vote. This would have excluded the union block vote and the vote of the Parliamentary Labour Party, but would have taken away the vote of what they considered to be unrepresentative constituency delegates in favour of a decision by all party members. At the Wembley Conference the universal ballot received derisory support and the conference adopted an USDAW resolution for a 30/40/30 split in which the unions were dominant.

The importance of this decision was soon obvious. It precipitated the departure of Williams, Rodgers and Owen from the Labour Party. It also proved exceedingly damaging in the subsequent election for deputy leader, when a number of the major trade unions failed to cast their votes in the way their members had indicated when they were consulted.

The advances made by extra-parliamentary groups in the campaign for inner-party democracy reflected a loss of authority and capacity by the party leadership, not only to dictate the terms on which the electoral struggle would be conducted but actually to control party life. In the first two decades after 1945, Transport House (Labour Party Headquarters) would intervene frequently in constituency affairs and imposed strict conditions for membership eligibility.

This began to change in the late 1960s with the movement of former Bevanites, such as Richard Crossman, into positions of power as Leader of the House. Ron Hayward, who became National Agent in 1969 and General Secretary in 1972 was the first incumbent of these posts not to be identified with the Right of the party. Perhaps even more importantly, the character of the trade union leaders on the National Executive Committee had changed as the unions became much less easy to control. The new generation of union leaders, such as Jack Jones and Hugh Scanlon, were often on the Left themselves, and they were much less ready to unite with the parliamentary leadership to discipline the Left. The National Executive Committee abandoned its strict monitoring of parliamentary candidates and curtailed its rôle in the review of deselection of sitting MPs to cases of procedural irregularity. Even more controversially, it virtually abandoned its control of membership eligibility. The easing of these rules made it relatively easy for members of Trotskyite groups to enter the Labour Party and a major theme in the 1980s concerned the attempts by the party leadership to deal with the most prominent of those groups, the Militant Tendency. In dealing with Militant the party leadership was constrained by three factors. Throughout the bulk of the 1980s the Left and Right on the National Executive Committee were fairly evenly balanced. The Left at all levels of the party were against the application of disciplinary sanctions to Militant. Party activists (see section on social composition, pp 91–2) were very resistant to central discipline.

> They [the party activists] lacked the reverence for established authority and the instinctive Party loyalism which had typified earlier generations of solidaristic members. One effect of this was to weaken the power and influence of Regional Organisations, who now lost advantages they had formerly enjoyed as they increasingly had to deal with an educated, articulate and politically more sophisticated membership.
>
> *(Shaw 1989, 299)*

The increasing intervention of the courts in the internal affairs of the party further reduced the freedom of movement of the party leadership.

The National Executive Committee had attempted to ban the Militant Tendency in June 1982 by proposing a 'Register of non-affiliated Groups to be recognised and allowed to operate within the party' after the Hayward-Hughes report had suggested that Militant was in conflict with Clause II, Section 3 of the Labour Party Constitution. The Militant leadership was able to counter this in October 1982 by pointing out that in a number of judgements, especially that of the Pembroke High Court, the courts had suggested that such devices offended against natural justice.

Gradually, however, the tide began to turn. The change of leadership from Michael Foot to Neil Kinnock was an important precondition. Kinnock had not supported Tony Benn in his bid to become deputy leader of the party in 1981, and the Left was increasingly divided between the soft and hard factions. The Labour defeat in 1983 concentrated attention on the electoral battle and Militant was seen as an electoral handicap. By the mid-1980s the actions of the Liverpool City Council had done much to undermine the credibility of Militant, and Neil Kinnock felt strong enough to stage a furious denunciation of Militant at the 1985 party conference.

From 1986 onwards the party executive acted decisively against the Militant Tendency. In 1986 a large number of prominent Militant adherents were expelled from the Labour Party. After the 1987 election the NEC launched a three-pronged offensive. Several Militant-dominated constituency parties were suspended. Selection procedures for parliamentary candidates were tightened up and funds to the Labour Party Young Socialists (a Militant stronghold) were cut.

By the late 1980s, the parliamentary leadership, which had lost much of its autonomy in the early part of the decade, had recovered its authority and capacity to act both in determining the party agenda and the control of internal party life.

THE SOUTHERN EUROPEAN PARTIES

The broad thrust of development in the Northern European parties in the 1970s and 1980s had been to restore a greater congruity between party statutes and actual practice in the direction of member sovereignty. Southern European socialist parties have been associated, since the time of Marx, with weak leadership, pervasive factionalism and their party statutes have conferred a very broad rôle on the party membership. This historic dichotomy of strong leadership/pliant membership in Northern Europe and weak leadership/assertive factionalised membership in southern Europe has largely been reversed in the 1980s.

The personalisation of party leadership

Greece The change towards a dominant personalised leadership was most pronounced in the case of the Greek Socialist Party between 1974-89. Papandreou was the uncontested leader of the Greek Socialist Party when the Colonels' regime collapsed in 1974, but faced a crisis in 1975 when the central committee rejected his view that subordinate party bodies should be nominated by him rather than being elected. Papandreou dissolved the Central Committee and expelled those party members who had refused to bow to his wishes. From then on until 1989 his authority was dominant and individuals were expelled without normal party procedures; the press simply being informed that 'the individual has placed himself outside our movement' (Featherstone 1987, 239).

Spain The battle was far more protracted in the case of the Spanish Socialist Party. Felipe Gonzàlez, who became leader in 1974, suffered several revenues at the hands of the so-called *sector critico*, headed by Castellano and Gomez Llorente. The decisive break came in 1979 when Gonzàlez was at odds with a number of leading party members on the issue of instituting changes through the press without reference to party procedures. Gonzàlez resigned after the May party conference, where he had tried to secure backing for his proposal that the party end its formal adherence to Marxist principles. Gonzàlez was the major electoral asset of the PSOE, however, and after the sector critico (the Left) was decisively defeated at an extraordinary conference in September 1979, Gonzàlez returned. His dominance was made totally secure by his electoral victory in 1982, and he was able to secure Spanish membership of NATO against the strongly expressed opposition of party activists.

Portugal In Portugal Mario Soares initially dominated the party and he derived immense authority from his rôle in founding the party and his skill in steering the party through the revolutionary period of 1974-6. Soares stepped down as party leader in 1980 and returned in 1981, but without the undisputed authority that Gonzàlez exercised in Spain. Since then he has operated as the leader of the majority faction rather than monolithic leader of the party.

Italy The personalised style of Bettino Craxi's leadership of the Italian party led many to dub him Benito Craxi. Craxi led the majority 'reformist' faction in the PSI which won 70 per cent of the votes at the Palermo Conference in 1981, but it was only after he became prime minister in 1983 that his dominance of the party became complete. In 1984 at the Verona Conference the party dispensed with any election and simply acclaimed him as leader. Claudia Martelli, the party Vice Secretary, declared in a 1987 interview: 'I check with Craxi first, then make the speech and afterwards confront the party. I have learned from Craxi that if you give a lead then others will follow' (*Financial Times*, 23 May 1987).

The decline of membership sovereignty in southern Europe

The erosion of membership sovereignty in southern European parties can largely be explained by eight main factors.

Firstly, the strength of the personalities of the major leaders and their electoral appeal. Secondly, there is the question of political culture. Public expectations in southern Europe are geared to a heroic style of political leadership, which militated against those who argued for collective leadership. The experience of clandestine activity and exile was a third factor which strengthened the appeal of unity behind the leader. Most important, perhaps, was the fact that these parties, unlike their northern European sister parties, were in government during this period. The leadership position is almost inevitably strengthened when the party is in government and this was heightened by the fact that governments in southern Europe enjoy considerable powers of political patronage, e.g. at the PSOE's 1988 conference 70 per cent of the delegates either held elective office or were employed in the administration.

Fourthly, the party leaders made extensive use of public broadcasting to appeal directly to the voters. The electoral systems are a fifth factor which works in favour of the leadership. They are based on party lists of candidates who are chosen by the central leadership. Party financing also helps the leaders since only a very small proportion comes from individual party members. From the mid-1970s there was considerable support from northern European parties, especially the SPD, which remained largely at the disposal of the leader. The main source of support is now state subsidies, which again remain largely under the control of the party leadership.

All these factors taken together enabled the party leaders to transform the internal life of these parties. Hardliners were expelled, especially in Greece, Spain and Portugal. Conferences changed to acting as a forum for the projection of a personalised leadership. There was by now little consideration given to local branch resolutions and discussion revolved around the leader's set-piece speech and the leader himself would normally only appear at the conference to deliver his speech. Papandreou extended this practice to meetings of the Central Committee.

CONCLUSION

Social democratic parties in western Europe have traditionally been distinguished from bourgeois parties in terms of ideology, organisational form and social base. The traditional social democratic organisation with its high membership ratios provided a solid financial backing for political action. Even more importantly, they constituted an extremely potent instrument for party propaganda and electoral mobilisation. Where the party was dominant in an area or a state the mass membership provided the basis of a social democratic 'hegemony' in society at large.

> Where the party sustains a large army of militants, it can also rely on their ability to penetrate local communities and imbue them with the spirit of social democracy. This task is further aided by the movement's ability to saturate society with sister organisations such as culture centres, educational institutions, cooperatives and various associations that represent group interests.   (Esping-Andersen 1985, 120)

In most accounts of the historical development of social democratic parties, attention is focused on ideological changes reflected in terms of changing party programmes. Registering change in internal party life and social composition require a much more diffuse research strategy. In the immediate postwar period the classic social democratic parties had changed only marginally in organisation and social make-up from their origins over half-a-century before. Changes at the ideological level symbolised by the Bad Godesberg Programme, predated really major changes in social composition and party organisation. But the dominant theme of this chapter has been that changes in social composition and party organisation have been at least as dramatic as the more obvious changes in ideology and that social democratic parties have lost much of their distinctive character along these dimensions as well. This lack of distinctiveness has been heightened by changes in its historic rival on the Left. In the course of the late 1970s most west European communist parties followed the lead set by the Italian Communist Party (PCI) and rejected their authoritarian part in favour of Eurocommunism. More threateningly, given that communist parties have been declining as an electoral force, has been the rise of Green and alternative parties which have generally incorporated a very ambitious version of the concept of member sovereignty into their organisational structures. This has proved to be a major alternative pole of attraction to the highly educated and critical younger generations that social democrats have traditionally looked on as their own.

CHAPTER THREE

The Electoral History of Social Democracy

SOCIAL DEMOCRACY AND THE ELECTORAL ROUTE

Universal suffrage in western Europe was attained only in the interwar period but there had been a major extension of suffrage at the end of the nineteenth century. The emergence of the classic social democratic parties coincided with this extension of the franchise but their attitude towards electoral participation was at first ambivalent.

A motion to the Swedish Social Democratic Workers' Party Conference in 1890 for instance declared 'Since Sweden's Social Democratic Workers' Party is a propaganda party i.e. it considers its main objective to be the dissemination of information about Social Democracy, and since participation in elections is a good vehicle for agitation the Congress recommends participation' (Tingsten 1973, 357).

This ambivalence towards electoral participation reflected deep-rooted inhibitions about participating in government within the context of capitalist economic systems. In this early period most European socialists would have agreed with the characterisation of their view presented by Przeworski and Sprague.

'Participation in electoral politics is necessary if the movement for socialism is to find mass support among workers, yet this participation appears to obstruct the attainment of final goals.'

(Przeworski and Sprague 1986, 19)

The minority view, best articulated by Eduard Bernstein and the revisionists in the German party, was much more unequivocally in favour of electoral and governmental participation since tangible progress for the groups represented by the social democrats was much more important for them than 'the final goals'. Socialism for Bernstein was simply 'democracy brought to its logical conclusion'.

Although 'the solidarity community' (Chapter 2) served goals which transcended the electoral battle, it was very effective as an organisational form in mobilising the manual working class which in the classic industrial societies of western Europe grew to comprise approximately a quarter of the adult population in the years before 1914. This was reflected in a steadily increasing share of the vote best exemplified by the SPD whose share rose from 19.7 per cent in 1890 to 34.8 per cent in 1912. These spectacular electoral advances weakened the inhibitions about electoral participation and most socialists began to believe that they could come to power by the electoral route and would indeed constitute natural governing parties as the proletariat continued to expand.

The split in the socialist world after the Soviet Revolution of 1917 into communist and social democratic parties reflected, among other differences, a sharply divergent estimate of the route to power. The communists expected to have to use force to take over the reins of power in capitalist societies, while the social democrats believed that power would be attained through the ballot box.

The interwar period

The social democratic parties after 1918 had a much more unequivocal attitude to electoral participation than their prewar predecessors and were optimistic about the chances of attaining an absolute majority and thus being able to rule alone. In practice this goal largely eluded them. A central assumption shared by all the parties was that the manual working class would continue to expand as a proportion of the adult population; that it already constituted, and would always constitute, a majority of the electorate and that the socialist parties as articulators of the interests of that class would be the electoral beneficiaries of the majority position of the manual working class.

The central assumption was in fact incorrect. The proletariat had not been, and never in fact became, a numerical majority in any of the industrialised societies of western Europe.

'The proportion of the population manually employed as wage earners in industrial activities at no time surpassed 50 per cent in any country. Even if agricultural workers are added to this group, the proportion of the workers in the adult population never approached one half in the four countries for which detailed information on the class structure can be reconstructed – Sweden, France, Denmark, Belgium'.

(Przeworski and Sprague 1986, 34).

The percentage of workers in the electorate typically declined in the interwar period with the extension of the franchise to women voters.

'Since workers and adult dependants of workers were typically more numerous among males than were workers and dependants among women, the effect of extending the suffrage was always adverse to the workers' share of the electorate.'   *(Przeworski and Sprague 1986, 37).*

There were two other obstacles to a strategy of securing an electoral majority through mobilising the votes of a united proletariat. The first had been present since the formation of mass socialist parties in the last quarter of the nineteenth century. The Roman Catholic Church under a succession of Pontiffs had encouraged the formation of catholic parties to defend the interests of the church where they appeared to be threatened, as in Germany during Bismarck's anti-Catholic *Kulturkampf*. It had also consistently expressed strong hostility to socialism and to socialist parties. The result was that sizeable proportions of the working class in a number of European countries had been mobilised behind the electoral aspirations of organised catholicism and were simply not available for mobilisation by socialist parties.

The second barrier was a product of the great split within the socialist movement in 1917. Social democratic parties now found themselves competing for the votes of the proletariat against the newly formed communist parties. The communist parties, while clinging to a revolutionary ideal, fairly quickly abandoned insurrectionary practice in western European societies and proved themselves to be formidable competitors for the votes of the manual working class, especially in France and Germany.

The failure to transform an assumed working-class majority into an actual electoral majority should not be read as indicating a record of complete electoral failure of the social democrats. A sizeable proportion of the parties consistently polled over a third of the votes cast and the Scandinavian and Austrian parties broke the 40 per cent barrier. The British Labour Party secured 37.1 per cent in 1929 and 37.9 per cent in 1935.

Factors underlying electoral appeal of social democracy

The reasons for the relative electoral success seem to be two fold. Firstly, the organisational form of the social democratic party proved well adapted to electoral mobilisation, and organisational strength was generally reflected in electoral results. As we note in our chapter on the internal life of social democratic parties, the dense organisational network characteristic of these parties remained largely intact throughout the interwar period. The result was a continued and even enhanced capacity to mobilise support.

> 'Mobilization of working class support took time; workers had to be organised if they were to participate in politics. Indeed, only by the mid-1930's was the process of electoral mobilisation almost completed – the rates of voting participation reached the level at which they have rested ever since'.

> 'Thus the success of electoral socialism was due to political mobilisation, not to industrialisation.' *(Przeworski and Sprague 1986, 159, 163)*

The second reason for the relative electoral advance of the social democratic parties was their abandonment of an electoral strategy which concentrated exclusively on mobilising the votes of the industrial working class. From an early point socialist parties in practice had attempted to blunt the sharpness of their appeal to a relatively narrow class interest. This was generally only cosmetic, however, and failed to carry any great conviction with the groups to whom it was addressed, for example the German SPD's appeal among the peasantry in Wilhelmine Germany was severely restricted by its adherence to the Marxist view of the agrarian question which envisaged a less than brilliant future for the peasantry.

Changing class alignments

Revisionists including Bernstein had tried to alert the parties to the unlikelihood of constructing an electoral majority on the basis of the proletariat, and the consequent importance of securing allies, but with relatively restricted effect before 1918 since socialists continued to believe, against the evidence but in line with Marx's immiseration thesis, that the old middle class would shrink and that its displaced members would join the ranks of the proletariat and the unemployed.

This view had simply become untenable by 1918 and the social democratic parties began to make serious appeals beyond the working class. They were prepared to alter their analysis and their programmes to find some space for selected groups, notably lower-grade office workers. In making these adaptations the social democratic parties were reacting belatedly to social changes, especially the vast expansion of a service class, 'a new middle class' of salaried employees in offices who came to constitute roughly a tenth of the working population in advanced industrial societies by the 1930s.

The pace of adaptation was subject to wide variations and the general picture was one of incremental adaptation rather than the wholesale and explicit alteration of doctrinal views. It went furthest in Belgium where the Socialist Party had a notorious revisionist bias and had always attempted to appeal to the lower middle class and the intelligentsia. The Belgian endorsement of a 'superclass' strategy culminated in its adoption of Hendrik de Man's Labour Plan, which advocated an explicit alliance with the middle classes in 1933. The Swedish party also adopted a multiclass strategy in 1920. Other parties made lesser adjustments, for example in Germany the SPD in 1927 adopted a strategy designed to appeal to salaried employees.

The search for allies beyond the manual working class was not restricted to adjustments in the electoral appeals of the social democratic parties. It also included the search for class allies outside the parties with whom long-term electoral coalitions could be built. This was most obviously the case in Scandinavia where the social democrats responded to the World Depression by forming coalitions with the farmers. The basis of these coalitions was an agreement on a policy of agricultural subsidies and full employment in return for which the trade unionists would guarantee restraint on the wage front while the farmers would support the interventionist policies of social democratic led governments. This Red/Green formula was very appealing electorally and provided the basis of social democratic domination of the Swedish and Norwegian governments in the 1930s.

POST-1945

Rudolf Breitscheid's famous cry '*Nach Hitler Wir*' (after Hitler us) was not untypical of the hopes that social democratic parties entertained about their electoral future in the postwar world. This rosy view was based on the assumption that the collapse of fascism would discredit not only the eponymous parties but many of their conservative and liberal allies. It was assumed that the communists would remain formidable competitors on the Left, but Keynesian economics with its promise that full employment could be secured seemed likely to render social democracy electorally more attractive.

In particular, it offered a way out of the representational dilemma, i.e. the view that, in developing a 'superclass' electoral appeal, social democracy would be less and less able to mobilise its core working-class constituency. Since full employment, the key interest of the industrial working class, would be safeguarded by Keynesian demand management, the expectation was that the parties could safely extend their appeal to other groups without losing support in the key group.

The result in practice was somewhat more mixed. Where Keynesian-type economic policies were practised, as in the Scandinavian states and the United Kingdom, the social democratic parties did very well. The Scandinavian combination of the economics of full employment and welfarism was an especially potent electoral appeal and the Swedish and Norwegian parties consistently polled well over 40 per cent. The Danish party had less support and always governed in coalition with the Radical Liberals. The Scandinavian parties were also aided by the strength of their organisational networks and their close relations with the trade unions.

The British Labour Party had a stunning victory in July 1945 when they polled 47.8 per cent of the votes as against 39.8 per cent for the Conservatives. Any full explanation of the Labour victory in 1945 must rest on a number of factors, but a central element was a rejection in retrospect of the 1930s and support for the Labour Party's policy of full employment.

Elsewhere in western Europe the electoral picture was less hopeful for the non-communist parties of the Left. Dutch politics were still constrained by the impress of the religious cleavage and the Dutch Labour Party was able to poll only just over a quarter of the votes in the first postwar elections (1946, 28.3 per cent; 1948, 25.6 per cent). In France and Italy the results were extremely disappointing. In both countries the communists had played a leading rôle in opposition to fascism and German occupation, and the communists emerged much more strongly than the democratic socialist parties. Support for the SFIO in France dropped away after 1946 and the disparity with the Communist Party (PCF) narrowed only at the very end of the IVth Republic. The picture of a widening distance between the socialists and the communists in this period was replicated in Italy where electoral support for democratic socialism was further weakened by being divided between the PSI and a breakaway Social Democratic Party.

The electoral fortunes of the social democratic parties of Austria and Germany showed a marked discrepancy. Austria had always had a higher percentage of electoral support for the socialist party, which was concentrated largely in Vienna. Luckily for the Austrian party, the country, unlike Germany, was not divided and Vienna was able to continue to be the dominant source of electoral strength for the socialists, albeit on a reduced scale. It also reflected the immense organisational strength of the Austrian party. This pattern persisted and the party regularly polled over 40 per cent with the single exception of 1949 when it fell to 38.7 per cent.

In Germany, however, the SPD polled very disappointingly in the first elections after the war. With the division of Germany it lost some of its strongest areas of support in Saxony, Thuringia and East Berlin. Division also meant a change in the confessional balance from the traditional position where catholics had made up one third of the electorate to a roughly equal balance between catholics and protestants in the Federal Republic. The SPD had also been weakened by its decision to go into opposition in the Frankfurt Bizonal Council in 1947, while the christian democrats derived the benefits of incumbency especially after the successful implementation of the currency reform in 1948.

The 1950s – social democracy falters

In Scandinavia and Austria electoral support for the social democrats showed no evidence of weakening in the 1950s and the Austrian, Danish, Norwegian and Swedish parties consistently polled over 40 per cent. Outside Scandinavia there was a general slackening of support for social democratic parties which grew more marked towards the end of the decade. The decline was not of a very large order. In West Germany the social democrats actually increased their share of the poll from 28.8 per cent to 31.8 per cent between 1953 and 1957, but this small gain looked like a defeat in the context of the massive advances of the christian democrats which took them to a majority position (50.2 per cent) in 1957.

The general electoral trend as identified by analysts and party strategists, however, was downwards. The flavour of these analyses is well represented in M. Abraham and R. Rose, '*Must Labour Lose*' (Penguin 1959). Two main explanations were furnished for this trend. The first focused on the long and sustained boom of the 1950s. This boom was accompanied by the rapid spread of mass aspirations with regard to the possession of consumer goods, a development which led many analysts to talk of the embourgoisement of the working class. The other central explanation focused on the reduction in size of the manual working class, the traditional core clientele of the social democratic parties. This decline was balanced by a steady growth in the service sector. In particular there were new jobs for the sons and daughters of working-class homes in the expanding service sector.

The latter explanation was crucial in persuading a number of parties, most notably the German and Dutch parties, to move explicitly to a superclass strategy and to adopt a 'people's party model', a catch-all party which sought to attract voters not adherents, and which attempted to make some appeal to all strata of society, especially the new middle class. Of course, as we have pointed out, social democratic parties had attempted to respond to changes in the class composition of European societies in the interwar period; the difference this time was the explicit character of the shift which involved a change in party style, organisation and programmes (see chapters on Ideology and Internal Life of Social Democratic Parties). These changes went much further in the Austrian, Belgian, German and Dutch parties than in Britain and Scandinavia but, even where the programmatic and organisational changes were less striking, a superclass appeal was adopted or strengthened. The adoption of the wage earner and pensions fund strategy in the Scandinavian parties was designed to extend the appeal of the parties, and Hugh Gaitskell would have liked to bring about programmatic changes in the British Labour Party but was unsuccessful. His successor, Harold Wilson, made explicit appeal to the new middle class in his embracement, at a rhetorical level at least, of the new technology.

Decades of success

The 1960s and 1970s were in general electorally good years for the classic social democratic parties. By the late 1960s, however, there seemed to be a fairly steady trend in favour of social democrats, referred to in the Federal Republic as the Genosse (comrade) trend. Politics was not as polarised as at some points in the past, but class continued to play a dominant rôle in structuring voting preferences in the advanced industrial societies of western Europe. Indeed, there appeared to be some force in the argument that as other cleavages such as the urban – rural and religious became less important, class became more salient than in the past. This is the paradox to which Butler and Stokes (1969, 116) drew attention: 'the intensity of the class tie may have declined at the same time as its extent became

113

more universal'. The process in which people in western Europe moved from rural agricultural jobs to places in industrial and unionised factories was one which appeared to promise continual gains for social democracy.

In these decades the social democratic superclass strategy appeared to be working electorally. Keynesianism as a formula for political rule was more widespread than ever and was adopted at least partially in the Federal Republic. There was still sufficient class appeal to mobilise the core working-class constituency, but the accommodations represented by the adoption of a people's party model and a superclass strategy made an appeal to new groups, especially to those with careers in the public service in education, the new technologies and the caring professions. The electoral advance of social democracy in the 1960s and 1970s was reflected in a very high level of governmental participation.

The electoral appeal of social democracy in decline?

The intellectual appeal and coherence of the social democratic paradigm began to crumble in the mid 1970s and displayed signs of terminal exhaustion by the end of the decade, and the political discourse of the 1980s was dominated by rival political ideologies. Intellectual reach and electoral appeal are rarely identical, however, and the reverses suffered by social democracy on the intellectual plane and as a formula for political rule (Chapter 4) have translated imperfectly into electoral results. In particular, the pattern has varied and talk of the electoral decomposition of social democracy is exaggerated if applied without severe qualification. The electoral history of social democracy in the last decade is best treated by dividing the parties into three broad geographical groups, while recognising that there is variation even within the three categories of northern, central and southern European parties. The northern group comprises the Scandinavian parties; the central group includes Austria, Benelux, Britain and the Federal Republic; while the southern group comprises France, Italy, Portugal and Spain. Italy, Portugal and Spain are self-evidently southern parties. The French party lacks the relationship to the trade unions of the central and northern parties and it has usually preferred to see itself as a southern party.

Scandinavia The Scandinavian social democratic parties have had, along with Austria, by far the most consistent record of electoral success among social democratic parties in postwar Europe, and the factors ensuring their success have been essentially similar to these in Austria. The most important of these factors have been the very high level of unionisation and the organisational strength of the parties and the labour movement in general. Organisational strength gives the parties two important advantages.

'On the one hand it promotes political mobilisation. It may also help avert splits, cleavages and fragmentation. Powerful organisation affects broad solidarity, which in turn will be decisive when the party's policies are under strain – as in the EEC debate in Norway and Denmark. Where the party's organisational apparatus has collapsed, some differences and ideological splits will more readily translate into zero-sum confrontations precisely because the party will have no framework within which controversies can be debated and reconciled.'

(Esping-Andersen 1985, 120).

They have also profited from the division of the bourgeois parties which has enabled them to exercise a dominant influence in the shaping of these polities which, not surprisingly, has generally worked to their continued electoral advantage.

The high point of electoral success for the Scandinavian social democrats was reached in the 1950s and 1960s and some decline had already become apparent in the 1970s. The biggest reverse occurred in relation to the Norwegian Labour Party which was very badly split on the question of entry into the EEC and registered a historic low in the 1973 election when it polled 35.3 per cent. By the time of the next election in 1977 its share of the poll had risen to 42.3 per cent. Disquiet on the Left of the Danish party, especially in external issues, worked to the electoral advantage of the Socialist People's Party which polled 5 per cent in 1975, 3.9 per cent in 1977 and 5.9 per cent in 1979. The SD itself polled 25.7 per cent in 1973 when it lost votes to the Centre Democrats, a right-wing group which had broken with SD in the tax issue. It polled 29.9 per cent in 1975, 37.0 per cent in 1977 and 38.3 per cent in 1979. The Swedish Social Democratic and Labour Party polled 42.7 per cent in 1976 and 43.2 per cent in 1979.

In the 1980s there was a further marginal decline of support. Electoral support held up very well in Sweden. The Social Democratic and Labour Party polled 45.6 per cent in 1982, 44.7 per cent in 1985 and 43.2 per cent in 1988. The Norwegian Labour Party actually registered an increase from 37.2 per cent in 1981 to 40.8 per cent in 1985. The Danish party suffered a slight drop in support in the 1980s. It polled 32.9 per cent in 1981, 31.6 per cent in 1984, 29.3

per cent in 1987 and 29.8 per cent in 1988. The Socialist People's Party significantly increased its share in the 1980s as compared with the previous decade. It polled 11.3 per cent in 1981, 11.5 per cent in 1984, 14.6 per cent in 1987 and 13.0 per cent in 1988.

The most striking feature of the electoral fortunes of the Scandinavian social democratic parties is the weak electoral position of the Danish party as compared with its counterparts in Sweden and Norway. A major part of the explanation must relate to the disparity in organisational strength and the related dominance of social democratic values. A major feature of the Danish development has been the impact on the electoral share of the social democrats of the Socialist People's Party. Esping-Andersen suggests plausibly that this sort of fission is much less likely to occur where the party is organisationally stronger. There has also been a much stronger rejection of high tax policies in Denmark which caused the social democrats to lose votes to Mogens Glistrup's 'anti-tax' Progress Party and the Centre Democrats. The attachment to solidaristic values appears to be higher in Norway and Sweden, though there have been recent indications of a change in Sweden.

Esping-Andersen (1985) makes a convincing case in his classic work '*Politics against Markets*' for attributing differences in electoral performance between the Swedish, Norwegian and Danish cases to policy failures on the part of the Danish social democrats in office. In Esping-Andersen's account, classes are not the autonomous and immutable result of societal changes but constructs which can be affected by political decisions. Esping-Andersen identifies three policy failures which led to the electoral decomposition of the Danish party. In social policy the Danish social democrats had created 'a pervasively liberalistic welfare state that enhances social stratification and cleavages cutting across class lines' (Esping-Andersen 1985, 149). They were also relatively unsuccessful in controlling the business cycle (Esping-Andersen 1985, 244) and finally, and significantly for Esping-Andersen, they abandoned a housing policy which was advantageous to tenants to one that encouraged home ownership'.(Esping-Andersen 1985).

The Scandinavian parties had always been notable for the breadth of their class appeal and this feature has largely been preserved. All three parties have largely been able to hold on to working-class support but have lost some of the 'catch-all' quality they had in the past. This development has been most noticeable in Denmark where a significant proportion of middle-class employees in the caring professions and in the public services have moved leftwards and transferred their votes to the Socialist People's Party.

The central European group The dominant trend in the electoral fortunes of the parties in this group was of electoral decline. The 1970s had seen them on a high point electorally and this contributed to some of their electoral difficulties in the 1980s. The variations within this group are considerable, however, and even where the trend is similar, the factors behind it vary from party to party. The most striking feature in this group is, however, the electoral decline of the two major parties, the SPD and the British Labour Party.

Electoral support for the Labour Party had already begun to decline during the 1970s. Its share of the poll in 1970 at 43.0 per cent was not greatly different from its general level of postwar support which hovered around the mid-forties. The decline thereafter was quite steep to 37.2 per cent in February 1974 and then a slight rise to 39.3 per cent in October 1974 before falling to 37.0 per cent in 1979. This weaker level of performance was compatible with holding office between 1974 and 1979, given the Conservatives' even greater loss of support and the rise of support for third and alternative parties, though it left the Callaghan government of 1976–79 dangerously and, as it turned out, fatally dependent on the support of other parties.

If the decline in the 1970s had been serious, the electoral performance in the 1980s looked for a period as if it might be fatal for any hopes of future office. In 1983, after a disastrous campaign of muddle and ineptitude, on a programme described by a senior shadow Cabinet member as 'the longest suicide note in history' and with an electorally unappealing leader, the Labour Party polled an historic low of 27.6 per cent. This appeared to be especially threatening since it was only marginally larger than the 25.4 per cent scored by centre parties of the Social Democratic and Liberal Alliance, though the more concentrated nature of the Labour vote gave the party many more seats than the Alliance.

Under a new leader, the Labour Party recovered some support to poll 30.8 per cent in 1987 and, more importantly, the Alliance support fell to 22.5 per cent; the danger of the Alliance overtaking Labour receded and a period of intractable difficulties between the various Alliance groupings set in.

The roots of Labour's failure in the 1980s, from which it looked like emerging in the 1990s, are manifold and complex. The first is the obvious ability of the Conservatives under a new leader, who for some years at least was very skilful in exploiting populist issues, to recover the historic level of Conservative support. Perhaps the best example of such an issue is the sale of council houses. This reprivatisation of the housing market was popular with tenants and voters and was one which it was extremely difficult for the Labour Party to embrace. Perhaps even more crucial was the failure of the Labour Party leadership to prevent the damaging split with the Social Democratic party (SDP) which led to the formation of the Alliance. The dissolution illustrated the historic weaknesses of the Labour Party organisation with its reluctance to accept member sovereignty and its over-dependence on the unions. This over-dependence was both a precipitating factor in the split and an electoral liability, given unfavourable public perceptions of the unions. The political values of the Labour Party led it to under-estimate the popularity of a number of issues. In common with social democratic parties elsewhere, it assumed that the electorate would punish governments which gave a greater priority to containing inflation than to unemployment, and in this they proved to be mistaken. The Labour Party also found the defence issue to be a difficult one electorally. Michael Foot and Neil Kinnock were the first unilateralists to lead the Labour Party and this proved to be electorally damaging in both cases.

A decline in class voting?

There has been a great deal of discussion in Britain on the degree to which falling support for the Labour Party can be attributed to a decline in class voting, to a dealignment in which voters respond less to social cues. At first glance the decline in the proportion of the Labour electorate who can confidently be assigned to the working class is beyond doubt. Anthony Heath et al. (1985) have queried the view that this conclusively demonstrates a decline in class voting. They make one very important point which applies, of course, equally to other western European societies. The decline in class voting hypothesis underplays the marked changes in the relative size of social classes. The working class declined from 47 per cent of the working population to 34 per cent between 1964 and 1983. Such a reduction could be expected to produce a fall of 7 per cent in Labour's vote, even if the proportion of working-class voters sup-porting Labour remained constant. However, in 1979, 1983 and 1987 the Labour Party did suffer a real loss among working-class voters as some groups of skilled workers, resistant to higher tax rates, voted for the Conservatives.

Whether Labour's electoral decline was due to the shrinking size of the working class or to its declining ability to mobilise the votes of the working class as society loosened up, the electoral implications for the Labour Party were clear. It had to be seen to devise a strategy which would have much more of a superclass appeal, and it had to be oriented much more towards electorally popular issues than in the past. These considerations have formed the party's Policy Review which was initially successful in increasing Labour's rating in the polls, though the party will have to make considerable advances to take enough seats in the populous Midlands and south of England to form a government.

West Germany

The 1980s was a decade of electoral decline for the SPD at the federal level, though it started to pick up support at the state level in the last four years of the decade. The election of 1980 where the SPD faced Franz Josef Strauss, as electoral challenger for the christian democrats, proved to be a very misleading pointer to the real state of electoral support for the party. Helmut Schmidt was the most popular chancellor since Adenauer, while Franz Josef Strauss was widely distrusted in northern Germany. A more accurate view of the underlying level of support could have been derived from a whole series of state elections after 1980 and it was this evident decline that persuaded Hans-Dietrich Genscher to move towards ending the governmental coalition with the SPD.

The SPD vote in 1983 of 38.2 per cent was a major reverse since its average poll between 1969 and 1980 had been 43.3 per cent. In 1987 its vote fell further to 37 per cent, which took the SPD back to the level they had been before the breakthrough of the Bad Godesberg conference. The year 1983 was a double haemorrhage for the SPD. Many centrist voters had been alienated by the last years of the Schmidt government and the discord between party and government. Its greatest losses were in its middle-class electorate. Contrary to earlier speculation, it lost very little support among unskilled workers and its losses among the skilled working class were not disproportionate. Its greatest losses were among low- and medium-level employees and civil servants, among voters with intermediate and advanced educational qualifications, and among voters with very loose ties to the SPD. Losses were greatest among young voters.

The 1983 elections left the SPD in a very difficult position. It had succeeded in mobilising their traditional voters but the attempt to neutralise the threat by some 'greening' of the SPD programme had been a failure. The indications were of the existence of a fairly solid post-materialist constituency in West Germany which would not be easily integrated into the SPD. In terms of social composition the Greens were the most homogeneous of the parties. Predominantly young and well educated, centred in large towns and university centres, they had few supporters over the age of thirty-five and were overwhelmingly middle-class in background.

The 1987 result for the SPD was arguably worse than that for the CDU/CSU. The SPD vote declined only from 38.2 to 37 per cent, but 1983 was already a major reverse (its average poll between 1969 and 1980 had been 43.3 per cent), and 37 per cent took the social democrats back to the level they had been before the breakthrough of the Bad Godesberg Conference of 1959.

In 1987 the SPD losses largely accrued to the Greens who were estimated to have won 400,000 votes from the SPD. The strength of the Greens *vis-à-vis* the SPD was also reflected among young voters, traditionally a group in which the SPD had been very strong. Some four months after the election in Germany an official analysis was published based on analysis of a sample of completed ballot forms. The representative figures for 1987 indicate that of the eighteen to twenty-four year-olds who voted, 37.5 per cent voted CDU/CSU, 38.1 per cent SPD, 8.3 per cent FDP and 15.5 per cent Greens. The SPD polled above its overall percentage in three states belonging to the 'rust belt' and in which it had recently polled well in state elections. In the Saarland its share went down marginally from 43.8 to 43.5 per cent. In Lower Saxony it increased its poll from 41.3 to 41.4 per cent. Most importantly, in West Germany's largest state, North Rhine –Westphalia, the home state of Johannes Rau, the SPD share increased from 42.8 to 43.2 per cent. The SPD had run a special campaign in North Rhine–Westphalia which based itself more squarely on Rau, the Chancellor candidate, not the Minister President of North Rhine–Westphalia.

The electoral weakness of the SPD and the difficulty it had in devising an electoral strategy to win votes both at the centre and from the Greens was already a major feature of the 1983 election. The increasing strength of the Greens in 1987, especially after the Chernobyl nuclear disaster, merely exacerbated a pre-existing set of difficulties.

The electoral failure of the SPD in the 1980s was not a product of its failure to mobilise its traditional *Facharbeiter* (skilled worker) core, though the declining size of the working class was certainly a problem. The failure can be much more plausibly ascribed to two other factors. Firstly, and most obviously, the failure to contain the rise of the Greens, and secondly the failure of the SPD to make significant inroads or even to hold on to its gains in the new middle classes. The new party programme (see chapter 1) is designed to address the first of these deficiencies, and the candidature of Lafontaine will focus on trying to make good the failure in the second area.

The Austrian party suffered an electoral decline of the same order as the SPD and the Labour Party in the 1980s. Its share of the vote fell from 51 per cent in 1979 to 47.7 per cent in 1983 and to 43 per cent in 1987. This erosion of electoral support was reflected in its governmental position which changed from sole governing party (1970–83) to coalition with the Liberals (FPO) from 1983 to 1987 and to coalition with the christian democratic ÖVP since then. The electoral decline of the Austrian party reflects the difficulties the Austrian model of economic management had run into by the mid 1980s (see chapter 2) and the increasing electoral appeal of the liberals and their charismatic leader, Jorg Halder.

The major exceptions to the trend of electoral erosion among the central group are the Benelux parties. These parties were either in coalition government or out of office when recession and mass unemployment emerged, and they escaped the opprobrium which attached to parties in dominant government positions at the time. The Dutch Labour Party has benefited from the continuing secularisation of Dutch society and increased its share from 28.3 per cent (1981) to 29.4 per cent (1982) to 33.3 per cent (1986). The trend has also been upwards in Belgium, but the Belgian Socialist Party has been divided into its Flemish and Walloon components.

THE SOUTHERN EUROPEAN PARTIES

The electoral geography of social democracy was transformed during the 1980s. Social democracy had always been a weak plant electorally in southern Europe where the preconditions for success seemed to be absent. Industrialisation had come relatively late, and was far less extensive than in northern Europe. Historically, electoral support for social democracy correlated fairly closely to the level of unionisation, and this was much lower in southern Europe, including France. Moreover, the unions themselves were fragmented. Many of the most important unions were communist controlled, while in others there was a strong anarcho-syndicalist element (see chapter 5). The parties in that area were small and faction ridden and never really developed as 'solidarity communities' (chapter 4) in the northern European manner; they were therefore correspondingly weak as agencies of electoral mobilisation. The French and Italian parties had suffered from the competition of the much more electorally powerful communist parties throughout the postwar period, and the Iberian and Greek parties had endured long periods of illegality.

The newly legalised parties

The electoral performance of social democracy in Greece and Spain in the 1980s has approached that of the Scandinavian and Austrian parties. The grounds of this electoral success were quite different, however. Whereas the electoral strength of the Scandinavian and Austrian parties was the culmination of long years of organisational effort, the Greek socialist (PASOK) and the Spanish socialists (PSOE) had a mushroom-like growth and were strongly fixed on a personalist style of leadership. Moreover, both Gonzalez in Spain and Papandreou in Greece very skilfully identified electorally popular themes even when, as in Gonzalez's case, they sometimes ran against established party positions. In Spain there has also been a marked change in direction during Gonzalez' incumbency. Despite this, the PSOE was able largely to hold on to its vote and its share of the poll declined only marginally from 46.5 per cent (1982) to 44.3 per cent in 1986. In these years the PSOE achieved the social profile of a successful catch-all party. Its electoral support faithfully reflected the social composition of Spanish society, and in achieving this broad spread of support it did not have to sacrifice working-class electoral support but was able to eat into the working-class base of the Spanish Communist Party.

Greece The electoral record of PASOK was in many ways as impressive as PSOE. PASOK was led in an even more personalist style than PSOE and, for much of the 1980s, Andreas Papandreou proved to be extremely adept at identifying populist themes. The degree to which the party was mortgaged to Papandreou was vividly demonstrated as age and difficulties in his personal life began to affect his ability to spot populist themes and to fulfil the leadership rôle in the way that had compelled the admiration of the Greek electorate. Support for PASOK, which had peaked at 48.2 per cent in 1981, declined to 45.8 per cent in 1985 and fell further in the two elections of June and November, 1989, and the party left government after the November election.

Portugal The eighties were a difficult decade for social democracy in Portugal. The Portuguese party had emerged earlier than the other two parties and had played a major rôle in the transition to democracy. It had been rewarded electorally for this achievement in 1975 when it gained 40.7 per cent. This early success meant, however, that, unlike its more electorally successful counterparts, it was in power during the economically difficult years and saddled with the responsibility for problems to which it had no adequate answer.

> 'The PSP was thus harmed by not gaining the vital breathing space which enabled the Greek and Spanish Left to produce an organisation capable of assuming power and hammering out a strategy to cement its authority.'
> *(Gallagher and Williams 1989, 31).*

By the end of the decade its support had been almost halved and it polled 21.3 per cent in 1985 and 22.8 per cent in 1989.

France and Italy

The success of the French Socialist Party in the 1980's reflected Mitterrand's grasp of the politics of the Vth Republic. Mitterrand saw more clearly than anyone else on the Left the necessity of creating a broad coalition of the Left in order to capture the presidency, and he had worked consistently and effectively to that end. Mitterrand also calculated correctly that an alliance of the Left would work to the benefit of the PS and that the communists (PCF) would lose greatly as a result of being in office.

The electoral history of the 1980s largely bore out Mitterrand's insights. In the 1981 presidential election the PS had its best (first-ballot) result since the war (25.8 per cent with 2.2 per cent to a close ally). George Marchais, the communist candidate, was very comprehensively defeated. The presidential victory provided a platform for the even more striking legislative success in June 1981 when the Socialist Party vote increased from 24.9 per cent (1978) to 37.2 per cent. The electoral support dipped to 32.7 per cent in the legislative

123

election of March 1986 as a result of the economic policy difficulties of the PS government (see chapter 2) but climbed again to 37.6 per cent in June 1988. Mitterrand increased his share of the vote in the presidential election of 1988.

The electoral position of the PS had been transformed in the 1980s. The party was able to increase its vote significantly among lower-managerial and white-collar workers, but it derived even more satisfaction in 1981 when it took two-fifths of the working-class vote in legislative elections as against one-quarter that went to the PCF.

'Thus the PS achieved the double distinction of being a 'catch-all' party with a deeper penetration of the working class than the country's leading working-class party'.   *(Bell and Criddle 1988, 199)*

The success of the Italian Socialist Party (PSI) in winning control of government under the premiership of Bettino Craxi has tended to obscure the fact that the PSI secured relatively small electoral advantage. Unlike the French presidency, the Italian prime ministership does not provide an institution around which electoral support can be rallied. Moreover, the Italian communists (PCI), unlike the PCF, had initiated the strategy of Eurocommunism and indeed proceeded beyond it to occupy many of the policy positions which elsewhere in western Europe would have been the preserve of the social democrats.

In the 1980s the PSI was able to push its vote up from 11.4 per cent (1983) to 14.3 per cent. The social composition of the party's electoral support had also changed, with a steep decrease in the proportion of its support which could be identified as working class and, as in other parties, a steady increase in the proportion of white-collar workers.

'More than any other party, it reflected the overall profile of Italian society – a matter of satisfaction, perhaps for a party which by then claimed in Craxi's words, a 'centrist vocation', but a position which also left the party with no core constituency on which it could rely when times were difficult, and indeed left it with a far less stable electorate than either of the two major parties'.   *(Hine 1989, 112)*

CONCLUSION

After some initial hesitation, social democratic parties embraced the electoral route to socialism confident in the belief that, as societies become increasingly industrialised, industrial workers would constitute an overwhelming majority of the population. They were confident, too, in their ability to mobilise these workers.

It quickly became apparent that further industrialisation was associated not with increasing homogeneity but heterogeneity and the rise of new groups and further fragmentation of existing class structures. Social democrats adjusted to these changes slowly, but they did all come to adopt a superclass strategy and, particularly after the advent of demand-led economics, they were convinced that the representational gap could be bridged and that it would be possible to continue to mobilise working-class votes and reach out to new groups. These hopes appeared well founded in the classic years of postwar growth.

From the mid 1970s onwards the electoral obstacles confronting social democracy appeared much greater. Keynesianism proved an increasingly inadequate basis for the electoral work that had been allotted to it (see chapter 1). By this time the social composition of advanced industrial societies and the organisation of work were undergoing accelerated change. While it had been one thing for the social democratic parties to accept that the workers did not constitute a majority by themselves, it was quite another to see them threaten to become just another minority interest.

The combination of these two factors led many to predict the electoral demise of social democracy (i.e. the social democratic parties)

> ...as long as they continue to be concerned with the class composition of their electorate, they will bear electoral losses. And they do not have much of a choice: their organisational links, their ideological commitments, their daily habits, and their political projects tie them to their working-class roots. They are thus more likely to turn inward, to their working-class base, and suffer the electoral consequences. Thus the era of electoral socialism may be over.'
>
> (*Przeworski and Sprague 1986, 183–5*).

The historical record has not borne out these predictions. There has been some electoral decline, especially in the central geographical area, but it has not proved to be terminal and the record in the southern area has been one of electoral advance.

In chapter 1 we stressed the looseness and fluidity of social democratic ideology and it is this that has given social democrats the capacity to adapt and weather these changes. Much will depend on the present wave of rewriting of party programmes but there is no evidence either in the record of the 1980s or in various attempts at programmatic renewal of them 'turning inward to their working class base'. (Przeworski and Sprague 1986, 184).

CHAPTER FOUR
Social Democracy in Power

POSTWAR RECONSTRUCTION AND THE CHALLENGE TO *LAISSEZ-FAIRE*

The postwar settlement

Social democratic government in the early postwar years was concerned with the reconstruction of an economic and social order discredited by the interwar depression and decimated by the Second World War. The opportunities for reshaping national life were great, but so too were the practical difficulties of restoring the basic fabric of society and overcoming the shortages of raw materials, fuel, housing and food. Moreover, the renewal and regeneration of national life was inextricably entwined with a reconstruction of the international economic order which was led by the United States. Increasingly, social democrats found that their room for manoeuvre was restricted by external circumstances in the international economy.

Social democrats had a model, albeit a skeletal one, of the sort of social order which they wanted to construct. Their vision occupied the ground between the liberal capitalism of the western world and Soviet communism. It involved a new relationship between the state and the economy. In short it was a blueprint for interventionism with the state participating much more fully in economic life – a form of state collectivism, with governments accepting responsibility for general economic and social security. Politics in the immediate postwar years tended to revolve around the conflict between interventionists and *laissez-faire* liberals. To a large extent the character of postwar order in the western European states was determined by the relative strengths of social democratic interventionism and market liberalism. In most cases the outcome was a compromise, but the terms of the compromise differed quite widely often reflecting the political balance between the social and political forces of the Left as against those of the Right.

From 1945 to 1947 social democrats had a voice in government in most western European countries and the first steps towards reconstruction were taken on interventionist, collectivist lines. In Britain and Norway, majority Labour governments from 1945 meant that the foundations of the postwar order were laid in accordance with these philosophies. Nationalisation and government controls played a large part in economic programmes. Elsewhere where socialists or social democrats shared power in coalition governments, the political bargaining process was often protracted, and decisions about the future economic and social order were postponed. The significance of this delay was that after 1947 the political balance swung to the Right, as the entrepreneurial middle classes gained political confidence and bourgeois parties seized the initiative. In Italy and Western Germany, for instance, the Right was in control by the time the decisive moves towards a postwar settlement took place, and for the most part they dictated its terms. In France and the Benelux countries the political balance was rather more even, and the postwar order emerged as a hybrid of interventionism and *laissez-faire* liberalism.

Quite apart from the political balance between Right and Left, there was a further influence on the emerging postwar order in the western European states. It was difficult to reconcile economic interventionism in the form of statutory government controls with the free and open, international economy which was taking shape under US tutelage. 'Paying the piper, the United States felt entitled to suggest at least some of the tunes' (Mayne 1970, 121). It was an inescapable fact that Marshall Aid and the European Recovery Programme which it financed were based on the objective of a liberal order in the world economy.

From the liberal viewpoint, socialist interventionism was anachronistic and alien to American values. 'The purpose of Marshall Aid was, through furthering the process of economic recovery in Western Europe, to develop a bloc of states which would share similar political, social, economic and cultural values to those which the United States itself publicly valued and claimed to uphold' (Milward 1984, 123). In those countries where social democratic interventionism was politically dominant this posed a dilemma of 'how to reconcile the aims of full employment and socialist change with the necessity of a liberal world economic system' (Grosser 1980, 16). The British Labour governments of 1945-51 epitomise both the vision and the dilemma of government social democracy in the early postwar years.

Britain Many of the participants in the Attlee government were initially of the conviction that they were harbingers of a social revolution. 'That first sensation, tingling and triumphant, was of a new society to be built; and we had the power to build it. There was exhilaration among us, joy and hope, determination and confidence. We felt exalted, dedicated, walking on air, walking with destiny' (Dalton 1962, 36–8). Some historians reflect Hugh Dalton's perception that he was a part of an epoch-making government. The Attlee government wrenched the course of British history into significant new directions...its legacy lived on in a broad influence over political and economic thought, and indeed over much of British intellectual and cultural life for a full quarter of a century after 1951' (Morgan 1984, vii). Here was an example of a vigorous programmatic party in power: 'to an extent unprecedented in British political history the legislation of a government was dictated by party programme' (Beer 1965, 179).

The evidence for the 'social earthquake' view arises largely from the remarkable legislative record of the government's first two years. Attlee was surrounded by men who already had considerable experience of government. The 'big five' (Attlee, Ernest Bevin, Herbert Morrison, Stafford Cripps and Hugh Dalton) constituted a cohesive group united around common purposes. They were able to exploit an overwhelming parliamentary majority to create a sizeable economic sector owned and administered by the state. Coal, railways, air transport, electricity, gas, broadcasting and the Bank of England – all had been taken into public ownership by 1947. A new conception of economic management emerged – an admixture of planning and budgetary control, *dirigisme* and Keynesianism in which full employment was a major priority. As Chancellor of the Exchequer, Dalton was committed to the principle of economic planning, and set about the creation of a broad range of planning controls and agencies (Cairncross 1985, 446–8). In his view, planning was more than merely a set of instruments for promoting economic rationality and efficiency. A comprehensive planning machine would allow government to guarantee full employment and to redistribute income and wealth (Pimlott 1985, 472). As a step towards the latter the tax structure was reshaped, strengthening its progressive character.

The principle of equality which lay behind Dalton's tax changes was also uppermost in Labour's thinking on the welfare state. Under Aneurin Bevan at the Ministry of Health a comprehensive National Health Service was brought into being. Moreover, the National Insurance Act of 1946 created a comprehensive and unified system of social security benefits. Financed heavily through National Insurance contributions it nevertheless drew on tax revenues. Hence the drive to provide a minimum standard of freely available health care, medicine and welfare was coupled with Labour's attack on concentrated wealth. 'Inequality was to be attacked at both ends of the social scale' (Cairncross 1985, 118). In addition, trade union law had been reformed, and large strides taken by 1947 towards the decolonialisation of India. All of this was the achievement of ministers who were also occupied by day-to-day survival in the face of the rigours of postwar reconstruction. Taken together it is not difficult to conceive of these measures as at least a platform for social transformation.

By 1948 however, 'the major acts of nationalisation had taken place, the state had acquired a commanding position in a crucial sector of industry and the...advance in social welfare had reached its climax' (Shonfield 1958, 160). Thereafter the government embarked on what it called a phase of 'consolidation'. The circumstances of the retreat into consolidation are too complex to detail fully here, but they were closely bound together with Britain's growing economic dependency on the United States. Labour ministers did not enter lightly into this relationship of dependency, but they came to believe at an early stage in the government that the alternative was austerity, unemployment and a consequent threat of social unrest. Moreover, they were persuaded that their plans for a new social order could not be accomplished without American aid. The British government was not alone in its susceptibility to US influence. Dollar shortages weakened the capacity of western European economies for recovery. The conditions of American aid meant a commitment on the part of the recipient governments to progressive fulfilment of the 1944 Bretton Woods vision of a free and open international monetary and trading system – the foundation of the postwar western economy. Step by step, beginning with the Loan Agreement of 1945 and culminating in the acceptance of the conditions attached to Marshall Aid, the British government forfeited its ability to pursue an independent economic course. Any aspirations which it might have harboured towards carving out a 'third way' between communism and capitalism (Paterson and Thomas 1977, 13) were effectively stifled.

The financial crisis of 1947 was a watershed in this process. It was precipitated by the return to free convertibility between the pound and the dollar, but its roots were in the underlying weakness of the postwar economy. Sterling convertibility left the British economy much more open to external forces, reducing the effectiveness of economic controls over foreign exchange, investment, consumption and the labour market. Although these controls remained in place, there was a marked trend towards fiscal policy as the central instrument of economic management. Hugh Dalton's budget of October 1947 also marked a transformation of fiscal policy, as the control of inflation became the government's overriding concern. When Stafford Cripps became Chancellor of the Exchequer the following year, he maintained this policy of surplus budgeting for deflation. An erstwhile advocate of economic planning, Cripps now saw direct economic controls as anachronistic in a free society. For him the budget was now 'the most powerful instrument for influencing economic policy which is available to the government'. Thus the drift from planning to Keynesianism and the shift from reflation to deflation were in part at least, bound up with the growing realisation of the American vision of the postwar international economy. With the heightening of Cold War tensions, the tendency of the government to identify with the United States was greatly reinforced. The only resistance to Atlanticism and economic liberalism now came from Hugh Gaitskell, and he fell into line soon after he succeeded Cripps as Chancellor in 1950 (Williams 1983, 171–2 ff.).

It would, however, be a mistake to ascribe these developments solely to American influence and economic weight. By 1947 the main elements of Labour's programme had been fulfilled, and the government lacked the political will to go further. It has been argued that consolidation was built into the thinking of the Attlee government from the outset. According to this view, for most members of the government a planned economy was a temporary expedient to facilitate the transition to peacetime normality. Equally, nationalisation was seen as a necessary step in the restoration of vitality in the capitalist economy. Neither planning nor national-isation was regarded as a vehicle of socialist change (Miliband 1972, 272–317; Coates 1975, 47). It has also been argued, in contrast to the 'social earthquake' view that the 1945–51 Labour governments simply realised a vision of the postwar order which had gained broad political acceptance during the war. 'The Attlee govern-ments...completed and consolidated the work of the (wartime) coalition by establishing a peacetime managed economy and the expanded welfare state envisaged by Beveridge' (Addison 1977, 273). We shall postpone our evaluation of these rival conceptions until the end of this section, when it will be possible to judge the performance of the Labour government in the wider European context.

Norway The Norwegian Labour Party (DNA) closely mirrored the policies and experience of the British Labour government. As in Britain there was consensus backing for the politics of full employment, embodied in the all-party London Agreement of 1944 and formalised in the *Work for All* programme of 1945. There was also a ready-made case for nationalisation and planning. State-run enterprises had been developed under Nazi occupation, and in key industrial sectors (metals, electricity generation) there were weaknesses which cried out for state intervention (Esping-Andersen 1985, 217). Social democrats saw the state sector in a wider context. They were convinced 'that national income accounting and improved knowledge of the economy would enable the Norwegian Labour Party to pursue a radically different set of reconstruction policies in which full employment would be a first objective and some measure of gross overall planning of resources and rewards a second' (Milward 1984, 68).

Like Labour in Britain, the Norwegian Labour Party was able to rely on a parliamentary majority to back its policies. The Einar Gerhardsen government proceeded to establish state-owned enterprises in iron and steel, aluminium production and electric power generation. Keynesian techniques of economic management were geared to the maintenance of full employment at the cost of budget deficits equivalent to the entire state budget of 1938/9. In order to contain the threat of inflation and trade imbalance, a formidable battery of price ceilings, import licences and trade tariffs were employed. Agreements concluded between trade unions and employers, and supervised by a Public Wage Board, ensured that wage levels were simultaneously restrained and equalised. Planning councils and production committees were intended to promote participatory planning in matters of investment and industrial organisation. Although these were never fully effective, state investment banks for industry, housebuilding and agriculture were successful in taking rapid strides towards reconstruction and modernisation through low-interest credit and subsidies (Hodne 1983, 130–52).

131

However, it was impossible to escape the fact that much of the investment credit and subsidies went to finance imports – especially of capital equipment from the United States. As imports outstripped the export performance of the Norwegian economy there was an alarming drain on (dollar) currency reserves. By the summer of 1947 Norway faced a financial crisis of similar proportions to Britain's. The response of Finance Minister Erik Brofoss was to attempt to stem the flow of imports by boosting controls. Both Brofoss and Foreign Minister Halvard Lange were opposed to the conditions (trade liberalisation) attached to Marshall Aid. Lange told the Cabinet in June that it would be better not to participate in the programme if this was economically possible (Pharo 1976, 134). The government hesitated until spring 1948 before acquiescing, and it remained resistant to moves within the framework of the Organisation for European Economic Cooperation towards liberalisation of the European economic order. Asked in a meeting with the Americans in 1949 if he did not feel that monetary and financial liberalisation would contribute to Norwegian objectives, Brofoss replied bluntly in the negative (Milward 1984, 304). However, as in Britain, the Labour governments were forced by imminent economic collapse into acceptance of a US-inspired liberalisation of the economic regime. The decision to participate in the Marshall Plan meant 'in effect a trade-off of socialism in return for economic growth' (Hodne 1983, 162).

Britain and Norway in the immediate postwar years are examples of majority Labour governments with relatively clear-cut policy orientations and a determination, at least at the outset of their terms of office, to set their stamp on the new economic and social order. Nationalisation, planning and welfare made up the collectivist trinity of programmatic themes running through government social democracy in these countries. Where socialists shared power in coalition governments, as in France and Italy, collectivist prescriptions figured prominently in the early peacetime policy agendas. Here, however, social radicalism was more rapidly overtaken by the priorities of monetary stability, inflation control and trade balance. There was less resistance to the twin pressures of economic crisis and US political hegemony. In practical terms this meant the speedy restoration at the heart of government policy of the economic orthodoxies of liberal capitalism.

France and Italy France's first post-liberation government proceeded to nationalise key economic sectors including the utilities, railway and air transport, cable and wireless, oil, the Renault motor works and some major banks. Steps were taken towards the institutionalisation of a fairly comprehensive social security system. In Italy, the machinery of state intervention which had been created in the interwar years was consolidated. The *Instituto Per La Riconstruzione Industriale* (Institute for Industrial Reconstruction), had holdings in steel, engineering, electricity, telephones, armaments and some large banks. The banks themselves possessed important industrial holdings. Overall, the state had a substantial stake in the economy, and the socialists saw this as an instrument of a state-led economic reconstruction. The first postwar government, a six-party coalition which included the Socialist Party, introduced a number of economic controls: indexing wages to prices, protecting employment and regulating the resumption of production through controls on the availability of foreign exchange. However, in both France and Italy, circumstances conspired to frustrate major socialist reforms.

Firstly, socialists were generally restricted to ministries of relatively minor importance which left them without great influence over the reconstruction of the national economy. Secondly, in both France and Italy, the socialist parties failed to present a concrete alternative strategy for reconstruction (Hine 1978, 315; Williams 1958, 90). Thirdly, coalition governments in both countries were plagued by political differences which widened as the radicalism attendant upon the end of the war was dissipated. Deadlock between the coalition partners negated any moves towards clear-cut policy positions. Coalition differences centred on conflict between interventionist and *laissez-faire* solutions to successive economic and financial crises. By 1947 the *laissez-faire* liberals had the upper hand, particularly in Italy where the expulsion of both communists and socialists from government meant that the Right was now free to stamp its own image on the postwar settlement. In France, the political deadlock of the immediate postwar years continued to characterise the Fourth Republic until its demise in 1958. Once the communists left government in 1947, the socialists lost any chance they might have had of winning support for their policies. Economic development took place outside the arena of party politics, led by technocrats like Jean Monnet.

Interventionism was not eradicated in either country. In France there was the *Commissariat du Plan*, in Italy the Institute for Industrial Reconstruction was preserved and the state led a large-scale modernisation and rationalisation of the industrial infrastructure in the early 1950s (Sassoon 1986, 41). However, government intervention on the French and Italian model differed from the social democratic or socialist conception. It took the form of partnership between the government and the private economic sector in which the government's rôle was largely limited to coordination. Private-sector entrepreneurship was the motor of economic recovery, and there was little attempt to make the economy responsive to social need.

West Germany The same was true to an even greater extent in western Germany. Here too, circumstances at the end of the war generated a mood for radical economic and social change. In the aftermath of National Socialism there was a vacuum on the Right, and almost all the important political forces looked to some form of social control, public ownership and state intervention as the foundation of the new economic order. However the sharp take-up in economic activity which accompanied Marshall Aid and the currency reform of 1948 reawakened the political self confidence of the entrepreneurial middle classes. The political climate moved to the Right as the Berlin blockade and the relief of the city by an airlift spearheaded by the United States forged a bond between West Germany and the western powers. Allied occupation had provided the Right with a breathing space in which to reassemble its forces. By the time the Western Allies restored self government to the West Germans, the Christian Democratic Union had committed itself decisively to economic liberalism and the market economy. As in Italy, christian democracy emerged as the overwhelmingly dominant political force and the social democrats were left isolated and powerless.

The Benelux countries In the Benelux countries there was a far more even balance between Right and Left, and consequently social democrats were able to make more of an impact on government. A common feature of the Benelux countries was the extraordinary openness of the national economies. A high priority was therefore accorded to the restoration of free trading relations, the renewal of export industries and the gearing of national economies to their international rôle. The drive for international competitiveness overshadowed domestic structural reform, and social democrats sharing power in both the Netherlands and Belgium did not resist. In a variety of other ways, however, they were able to exert an influence on the postwar settlement.

Governments in these two countries followed quite different strategies for reconstruction. The Netherlands represented a half-way house between the British and Norwegian experience and that of Italy, West Germany and France. Dutch governments embarked on an emphatically *dirigiste*, interventionist road to reconstruction, albeit within the framework of a market economy in which business continued to enjoy a wide measure of freedom. A Central Planning Bureau was set up in 1947, armed with an array of controls over wages and prices (Abert 1969, 112). The planning exercise was based on the prewar socialists' *Plan for Labour*, the architect of which (H. Vos) was Minister for Trade and Industry. It was recognised, however, that 'ultimately the necessary industrialisation will not come about as the result of a plan, but...will have to be principally the fruit of private economic decisions' (de Vries 1978, 105). Economic reconstruction in the Netherlands took place on the basis of a sort of social partnership between capital and labour epitomised by the Labour Foundation created in 1945 as an expression of a will for unity engendered under Nazi occupation. The partnership was institutionalised in 1950 with the creation of the Social and Economic Council, a forum for consultation between the 'social partners' and government. In 1950 there was an attempt to integrate organised interests and government still further through a Statutory Trade Organisation Act, though this was only partially successful. All this was indicative of the remarkably consensual nature of Dutch society in the late 1940s and early 1950s, and this consensus was reflected in a relative balance and harmony between the socialists and the confessional and middle-class parties in the government. Hence there was a kind of social symmetry about the postwar settlement in the Netherlands.

In Belgium, socialist-led governments between 1945 and 1949 placed rather more reliance on market forces than their Dutch counterparts. In common with the Netherlands, interest group pluralism was highly developed, but the concentration of economic power in the hands of the banks allowed them to exert a disproportionate influence over reconstruction policy. Hugh Gaitskell remarked on the extraordinary power of Belgian bankers (Williams 1983, 191), and it was one of these, Camile Gutt (also a government official) who fashioned Belgium's recovery programme. Geared to strengthening individual purchasing power rather than state intervention, the programme rapidly placed Belgium on the road to recovery, though at the cost of relatively high unemployment. The Liberal approach to reconstruction also owed much to

Paul-Henri Spaak, a socialist and twice premier between 1945 and 1949. Spaak was close to the American administrators of the European Recovery Programme, with whom he cooperated to promote the idea of European integration (Grosser 1980, 76–7). Economic and social issues were overshadowed for Belgian socialists by the *Question Royale* which come to a head in 1950 with a socialist-inspired general strike, provoking the abdication of the wartime collaborator King Leopold (Fitzmaurice 1983, 46–7). Ultimately, in economic terms, social democracy made relatively little impact on the postwar settlement in Belgium.

Austria　To an even greater extent than in the Benelux countries, national circumstances dictated the course of postwar reconstruction in Austria. The Austrian nation-state had had a short and troubled history and there were severe doubts as to its political cohesion and, more particularly, its economic viability. Economic reconstruction was vital for political self-confidence, and the Austrians chose a form of state capitalism as their vehicle. A powerful state sector was created (Steiner 1972, 84–6) and the government mounted a massive investment programme out of Marshall Aid finance (Milward 1984, 481). Semi-formal institutions of economic concertation were established, embracing government and the organisations of capital and labour, and exercising control over aspects of economic activity.

Politically the Austrian social democrats (SPÖ) were weaker than their right-wing rival, the Austrian Peoples' Party (ÖVP). However, a *modus vivendi* between the two parties quickly developed out of an initiative by SPO leader Karl Renner (Scharf 1955, 31–4). The agreement was to form the basis of twenty years of coalition government, the counterpart to which was a parallel accommodation between the leaders of the trade union confederation and that of the employers, (mirroring in some ways the Labour Federation in the Netherlands). Thus the political order was characterised by a 'consociational' style in which party élites came to terms with each other (Steiner 1972, 412–17; Barker 1973, 166). The immediate postwar years in Austria appear to display some of the hallmarks of social democracy - nationalisation, state interventionism and an embryonic welfare state. However, the substance of economic and social policy was heavily tinged by the christian social traditions of the People's Party. Social democracy could not be said to have been dominant in early postwar Austria.

Sweden The Swedish social democrats in the SAP were more hesitant in settling their course than their Norwegian counterparts. Without either an overall *Riksdag* majority or a stable coalition partnership they were rather vulnerable, the more so after the death of the veteran party leader and premier, Per Albin Hansson, in 1946. Hansson's successor, Tage Erlander, was relatively young and inexperienced, having held only one senior Cabinet portfolio, and that only briefly. It was not until 1951 that the prewar red-green coalition with the Agrarian Party was re-established, providing a more stable basis for government.

From the outset, SAP governments eschewed nationalisation and statutory economic controls for the more liberal prescriptions of Keynesian demand management, although inflationary tendencies after 1947 forced the temporary introduction of wage and price controls (Lindbeck 1975, 30–1). Immediate postwar programmes followed orthodox demand management strategies, geared principally to monetary stability (Esping-Andersen 1985, 228). The distinctive and innovatory features which the Swedish social democrats were subsequently to introduce into the Keynesian economic system were not yet fully developed, and it was not until the mid-1950s that the celebrated Swedish model of government social democracy attained its full ascendancy.

The welfare state

An important element in the Swedish model of social democracy was the welfare state. As it developed in Sweden, this meant more than merely the provision of widely available welfare services – most of western Europe had moved in this direction by the early 1950s. The social democratic welfare state, or social citizenship state, has been defined firstly with reference to the principle of universal solidarity (Esping-Andersen 1985, 147–9). This meant, above all, a harmonisation of the interests of wage-earners and welfare beneficiaries in a broadly based welfare state which recognised the interdependence of wages and benefits. The wage–benefit equation had to be confronted since 'once states began to provide more social benefits they unavoidably affected wages and redistributed income' (Ashford 1986, 17). The consolidation of broad political support for the welfare state thus required a new set of assumptions about economic rights and rewards. The labour market, however, was inherently divisive and inimical to social solidarity. Consequently, for the welfare state to operate effectively, political devices had to be found which would suppress market forces or limit their divisive effects. This was the second working principle which has been identified at the heart of the social democratic welfare state. The fulfilment of these conditions required radical institutional changes in government and in the behaviour of the trade unions in the labour market, and it has been argued (Esping-Andersen 1985) that the success of the social democratic welfare state, and ultimately the political success of social democracy, depended on negotiating these changes.

The postwar Labour government in Britain proceeded between 1945 and 1948 to create the world's first welfare state. Close examination of the policy process, however, exposes the absence of clear thinking about the kind of state which they were engaged in bringing about. Not surprisingly, then, the launch of the welfare state did not entail any major changes to political institutions. 'To argue that Britain stumbled into the welfare state would be excessive, but...it is clear that avoiding political obstacles regularly took precedence over exploring new ideas or developing national priorities in a coherent way' (Ashford 1986, 279). A major obstacle to a truly innovative approach to welfare was the labour movement. Even in wartime, the TUC had resisted the suggestion that wages should be related to family need. For them a high-wage, full-employment economy was the ultimate guarantee of postwar welfare. Whilst accepting the general idea of state welfare, the TUC were ambivalent towards some aspects of the Beveridge Plan and harboured 'deep reservations...over building a coherent welfare state' (Ashford 1986, 266) in which social policy and wages could be integrated. In addition to negative trade union attitudes, the severe financial constraints of the immediate postwar years (articulated with some force by the Treasury) curtailed the government's room for policy manoeuvre. Thus in Britain 'the institutionalisation of the welfare state from 1945–1950 was a product of institutional constraints and a limited understanding of the ultimate aim of welfare states' (Ashford 1986, 189). In the final analysis Beveridge and Keynes exercised more influence over the creation of the British welfare state than those Labour leaders who put it on the statute book. Consequently, their 'reluctant collectivism' tended to 'absorb and neutralise the social democratic tradition' (Perry 1986, 158–9).

Less constrained by circumstances, and with a more favourable institutional environment, the Scandinavian social democrats in government in the 1940s and 1950s were able to fashion the welfare state in their own image. The governing principles were those of institutionalisation, universalism and unconditional entitlement. In short, institutionalisation meant that the state accepted responsibility for the welfare of its citizens. Universalism meant the complete socialisation of welfare provisions. Unconditional entitlement separated benefits from contributions, thus eliminating market criteria from social welfare (Esping-Andersen and Korpi 1984, 49–55). The Scandinavian model was a total break from the past, and surpassed provisions in other countries. 'Scandinavian developments as a whole diverged from those elsewhere. Whereas most countries extended social security by including new groups within existing insurance systems...Denmark, Sweden and Norway explicitly broke with the liberal tradition by introducing universal non-contributory programmes. In principle the Beveridge plan was a guidepost; the Scandinavian reforms, however, went further' (Esping-Andersen 1985, 157).

Sweden was the leader in welfare state innovation. One of the keys to SAP success was its close relationship to the LO trade unions and the readiness of the latter to see the welfare state, wages policy and wider economic goals as inter-related. Thus the solidaristic wages policy designed in the LO economic bureau in the 1940s reinforced the solidaristic principles of the welfare state, and prevented the latent conflict between wage-earners and benefit recipients from breaking out in damaging and divisive political conflict. At the heart of the economy/labour market/social security network was the Labour Market Board, reformed in 1948 to gear it to its new rôle (Olsen 1986, 8–10). We shall deal at greater length with the practice of solidaristic wage bargaining, and the operation of the Labour Market Board later in this chapter. For present purposes it suffices to say that here was the foundation for the success of the Swedish model of the social democratic welfare state.

A new social order?

We can now evaluate social democratic government in the postwar years in a wider European context. Majority social democratic governments exhibited a stability and, at least initially, a unity of purpose absent from coalition governments elsewhere. Cohesion bred a relatively clear-cut policy orientation, as social democrats embarked upon a broadly collectivist road to reconstruction which drew on the traditions of working-class socialism outlined in the previous chapter. It represented an attempt to reach a postwar social settlement in which economic and social benefits would be

139

conferred rather more widely than under the prewar order. Social democratic governments redefined the nature and scope of government, the relationship between the state and the economy, and the rôle of the state as guarantor of general welfare.

Undoubtedly, political and social change was confined within the limits of a society which continued to be governed by market capitalism, and these limits narrowed in the late 1940s. It is also certainly true that the new thinking had been prefigured in a wartime consensus which embraced social and political forces beyond the social democratic parties. However, the rapidity with which non-socialist governments recoiled from the radicalism inherited from the war years suggests that in Britain and Scandinavia too, non-socialist governments would have backed off from wartime commitments.

Ultimately, all the democratic countries of Europe found themselves following similar, though not identical paths of political development in the postwar era. This was due in no small measure to the parallel evolution of the increasingly integrated European economies within the framework of the European Recovery Programme and under US hegemony. Nevertheless, it is possible to distinguish the social democratic countries by their predisposition towards full employment, state interventionism and welfare collectivism. This was reflected, firstly, in a marked increase in the social democratic countries (or in those where the Right was weak and divided) in the share of national income taken up by government expenditure. In Sweden and the Netherlands the increase from before the war was 50 per cent; in Britain, Denmark and Norway it was one-third. Elsewhere, the increase was negligible (Milward 1984, 485). An important element in the increase in government expenditure was the welfare state. Most of western Europe was covered by some form of social welfare provision, but Britain and Scandinavia adopted the most comprehensive systems. For all the limitations of Labour's welfare state, it was pushed further and faster than in any other western European country in the immediate postwar years. Labour also made an assault on inequalities of income and wealth, attempting to redistribute consumption through progressive income tax: 'it was not until after 1951 that these inequalities were allowed freer play' (Cairncross 1985, 505).

Within the machinery of government in the social democratic countries, a new institutional framework and policy style was evolved, destined to play an influential rôle in the postwar order. Having backed away from regulatory interventionism, British Labour governments adopted the Keynesian instruments of a fiscal policy geared to full employment which prefigured the style of economic management of the next two and a half decades. The planning exercise of the immediate postwar years had ploughed up the ground for subsequent exercises in economic management. One has only to look at countries where the Right was dominant in the crucial formative years to see, by way of contrast, the entrenchment of liberal economic orthodoxy in the institutional fabric of public life. The Italian constitution, for instance, contained stern strictures against the use of deficit budgeting which struck at the heart of Keynesian economics (Sassoon 1986, 53). In Italy and West Germany, central banks and finance ministries acted as bastions of economic liberalism, resistant to demand management policies.

In terms of public attitudes too, government social democracy played an important formative rôle, reinforcing expectations that government would exercise itself in the economic realm and as guarantor of full employment and general welfare. The ethos of interventionism and collectivism contrasted sharply with West Germany, where the 'miracle' of rapid and sustained growth bred a mythology, nurtured by christian democratic government, of the market economy. Whether or not the miracle was, in reality, the child of the market economy, the myth became a potent political symbol before which the social democrats were forced to yield.

In the light of these contrasts it might well be argued that social democratic governments did indeed exercise a degree of hegemony over the political system and social order. As one commentator on the British postwar experience has put it, 'the government knew where it wanted to go and led the country with an understanding of what was at stake' (Cairncross 1985, 509). Its chosen direction was not that of socialism as it had previously been conceived. Nevertheless, government social democracy had struggled free of the political economy of classical liberalism which had ruled the prewar order.

THE HEGEMONY OF SOCIAL DEMOCRACY IN THE ERA OF MANAGED GROWTH

New tasks, new instruments

Government social democracy had made a significant contribution to the secular trend from a liberal order towards economic management and to the intellectual ascendancy of the political economy of Keynesianism in western Europe. However, it was a minimalist model of economic management which took root over . most of the Continent in the 1950s. Favourable economic conditions and high growth rates meant that governments were able to manage the economy at arms length, relying on the most basic instruments of intervention to keep the ship on course.

The only major country to go far beyond this minimalist model of economic management was France. As we have seen, the foundation of the French model of technocratic planning had been laid in the immediate postwar years (Kuisal 1981, 272–3). In the 1950s, successive plans developed the planning experiment, driven by a sense of national economic backwardness and the belief that 'only through economic and social change could France hope to rescue some of her international prestige and power from the shipwreck of 1940' (Hoffman 1963, 75). Economic modernisation and national aggrandisement were the main objectives of French planning. The SFIO took little interest, and in any event was only briefly in government in the 1950s. France, like most of western Europe in this period, was governed by the Right.

Conservative, christian democratic and liberal parties had accommodated themselves to the terms of the postwar settlement, despite the fact that it was not of their making. In many ways they had adjusted better than the social democratic parties, many of which still hankered after more *dirigiste* forms of economic regulation. Social democrats in some countries were rather slow to recognise that the Keynesian style of economic management had made a greater impact on postwar political economy than had the impulse to seize into state ownership the commanding heights of the economy. By the early 1960s, however, as we have seen in the previous chapter, the parties had come to terms with the political consequences of a decade of postwar growth.

The robust growth of the 1950s however, had concealed incipient problems in the Keynesian model, foremost of which was the dilemma of reconciling full employment and the control of inflation. When the growth miracle of the 1950s began to falter, the employment–inflation dilemma was intensified. The attempt to control inflation within the full employment economy (Skidelsky 1979, 67–71) led governments towards intervention on an increasing scale. Social democrats were able to exploit these circumstances, advocating a change of emphasis in the synthesis which had come about between neo-liberalism and Keynesian interventionism. In short, they called for more state intervention to rectify the short circuits which had arisen in European economies. They also advocated measures to even out the social inequalities which had persisted through the growth era, presenting these initiatives as a modernisation of the economic infrastructure and social order. These themes boosted the political stock of social democracy, and the parties entered government in Italy (1963), Britain (1964), West Germany (1966) after long periods of christian democratic or conservative government. Here, and in those countries like Sweden or Austria where the parties were already in power, the state machinery was geared up to play a more prominent rôle in the economy. New institutions were created to act as instruments of intervention. Ministries were reshaped to meet the demands of managing the economy.

The success which these endeavours ultimately met depended on a number of factors. The institutional and attitudinal environment of political and economic life was of primary importance. In Sweden, after a long period of social democratic government, the institutional fabric and a supportive consensus already existed, and it was relatively easy to strengthen it. In Italy, Austria and West Germany, where christian democracy had been the dominant force, neither the institutional arrangements nor élite or popular attitudes were very accommodating. A second factor was the balance of power between capital and labour. Where large-scale capital was strongest, or where bourgeois parties retained a foothold in government, capital was able to set the terms for government intervention and veto any radical social programmes. Where trade unions were strongest – i.e. where they encompassed a large percentage of the workforce, were highly centralised and where they already had powerful presence in the political domain – government social democracy was able to encroach furthest into the economic and social sphere. Thirdly, the capacity resources and traditions of the state, were a decisive influence (Hayward 1975, 6–16). It was the strong tradition of the centralised state in France (along with the weakness of capital) which allowed the French model of technocratic planning such scope. Italy, on the other hand, was an example of a country where the public administration or bureaucratic apparatus of the state was just not capable of meeting the demands of large-scale economic and social programmes. In Sweden there was a long tradition of the interventionist state acting for collective goals. In Britain an entrenched *laissez-faire* philosophy pervaded key sectors of the public administration. A final factor at work was the underlying strength and resilience of national economies. Growth management on social democratic lines involved long-term strategies for the restructuring of the economy. If short-term calculations became the order of the day, as they inevitably did in weak or crisis-torn economies, then long-term strategies were bound to suffer. Another quite fundamental reason why government social democracy depended on growth was the absolute dependency of social programmes on 'surplus' economic capacity. Thus growth, naturally enough, was the key to growth management. The failure of the 1964-70 Labour governments was bound up in the weakness of the British economy. Though neither succeeded in changing society in any really significant sense, the record of social democratic governments in West Germany and Austria, for example, was altogether more favourable, simply because of the underlying stability and resilience of the national economies. The growth factor was particularly significant in Sweden, which shows the most successful example of government social democracy in this era.

Sweden　Here the SAP began, in the middle 1950s, to develop the distinctive and innovatory forms of government social democracy for which it was to become renowned. The initial breakthrough in policy innovation was the development by labour movement economist, Gösta Rehn, of a novel strategy for regulating the economy. The Rehn model provided a solution to the employment–inflation dilemma. It also served to resolve the dilemma of how to rationalise and modernise the structure of industry, channelling resources into the most productive and profitable sectors, without the use of coercive instruments which the social democrats had long ago foresworn.

Rehn's scheme (Esping-Andersen 1985, 229–31; Lindbeck 1975, 39–41) entailed a system of solidaristic wage bargaining, by which negotiation took place on a national scale, across different industries and regions, between the central organisations of capital and labour. Thus the level of wage settlements would be determined by the level of profitability prevailing in the most productive companies and industrial sectors. Weak firms would be unable to protect themselves through artificially depressing wages. Competition from more productive firms would also prevent them from making inflationary price increases. In short, the industrial deadwood would be driven out of the market. Here was a formula for high wages, low inflation and the rationalisation of industry, without cumbersome and, Rehn believed, counterproductive wage–price controls. However, it would inevitably entail corporate closures and job losses, with unemployment concentrated in certain industries and regions. It was here that the counterpart to solidaristic wage bargaining came in. An active labour market policy, orchestrated by the state through the prewar Labour Market Board, would include large-scale retraining and labour mobility programmes in order to relocate labour from defunct to profitable industrial sectors.

Rehn's technically brilliant scheme reconciled the requirements of profitability and rationality in a capitalist economy with the demands of the trade unions for full employment and high wages. It was adopted, cautiously at first, by a social democratic government which breathed new life into the previously moribund Labour Market Board from 1956 onwards. It was the precursor of the emerging style of SAP government, bearing all its hallmarks. Firstly, it was a pragmatic, non-ideological solution to a set of economic problems. Secondly, it increased the government's leverage over the economy without involving the state in the exercise of statutory controls. Thirdly, it embodied a trade-off between government and the private economic sector, based on the maintenance of profitability in a socially responsive economy. Finally, it established the Labour Market Board as the nexus of the growing inter-relationship between the state and the capitalist economy.

A further step down this road was the introduction in 1959-60 of earnings-related pensions. The Supplementary Pensions Scheme represented the consolidation of an earlier initiative, and the enhancement of a welfare system which already included child benefits and state medical insurance. The Swedish welfare state had been brought into being piecemeal and not, as in Britain, at a stroke. It was based on the social citizenship philosophy referred to in a previous chapter, and rivalled the British model in its scope and open accessibility. However, the significance of this latest innovation went beyond its immediate social purposes. In economic terms it meant the accumulation in the pension funds of a massive reservoir of public capital which added greatly to the state's capacity for directing investment (Esping-Andersen 1985, 160–1).

This aspect of the pension reform aroused fierce opposition from the employers and bourgeois parties, and abruptly terminated the end of ideology, consensus politics of the 1950s. In the resultant realignment of political forces, the white-collar trade unions, formerly politically independent, swung behind the Social Democratic Party. The conflict liquidated the red-green coalition with the Agrarian Party, which had by now outlived its usefulness.

After a referendum in 1957 and elections in 1960, the SAP emerged ideologically reinvigorated and electorally strengthened, whilst defeat on the pensions issue left the bourgeois parties badly divided. Thus the pension reform represented an 'historical crossroads' for Swedish social democracy, liberating it from coalition with the agrarians and helping to cement a broad voting alliance of manual worker wage-earners and large sections of the salaried, white-collar middle class (see chapter 5). On this basis, the SAP 'marched through the decade with a recast programme emphasising extended public regulation and control of the economy, rapid structural modernisation of industry, active state direction of investment and housing development and, finally, wage solidarity and income equalisation' (Esping-Andersen 1985, 109).

The Labour Market Board was at the heart of government policy in these areas. In the late 1950s its activities had been extended. It had served as an instrument of counter-cyclical policy – intervening in the economy to even out the fluctuations in activity. The *modus operandi* of labour market policy was through the investment funds system. Private-sector companies were induced by tax concessions to set aside sums of capital out of profits as investment funds. A proportion of these funds was held in blocked accounts at the central bank, to be released at the behest of the AMS as and when its forecasts detected downturns on the economic horizon (Lindbeck 1975, 98–102). It had intervened in 1958 to counteract a minor recession, but the exercise had been only partially successful. The next downturn in the economy, in 1962, was met with greater preparedness and refinement of technique, and to better effect, and the operation was repeated in 1967 and 1972 (Jones 1976, 152–4). The effect of the national pension funds, then, was to add to the resources the state already possessed for economic control.

A high proportion of public investment capital was channelled into the construction industry which government saw as a sort of locomotive to generate growth elsewhere in the economy. However, housing was also a particular target of social policy. Social democratic governments made a great impact on housing finance and house building, manipulating market forces and effectively 'socialising the market' or else supplanting it altogether (Headey 1978, 66–99). Concerted and planned development over a period of time under Housing Minister Alf Johansson, made high-quality, low-cost housing widely available by the late 1960s. Housing policy typified the ability of SAP governments to win political control over markets and the market economy, rendering them responsive to collective needs as defined by the state. The concept of control was a central element in the political philosophy of government social democracy in Sweden. Economic planning was allocated little priority – state ownership still less. Moreover, government made no attempt to regulate the concentration of private ownership, which became concentrated to a remarkably high degree. This was one of the defining characteristics of Swedish social democracy. Leaving the ownership of private capital untouched and turning a blind eye to its concentration, government developed a contract with capital (see chapter 3). In return capital acquiesced in the exercise by governments of the guiding hand – the leitmotif of the Swedish model.

Austria A superficial view might place the experience of government social democracy in Austria alongside that of Sweden. In terms of its ability to maintain a rôle in government over a sustained period of time, the Austrian party (SPÖ) was not far behind its Swedish counterpart (Pelinka 1983, 80). Like the Swedes, the SPÖ had the benefit of a close relationship with a strong and centralised trade union confederation. The postwar order exhibited a certain superficial similarity with Sweden's in as much as it was built on an informal, contractual agreement between capital and labour. Growth management was the dominant theme of Austrian government, particularly in the 1970s when the SPÖ exercised majority power for almost a decade. Indeed this decade is often regarded as a period of outstanding success for Austrian social democracy, and is commonly known as 'the Kreisky era' after Party Chairman and Chancellor Dr Bruno Kreisky. Combining social democratic idealism with the realism required of a national leader, Kreisky became associated with the unprecedented affluence, high employment and progressive reform of these years.

However, Austrian social democracy was a much less dynamic force than its Swedish counterpart, unable to liberate itself from a conservative and rather complacent political culture which placed a premium on consensus and compromise. The postwar period had seen the institutionalisation of accommodation in political life. Cartel arrangements had developed between the SPÖ and its main rival the ÖVP, and between the peak organisation of capital and labour an elaborate, corporatist, para-coalition relationship had evolved (Steiner 1972, 311). The left being the weaker partner within this political order, 'the mandate for a social democratization of Austria was strictly circumscribed' (Esping-Andersen and Korpi 1984, 204).

The result was 'policy immobilism' and the politics of 'conflict avoidance'. Innovation, when it came, was slow and piecemeal. Significantly, the introduction of Keynesian instruments of economic steering and concertation in the early 1960s was at the initiative of the employers and trade unions rather than the SPÖ (Steiner 1972, 312–7). It was confined within the institutional framework of the 'social partnership' and did not involve any fundamental change in the balance of power between politics and the market. In the 1970s, majority social democratic governments pursued more aggressive Keynesian strategies which were successful in maintaining growth and avoiding unemployment (Scharpf 1984, 264). Still, however, the innovation which we have observed in Sweden was largely absent. The precondition for full employment was the labour movement's willingness to let market forces dictate wage behaviour, and politics were still not permitted to interfere in markets.

In social policy, the 1970s saw a series of reforms – the consolidation of child allowances, a rationalisation of social insurance, and improvements of sickness insurance benefits for wage-earners. The net result of these reforms was to introduce an element of progressiveness into welfare contributions and benefits, to extend the scope of the welfare state and to equalise employment conditions between wage and salary earners. However, these reforms were confined within the framework of an essentially conservative welfare state, largely governed by the christian social principles of social solidarity to which the Peoples' Party subscribed. The principle of social citizenship was absent from the Austrian model of welfare. No serious attempt was made to challenge the inequalities resulting from the play of market forces, and Austria remained one of the most inegalitarian societies in western Europe (Esping-Andersen and Korpi 1984, 190–4).

In summary, then, the impact of the Kreisky era was distinctly limited. It amounted to little more than a marginal readjustment in the policy framework of consensus corporatism and a market-oriented welfare state. In spite of its bland appearance, however, government social democracy in Austria enjoyed an unusual degree of longevity, outliving the more innovatory social democratic government in Sweden. Although the SPÖ lost its majority status in 1983, it continued to lead government into the late 1980s. The persistence of social democratic government in Austria reflected the capacity of the economy to withstand the worst effects of the recession, and the ability of government to reconcile economic stability with near full employment. The consensus politics of social partnership in a growth economy sustained social democratic government, even though the terms of the consensus prevented the social democrats from making a major impact on Austrian society.

West Germany A similar verdict may be delivered on the West German Social Democratic Party (SPD) in power between 1966 and 1982. As we have seen in the previous chapter, by the time the SPD entered government (as junior partner to the christian democrats in the Grand Coalition), it had become a party of pragmatic reform. It was now reconciled to an institutional and cultural environment which had been defined in the main by its christian democratic rival. It differentiated itself from its rival by its advocacy of Keynesian economics, a liberalisation of the social order and a more accommodating relationship to the East in foreign policy. As Economics Minister from 1966 to 1972, Karl Schiller was successful in introducing a form of 'arm's-length steering' into an economy which had hitherto been managed on neo-liberal lines. However, the strength of the 'market economy' ethos prevented the SPD from developing the institutionalised networks of state–economy relations which we have observed in Sweden. Nor were political conditions propitious for the implementation of SPD programmes for the democratisation of economic life, or the liberalisation of social or family law. The constraint of coalition government, the ability of organised capital to exert political muscle, the relative weakness of the trade unions, and the political influence of the Catholic Church all militated against a 'social democratic revolution' in policy terms. In many policy areas, commentators have drawn attention to the continuity between the era of christian democratic government and that of the Social Liberal coalition (von Beyme 1985, 21–2). The major exception was foreign policy, where the Brandt-Bahr programme of *Ostpolitik* amounted to a thorough reorientation of the policy framework (see chapter 5).

In 1974 the hard-headed pragmatist Helmut Schmidt replaced the reformist Willy Brandt. The maintenance of economic security was now given almost absolute priority over social and economic reform. Policy was constrained by a general restriction on public expenditure and the exercise of monetary caution. Periodically the government embarked on spending programmes designed to stimulate growth and employment. The volume of these re-flationary packages was carefully set, and they were targeted to achieve the maximum effect whilst minimising their inflationary consequences. Economic discipline meant a retreat from some long-standing party commitments. Proposals for a comprehensive vocational training programme, an extension of co-determination legislation, a wage-earner shareholding scheme and pension reform were either shelved altogether or decisively weakened in their implementation.

Although the government sought to strike a balance between an employer-oriented economic policy and measures favourable to wage- and salary-earners, it was towards the former that the balance tilted (Webber 1984, 61–86). Income from investment capital rose faster than that from wages and salaries. During Schmidt's second term of office (1976-80), the inner circle of the Chancellor's advisers and confidantes in economic policy was dominated by businessmen and bankers from the private sector. In short, the precarious balance between pragmatism and reform which the SPD had achieved at Bad Godesberg slipped decisively towards the former. The Schmidt Chancellorship was an exercise in growth management within very tight limits. There was little scope for deploying political instruments, on the Swedish model, to counteract market forces. Nor was Schmidt inclined to adopt such a strategy, looking as he did to the private economic sector, not the state, to generate growth. Moreover, as we have seen, the institutional and cultural environment of West German politics was not conducive to government social democracy along these lines (Scharpf 1984, 283–6).

Britain British Labour governments had met the problem of low growth a decade earlier than the West Germans. The experiences of Harold Wilson's administrations in the 1960s underline the dependency of government social democracy on vigorous and sustained economic growth. By the time Labour took office in 1964, the weak performance of the economy had already stimulated British interest in the French model of indicative planning (Wright 1979, 155). The Wilson government immediately created a Department of Economic Affairs (DEA) which drew up the National Plan, a document of some 500 pages presented to parliament in 1965. In his introduction to the plan, the head of the new ministry, George Brown, asserted that it represented 'a statement of government policy and a commitment to government action' (Liebermann 1977, 230). In fact, the plan on its own was more of a sketch of how the government would have liked to see the economy developing than it was a blueprint for action. 'The reluctance of the government to assume greater powers of control was striking.' Proposals for the direction of pension and insurance funds into investment were dropped for fear of damaging confidence in the City at a time when the pound was weak. The Industrial Expansion Bill, allowing the state to take up shares in private-sector companies, was diluted in the face of opposition from the CBI. The Industrial Reorganisation Corporation was intended to direct state investment into corporate enterprises, thereby giving the government leverage over the private sector. However, its influence was largely limited to encouraging corporate mergers and it contributed little to 'bringing the private sector in behind strategic public policy choices' (Jones and Keating 1985, 87–9).

One reason for the failure of Labour's planning strategy then, was that it was not backed up by sufficiently forceful or persuasive instruments of intervention. This introduces a second reason for failure, the political power of capital, and the concomitant inability of government to impose its will on the private economic sector. A third factor was the chronic weakness of the pound, the devaluation of which Wilson steadfastly refused to countenance for political reasons. Devaluation was not carried out until 1967, by which time the plan had been abandoned. Consequently the Treasury was repeatedly forced to defend the value of sterling through deflationary measures which were directly counterproductive against the DEA's growth policies. Under these conditions, planning disintegrated into a series of holding operations involving expenditure cuts and statutory pay restraint under the auspices of the Prices and Incomes Board. A fourth underlying reason for the government's failure to induce growth was the relatively low level of profitability in industry, which meant a low propensity to invest. Instead of producing investment and increasing output, the government's attempts to speed growth through stimulating demand simply produced an inflationary spiral. In turn, inflation aggravated balance of payments and exchange problems, the inevitable response being deflationary policies which only served to curtail growth further. In economic policy, then, Labour was caught in a vicious circle of inflation and stagnation.

The assumption of 1964 had been that 'the mixed economy could be operated efficiently by a Labour Government and this efficient operation would permit the provision of substantial benefits to Labour supporters' (Howell 1976, 251). Profitability and growth were therefore key elements in the government's social policy. However the growth target of 25 per cent between 1964 and 1970 was wildly optimistic, actual growth amounting to no more than 14 per cent. The shortfall curtailed the government's ability to meet its commitments to welfare and equality. The guaranteed minimum wage was shelved, as were Richard Crossman's radical pension proposals. One critical observer has written that 'Labour made ambitious and radical policies in opposition but had feet of clay when it came to their implementation in government' (Whitely 1983, 179). To be sure, the period saw an increase in social welfare benefits and the Social Security Act of 1966, which rationalised family poverty benefits and abolished the means test for family allowances. Even the most well-disposed observers, however, were unable to argue that Labour made any positive impact on the distribution of income and wealth (Beckerman 1972, 38–43). As we shall see in a subsequent chapter, it was the economic and social policy failures of the 1960s which began the process of political decomposition in the Labour Party, culminating in the formation of the breakaway Social Democratic Party in 1981.

Italy   In West Germany, the entry of the SPD into government came about partly as a response to a retardation of growth rates, the appearance of structural defects in the economy and the inability of the non-socialist parties to agree on a remedial programme. A similar, though more acute pattern of circumstances prevailed in Italy, where flaws in the economic miracle, which had been apparent in the late 1950s, reached crisis proportions in the early 1960s. Postwar growth had exacerbated the longstanding disparity between the relatively affluent, industrial North and the poor agrarian economy of the South. It had also tightened the labour market in the North, leading to labour militancy, wage increases and a squeeze on profits. The result was a crisis of profitability amongst the small firms which had in large part acted as the motor of the miracle. Inflation and balance of payments problems compounded the picture of economic instability. A political crisis in 1960 compelled the christian democrats to look to cooperation between political and economic forces in order to tackle the crisis (Sassoon 1986, 48–9). This was the background to the multi-party Centre-Left coalition, formed in 1963, of which the major participants were the christian democrats and the socialists.

The motives of the Italian Socialist Party (PSI) for joining the coalition were rather complex. In the background was the party's commitment to the liberal democratic regime, which appeared to be in jeopardy in the early 1960s. Political calculations also played a part. Here was the opportunity for a realignment of party politics from which the PSI might establish itself as a pivot in the party system, marginalising its communist rival. Finally in programmatic terms, there were those in the PSI who believed that by forging an alliance with left-wing christian democrats, they might be able to carry through reforms in the social structure. They had been encouraged by policy initiatives already underway – the nationalisation of electricity supply, modest reforms in education, agriculture and taxation, and above all, an undertaking by the Budget Minister to initiate a comprehensive system of economic planning (Hine 1978, 45-6; Sassoon 1986, 52–4).

In the event, however, this was the extent of the reforming achievements of the centre-left coalition. The planning initiatives were smothered by the Bank of Italy, a bastion of liberal economics, whose restrictive monetary policy effectively undermined the objectives of long-term economic restructuring (Hine 1978, 234). Moreover, to be successful, a planning exercise would have required the cooperation of the trade unions in pay restraint, and this was not forthcoming (Hine 1978, 243–6). Proposed reforms in urban policy and housing failed due to the weakness of the state bureaucracy. Not only were urban programmes under-funded, but they also fell prey to the extensive patronage and clientele networks of the Italian public administration. The experience of the centre–left coalition underlines the importance of the strong state to the success of government social democracy. A further factor in the ineffectiveness of the coalition was that the PSI's conception of structural reform was conditioned by its radical Marxist ideology. As we have already seen, the incremental reformism of government social democracy elsewhere in western Europe was foreign to the Italian party. It was thus unprepared to make the sort of compromises necessary to build consensus support for change. As it was, the modernisation of Italian society did not come about until the early 1970s, by which time the PSI had begun to think about alternative coalition formations. Social change occurred largely independently of party politics, provoked by economic advance and the social discontent expressed in the hot autumn of 1969 (Spotts and Wieser 1986, 218–9).

Politics against markets

The 1960s and early 1970s was a period of political hegemony for government social democracy. Party leaders – Brandt, Palme, Kreisky, Wilson – strode the stage of national, international and European politics. Success was based in large part on a convergence between social democracy and the economic orthodoxies of the day, growth management and Keynesian interventionism. One influential and valuable addition to the literature has suggested that social democratic government is geared to the exercise of 'politics against markets' (Esping-Andersen 1985). Without attempting to suppress market forces, governments in this period deployed political instruments to make market forces work more effectively and to harness them to social and indeed political purposes. From this perspective it is possible to identify some notable successes – labour market policies in Scandinavia and Austria, and Swedish housing policy, for example. However, as we saw earlier, success depended on the fulfilment of certain conditions – a favourable institutional and attitudinal environment, labour movement strength and resilience of the economy. The corollary of the conditions of success were the limitations to which government social democracy was subject – narrower in some countries than in others.

There is no easy yardstick for assessing the impact of government social democracy on society. However, it is possible to maintain, without great fear of contradiction, that there was no sense in which it was system transforming. The persistence of entrenched inequalities in the distribution of economic rewards is sufficient testimony to this verdict. We shall give a fuller assessment at the end of the present chapter. For present purposes it will suffice to adopt the method of the preceding section where we assessed the contribution of social democracy to the mainstreams of historical developments in the immediate postwar years. We might also draw similar conclusions. Government social democracy made some important though not decisive contributions to the economic and social ordering of advanced capitalist society. In short, it reinforced the trend towards 'welfare capitalism'. If this appears to be a muted and modest accolade then we might reflect that it was a good deal more than could be said of its contribution to the era which followed.

GOVERNMENT SOCIAL DEMOCRACY IN THE RECESSION

The malign syndrome

The roots of the decline in Keynesian economies have been located in the destabilising effects of the breakdown in US hegemony over the international economy, and the emergence of the OPEC oil cartel. The syndrome of instability which resulted 'hugely complicated the task of macroeconomic coordination' both internationally and nationally. 'The speculation against the dollar was partly responsible for the hectic inflationary boom of 1972–3; the OPEC price rise of 1973–4 produced the worst recession since the 1930s, while exacerbating a 'cost push' inflation as western businesses and trade unions tried to maintain profits and wages in the face of escalating energy prices' (Skidelsky 1979, 76). Keynesian responses to this syndrome proved impotent, even serving counter–productively to exacerbate the conditions they were designed to cure.

It was ironic that social democrats should have been reliant, albeit indirectly, on the global economic power of the United States, since they had often been highly ambivalent or downright hostile to its exercise. However, with the collapse of the international economic system which the Americans had engendered, and the contingent disintegration of Keynesian economics, government social democracy entered a period of profound disorientation. It was no longer possible to rely on the compromise formulas of the previous era. Then, governments had been able to reconcile the profitability of capital with high and rising wage levels and full employment, to couple a stable, performance economy with a social or welfare state and to orchestrate market forces through state intervention. Now they were forced to confront a 'malign syndrome' of stagnation, inflation, rising unemployment, a spiral of state debt, and trade imbalance. These new circumstances defied the comfortable formulas of growth management.

Crisis management

The Wilson/Callaghan governments in Britain (1974–79) and the Schmidt administrations in West Germany (1974–82) were quite quick to respond. Emphasis was placed on economic discipline in the form of wage restraint, strict controls on public expenditure and fiscal and monetary policies geared to controlling inflation. Crisis management programmes were justified on the grounds that social democratic policies depended on a foundation of economic stability, the restoration of which had to be regarded as a first priority. Thus in 1975 Harold Wilson introduced the 'social contract' – a policy of pay restraint agreed with top trade union leaders – as an issue of 'whether this or any other democratic socialist government can survive and lead the nation to full employment and social justice'. Wilson's successor, James Callaghan, went further, identifying business profitability as the *sine qua non* of economic life which had to be restored at all costs: 'I mean they must be able to earn a surplus, which is a euphemism for saying that they must be able to make a profit. Whether you call it surplus or profit it is necessary, whether we live in a socialist economy, a mixed economy or a capitalist economy' (Lieber 1979, 181–209). Helmut Schmidt and Finance Minister Hans Matthöfer shared this view, the more emphatically after the deepening of the recession in the Federal Republic in 1980. In his presentation of the budget of 1981 Matthöfer argued that the state was no longer in a position to guarantee full employment, that its capacity to influence economic development had to be more modestly assessed, and that ultimately it was not state spending, but entrepreneurial vitality which was decisive for economic success (Webber 1984, 99–100).

The recognition that the state could no longer guarantee full employment was part of a wider break away from Keynesian orthodoxy. As Finance Minister in the Brandt administration, Schmidt had placed increasing emphasis on monetary policy as an instrument of economic stabilisation. As Chancellor he went further down this road in step with the *Bundesbank,* which had decided to switch from a Keynesian counter-cyclical policy to an explicitly monetarist strategy in the summer of 1974 (Scharpf 1984, 284). As we have seen, Callaghan's renunciation of Keynesianism came in 1976 (chapter i). After the crisis of that year, and the recourse to IMF credits, the Labour government's thinking switched decisively towards monetarist solutions. A profound change of attitudes took place, in which the goal of controlling inflation eclipsed that of reducing unemployment (Holmes 1985, 181–2), even after unemployment passed the politically sensitive one million mark.

The crisis management model of government social democracy enjoyed a certain amount of success, particularly in the first two Schmidt administrations, when the Federal Republic became Europe's leading economic power. Nor was the Callaghan government entirely devoid of success. By 1978–79, inflation had been reduced from over 20 per cent to single figures, and the balance of payments restored to surplus. Ultimately, though, Callaghan's record was tarnished by the outbreak of industrial disputes in the winter of 1978–79, the inflationary explosion which followed, and the Machiavellian manoeuvring in which his government had engaged in order to maintain its parliamentary majority.

More fundamentally, however, the British and West German experiences revealed the limits of crisis management under social democratic government. Firstly, the piecemeal surgery which both governments applied to social expenditure did not resolve the crisis of social or welfare states which had expanded faster than the capacity of the economy to sustain them. Secondly, formal or informal agreements between governments and trade unions contravened the cherished principle of free collective bargaining (or *Tarifautonomie*), and placed strains on the unions which even government-loyal leaders were unable to contain. In Britain the result was the 'winter of discontent'. In West Germany, only the fall of the social-liberal coalition saved the social democrats from an open rift with the trade unions. Thirdly, social democratic governments were unable in the long term to sanction the breach in the postwar promise of full employment.

Many commentators envisaged the economic crisis spilling over into political crisis. According to this view, low-growth or no-growth economies no longer possessed the capacity to satisfy the demands generated within the democratic system. As a result 'an excessive burden is placed on the "sharing out" function of government' (Brittan 1975; Moss 1977). The maintenance of the process of capital accumulation required changes in the political landscape – a restructuring (contraction) of the welfare state, curbs on entrenched union powers, a reduction of popular demands and expectations concerning economic security and employment. Social democrats could not, however, relinquish the government's distributive rôle to the market for long. Neither could they acquiesce in a shift in the balance of power between capital and labour towards the former. Finally, they could not renounce the demands and expectations which they themselves had articulated. The welfare state, free collective bargaining and full employment were so closely entwined with social democratic traditions and the parties' postwar identities, that any retreat from these institutionalised principles precipitated a profound crisis within the parties and labour movements. Consequently, crisis management under social democracy increasingly resembled a series of unsatisfactory and frequently contradictory expedients, as governments fought desperately to reconcile assumptions carried over from a previous era with new economic realities.

The erosion of the capacity of social democratic parties for government was exposed most dramatically in Britain and West Germany. The Labour Party no longer had the cohesion and sense of purpose required of a party governing alone. The German party was also subject to internal disintegration. Moreover, it was not easily compatible on major policy issues with either of its potential coalition partners – the liberal Free Democratic Party or the postmaterialist, leftist Greens. For a party condemned by virtue of structure of the electorate and the party system to permanent minority status in relation to its main rival, the inability to sustain coalition compromises meant exile in opposition. This incapacity for coalition compromise was a common syndrome amongst social democratic parties in the late 1970s and early 1980s. In the Netherlands the Labour-led coalition of Joop den Uyl had met the first oil price inspired crisis with relative success through a policy of wage restraint and deflation. However, it was unable to contain the growth of the public-sector budget – approaching 60 per cent of national income – which threatened economic stability (Peper 1982, 144). Nor was Labour prepared to acquiesce in breaking the well-established system of wage and social benefit indexation. Consequently it was left to a centre-right government to take these steps, and although the Labour Party returned to coalition government in 1981 its presence was short-lived.

In Belgium, coalition government had been the norm in the postwar period, but here too the recession placed great strains on the capacity for compromise between socialist and non-socialist parties. The result was the formation in 1981 of a centre-right coalition which immediately introduced a more draconian form of crisis management (Fitzmaurice 1983, 70). The socialist parties meanwhile, went into opposition, where they have remained. Similarly, the Danish party's time honoured rôle as centre of gravity of a broad coalition became untenable as interparty differences over incomes policy, public expenditure cuts, taxation and employment became irreconcilable (Fitzmaurice 1981, 34). The fall of Anker Jørgensen in 1982 signalled the end of the ascendancy of government social democracy in Denmark.

In those countries where the parties had been accustomed to governing alone a similar picture of decay was replicated. The Norwegian Labour Party policy formula of 'state bureaucracy, high taxes and Keynesian deficit planning...[now]...seemed to intensify problems rather than solve them' (Hodne 1983, 267). The year 1981 marked the formation of a bloc of bourgeois parties sufficiently cohesive to oust the minority social democratic government of Mrs Gro Harlem Brundtland. Returning to power without a parliamentary majority after the collapse of the bourgeois government in 1986, the new Brundtland government was confronted with an acute crisis in an oil-dependent economy suffering from a world price slide. The response was to renounce the commitment to an expansive programme of demand-led reflation in favour of a tough austerity package.

In Austria, the SPÖ government of Bruno Kreisky had been very successful in the 1970s and early 1980s in managing the economy on Keynesian lines. Growth rates had been consistently amongst the highest in western Europe, and between 1973 and 1982 unemployment had averaged less than 2 per cent (Clement 1987, 7). The key to Austrian success lay with the highly developed network of corporatist relations between government, the trade unions and the employers (the 'social partnership') which promoted wage discipline and suppressed the inflationary consequences which followed from Keynesianism in other countries. Nevertheless, in the early 1980s the gloss began to wear off the Austrian model.

Although the economy was still relatively stable, it was no longer especially dynamic. Moreover, public expenditure was growing rapidly in relation to the national product in the private sector. Austria was losing its competitive edge. In addition, the corporatist machinery surrounding the national economy – and particularly the public sector – began to take on the appearance of a sprawling bureaucracy, spawning inefficiency and inhibiting innovation (Clement 1987, 14-19). Economic inertia was compounded by political stagnation and decay. The Chancellor, Kreisky, was now over seventy, and his authority was impaired by clashes with his Finance Minister, Hannes Androsch. A corruption scandal concerning the latter further damaged the government's standing (Sully 1986, 162–3). With the election of 1983 (at which the SPO lost its absolute majority), Kreisky stepped down as Chancellor. His successor, Fred Sinowatz, was obliged to conclude a coalition arrangement with the small, divided Austrian Freedom Party. This makeshift government was ill-equipped to deal with the deteriorating condition of the national economy, rising unemployment and a crisis in the VOEST state undertaking – the flagship of the public sector and symbol of the national economy. The termination of the coalition with the election of 1986, and the formation of a grand coalition between the SPO and the conservative Austrian Peoples' Party brought about a major policy reorientation – a shift away from the practice of 'Austro-Keynesianism' (Luther 1987, 396). It also marked another step in the decline of government social democracy in its north European heartlands.

The adjustment of the Swedish model

In northern Europe, only Sweden stood out from the general picture of government social democracy in a state of decomposition. The SAP had returned to government in 1982 after a six-year absence committed to what they presented as a distinctively social democratic approach to crisis management. Olof Palme's government accepted that structural defects in the national economy required remedial surgery, and that economic constraints placed limits on the welfare state. It also accepted that private-sector renewal was a prerequisite of general economic recovery. This entailed a restoration of business profitability and an improvement in the international competitiveness of Swedish industry. These were the assumptions which the Callaghan and Schmidt governments had made a decade earlier, but the Swedes went rather further in their attempt to prevent the cherished principles of social justice and solidarity from being subordinated entirely to economic exigency. In short the new SAP government tried to reconcile these principles with economic realism and crisis management (Walters 1985, 356–69).

Remedial surgery on the economy took the form of a 16 per cent devaluation of the Krona, and an urgent call to the trade unions for pay restraint. A central element in the crisis programme was the reduction of the public sector deficit, and the government recognised that this would entail cuts in the overall level of social expenditure. Housing (cuts in subsidised loans and rents), health (increased consumer charges) and public-sector industry (phasing out of subsidies), were the main targets. However, cuts were selective, and attempts were made to cushion the less well-off against their effects. Moreover, the SAP's commitment to employment support in the form of labour market policies was largely unscathed. Expenditure cuts were moderate by the standards of some other countries. The government calculated that the general economic recovery induced by the crisis package would allow them to restructure the welfare state without a sudden breach in its principles. Above all it would allow them to retain the redistributive character of the welfare system. It has been pointed out that the crisis programme was in keeping with the traditions of government social democracy in Sweden, most notably the integration of business interests and economic efficiency on the one hand with social solidarity and the welfare state on the other (Walters 1985, 366). Continuity with this tradition was essential for the government to secure trade union support for its crisis measures.

Initially the trade unions backed the crisis programme and accepted pay settlements in line with the government's goals. They were 'sweetened' by measures – increases in wealth, inheritance and gift taxes, reductions in tax concessions to shareholders – designed to show that burdens were being distributed evenly across society. Above all, though, their compliance was conditional on the government's implementation of proposals for wage-earner funds devised by the trade union economist, Rudolf Meidener.

As we have already seen in chapter 1, the plan was part of an ideological renewal on the part of the Swedish social democrats. It had certain attractions for the government, promising to increase collective savings, channelling them into productive investment. It was hoped also that the profit levy from which the funds were to be drawn would have the effect of legitimising business profits, consolidating wage solidarity and restraint (Thomas 1986, 203). On the negative side, however, the scheme engendered fierce controversy and the government was faced with total opposition from the business sector. Consequently, although the plan had been included in the 1982 election programme, Olof Palme remained cautious and implementation (in 1984) came only under pressure from the LO. Even then the plan was introduced only for an experimental six-year period and Meidener's original formulation was diluted (Thomas 1986, 206).

Five funds were established, with revenue coming from one of the state pension funds and from the profit levy which impinged on about one in ten firms. Each fund was run by a nine-member board, with a chairman appointed by government and a built-in employee majority. Since private-sector firms refused to cooperate, the boards were manned by representatives of state-owned enterprises and by organised interests, with trade unions heavily dominant. It was estimated that by 1990 the funds' holdings on the stock market would amount to no more than about 8 per cent of all listed share capital. Holdings in any single company were restricted to less than 50 per cent, protecting company independence (Thomas 1986, 204–5). Although in the experimental period the funds were thus limited in their impact, both their advocates and their opponents saw them as foreshadowing a gradual transformation of Swedish capitalism (Aimer 1985, 45). In so far as this was true, it was in harmony with the tradition of Swedish social democracy, consolidating collective public control over the private sector by modifying, though not suppressing, market capitalism.

The Swedish economy responded quite positively to the crisis package with steady growth from 1982 to 1985. Then, however, the recovery faltered and it became increasingly difficult to maintain the pay discipline of the previous three years. Nevertheless, the 1985 election confirmed the SAP in power. The party's success owed much to Olof Palme, who fought a brilliant individualistic campaign. Palme had also played an energetic personal rôle in persuading the trade unions to toe the line on wages. His death by assassination, early in 1986, was a devastating blow. Ingvar Carlsson, his successor, was something of an unknown quantity, having made his career as a back-room party manager. Carlsson's first period in office was characterised by uncertainty in which doubts about the performance of the economy were compounded by threats of widespread industrial action. He was assisted by falling oil prices which eased the pressure on the economy, and the conclusion of a moderate two-year pay settlement enabled Carlsson's government to consolidate the recovery.

The success of government social democracy in Sweden in the 1980s was based on a number of factors. Firstly, the disciplined wage bargaining of the trade unions enabled the government to pursue a growth-oriented economic strategy, thereby safeguarding employment, without severe inflationary consequences. Secondly, the political culture was more favourable to government social democracy than in other countries. Surveys have revealed in the Swedish electorate an acute sensitivity to unemployment, coupled with a certain tolerance towards moderate levels of inflation. There was also a low level of tax resentment, positive support for progressive taxation, and a belief that the hand of the state was necessary to prevent an over-concentration of private economic power (Esping-Andersen 1985, 263–75; Webber 1986, 42–5). These attitudes, spanning all sections of society, contributed to a sense of social solidarity supportive of a social democratic approach to crisis management. Thirdly, the basic resilience of the Swedish economy provided a launching pad for an export-led recovery after the devaluation of 1982 which bolstered employment independently of the government's labour market policies. The unique combination of these factors enabled the SAP to adapt its model of 'welfare capitalism' to constrained circumstances, without the sudden wrenching of the mechanism experienced elsewhere.

By the end of the decade however, the preconditions of social democratic success began to disintegrate. For all its flexibility, it appeared now that the Swedish model was approaching its limits.

The French socialist experiment

The Swedish social democrats were alone amongst the northern European parties in their ability to govern effectively with a coherent programme consistent with their basic commitments to maintaining high employment levels and the protection of social citizenship rights within the framework of the welfare state. Even here, social democracy was on the defensive, hemmed in by the constraints of the national and international environment. Only in France was there an attempt by social democrats to break free of these constraints. The French 'socialist experiment' entailed an ambitious and ultimately miscalculated dash for growth, spearheaded by the state sector and fuelled by an expansion of consumer demand. Faltering after a year, collapsing altogether two years after that, the experiment might be regarded as the epitaph to the interventionist/Keynesian model of social democracy. There followed a retreat into the forms of crisis management with which the reader should be familiar from the foregoing pages – devaluation, deflation, wage discipline, expenditure cuts and a shift in emphasis from the state sector to private entrepreneurship.

Success in the presidential and parliamentary elections of May–June 1981 gave the French Socialist Party a much more formidable power base than those of social democratic governments elsewhere in Europe. The government of Pierre Mauroy (which included the communists) had a solid majority in the National Assembly, and Francois Mitterrand occupied a powerful and prestigious presidency. The Right was discredited after twenty-three years in office, and the electorate had given the socialists a mandate for *changement*. Moreover, a decade of programmatic activity had imported a sense of purpose to the Socialist Party, and the government lost no time in implementing some of the main elements in the *Project Socialiste* of 1981. These radical and rhetorical programmes, however, were by no means the only inspirational force behind government policy. The drive to implant a new dynamism in the national economy was reminiscent of de Gaulle, and the belief in the central rôle of the state in economic development was characteristic of the French tradition of *dirigisme*. Additionally, the Mauroy government incorporated into its thinking some of the nostrums of social democracy more familiar in northern Europe – Keynesian formulas for growth and employment, the redistribution of rewards, social justice and solidarity.

The main theme of the socialist government in economic policy was that of the growth, renewal and mobilisation of the nation's productive forces (Lauber 1983, 161). Nationalisation was seen in these terms (Holton 1986, 67–80). French entrepreneurs, so the Left believed, had been lethargic, over-cautious and short-sighted, shrinking from necessary investment decisions. They had not served

163

the interests of national economic development, and it fell to the state to take the rôle of 'dynamic entrepreneur' (Lauber 1985, 153), with the public sector acting as the investment motor of the economy. Economic and industrial activity in the public and private sectors was to be coordinated through a newly created Ministry of Planning, and a strengthened Ministry of Industry, with the objective of reinvigorating France's flagging industrial performance. One of the socialists' criticisms of previous conservative governments had been that their austerity policies had inhibited industrial performance. An important element in the new government's strategy was the fostering of a 'hothouse climate' for 'reindustrialisation' by inflating the economy on Keynesian lines (Wright 1984, 290). Increased social benefits to the value of five billion francs, a 10 per cent increase in the minimum wage and a programme of infrastructure spending, was a programme for reflation through consumption. A strategy for checking the inflationary consequences of this package included increasing productivity, sharpening France's export performance and reducing imports through energy saving. However, these were bound to be long-term undertakings. In the short term, the dash for growth was a gamble in which the odds were lengthened by the retrenchment and deflation being practised by France's rivals. Moreover, the success of Keynesianism in one country depended on an upturn in the international economic environment, as expected by the government in line with OECD forecasts (Wright 1984, 294). Its failure to materialise either in 1981 or the following year did not augur well for the socialist experiment.

In the first year of socialist government the economy performed extremely poorly. Investment fell dramatically, production levels stagnated, unemployment rose at an accelerated rate, inflation rates remained high and the budget deficit spiralled out of control. In June 1982 the franc had to be devalued for the second time since the socialists took office. From the spring of that year, ministers had begun to voice disquiet over the direction of policy (foremost amongst them Finance Minister Jacques Delors, whose stock within the government was increasing relative to the 'spending' ministers). In summer the *plan de rigueur* (austerity programme) was introduced. Step by step, a full-scale policy reorientation was undertaken. Growth targets were revised downwards and wage discipline was introduced. The resignation of the aggressive and committed (but increasingly frustrated) Industry Minister, Jean Pierre Chevenement, and his replacement by the pragmatist Laurent Fabius, signalled a reversal of industry policy. Increasingly the private sector was cossetted, whilst limits were placed on public-sector finance (Wright 1984, 297). The minimum wage was pegged down and social security benefits were reduced, whilst tax concessions were opened up to stock exchange investors (Lauber 1985, 152–7). Premier Mauroy continued to make gestures towards the radicalism of the first twelve months – it was simply necessary, he argued, to consolidate before further progress could be made towards the fulfilment of the government's programme. Mauroy's resignation, however, in 1984, the succession of Fabius as premier and the withdrawal of Communist Party ministers from government signalled entry into a new phase of full-scale crisis management.

By the parliamentary election of 1986 the Fabius government had succeeded in bringing inflation below 5 per cent, stabilising the external trade balance and restoring a respectable rate of growth, though at the cost of rising unemployment and government borrowing. The turn-around, however, had come too late to allow the socialists to relax the austerity programmes which had curbed reform and led the government into damaging conflict. The failure to fulfil the *changement* pledge, and mismanagement of conflict with important economic and social groups badly undermined the government's standing. The early years of socialist government had produced reforms of some significance. Apart from nationalisations in the banking and industrial sectors there were the far-reaching Auroux laws on workers' rights and industrial democracy, a reduction in working hours, flexible retirement, an additional week of paid holiday entitlement, a decentralisation of government to the regions, a liberalisation of the media and the abolition of the death penalty. With the exception of the last-mentioned, surveys showed that there was majority public support for these measures (Wilson 1985, 165–6). Moreover, a modest redistribution of economic rewards had taken place between 1981 and 1983. However, socialist policies generally exhibited a striking continuity with the past rather than a break from conservative administrations. The government had failed to fulfil the expectations and aspirations which its rhetoric had aroused on coming to power.

At the root of the failure of the French socialist experiment was an overestimation of the capacity of government to mobilise the resources of the state against the forces of the market (Cerny and Schain 1985, 13–41; Hayward 1986, 222–36). Nationalisation and planning had been ascribed a central rôle in the state-led exercise of generating growth and imparting dynamism into the stagnating

French economy. However, the nationalisations of the first twelve months failed to provide the 'economic strike force' which Mitterrand had envisaged. Moreover, with their 'heroic' or Promethean conception of planning, the socialists failed to recognise the inherent limitations on government intervention in market economies. 'In practice planning has more the character of getting into step with the world than of changing it' (Hayward 1986, 222, 227). The political failure of the government was its apparent inability to recognise 'a paradox which lies at the heart of all state-inspired policy making, the greater the desire for *dirigisme* the greater the need for societal compliance or consensus' (Wright 1984, 299). The needless antagonism towards important economic and social groups – farmers, doctors, business, white-collar trade unions, Catholics – undermined the already fragile support for the socialist experiment. Both of these failures underlined important lessons for government social democracy. The first was the extreme difficulty which governments experience in making market economies behave in accordance with predetermined political strategies. The second was the necessity for social democratic parties to forge alliances of social and political groups to sustain them in power.

These lessons were quickly learned. When the French socialists returned to government under Michel Rocard in 1988, the emphasis was firmly on pragmatism, eschewing any grand strategic policy design, (partly out of necessity since Rocard's minority government was only sustained through some delicate political manoeuvres). As president, re-elected in the same year, Mitterrand put the projection of personal image and the symbols of national purpose before party ideology or programme as the rallying point for broad electoral coalitions.

Italy: the quest for 'governability'

A similar formula was employed by Bettino Craxi in Italy. His elevation to the premiership in spite of his party's electoral weakness (only 11 per cent of the vote in 1983) was due to his clever manipulation of the weaknesses of and divisions within the two major parties of Right and Left. His appeal lay not in any grand programmatic design, but in his claim to be able to find a way through the impasse in the Italian system, and thereby to solve the problems of national economic and political life. His themes were simple ones – governability and *decisionismo* (decisiveness), (Pasquino 1986, 125).

In the Italian context, 'governability' meant cutting through the tangled morass of party politics, and breaking the stranglehold of entrenched interests and practices in the public administration in order to undertake measures to resolve major structural defects in the economy. There was general agreement in Craxi's five-party coalition over the general direction of economic policy. The main objectives were a reduction in the public-sector deficit, liberalisation, privatisation and deregulation of economic life in order to stimulate investment in growth sectors, and a fundamental change in the balance of labour market power. Reversing the strategy of conciliation and inter-group bargaining of his predecessors, Craxi adopted an aggressive and confrontational approach to government, taking on 'almost all the major elements of the Italian political establishment' (Hine 1986, 107). The bitterest confrontation was with the trade unions over the dismantling of the institutionalised practice of wage–price indexation. The ultimate victory of the government on this issue marked a sea change in national economic life, resulting as it did in a permanent weakening of the trade unions in relation to capital (Lange 1986, 43).

Craxi set out to change Italy's political landscape to accommodate the new circumstances of the low-growth era. Whilst social democrats in northern Europe embraced the 'new realism' of politics in the 1980s with reluctance and somewhat apologetically, Craxi seized it with enthusiasm, making a virtue of necessity. He deliberately cultivated the style of new realism politics, projecting an image of dynamism and force, and turning *decisionismo* into an ideology (Tarrow 1986, 4). It was part of his strategic design for the Socialist Party – to heighten his own personal profile in the (mistaken) belief that his prominence and populist appeal would boost his party's electoral fortunes. It was also part of a secular trend. As its centre of gravity swung from northern to southern Europe, government social democracy was progressively redefined. It came to stand for economic 'realism', governability (the terms of which differed according to national circumstances) and political modernity – the sweeping away of archaic, inefficient and frequently corrupt bureaucracies.

The new Mediterranean democracies

Whilst decomposition, stagnation and electoral defeat were the predominant characteristics of government social democracy in its north European heartlands, and whilst the socialist experiment collapsed in France, the parties of the new Mediterranean democracies flourished. By the early 1980s, Spain, Greece and Portugal were ruled by socialists. The parties here had certain advantages denied to governing parties in more mature democracies. Firstly, they were closely identified with the new democratic regimes, and were seen as rallying points for national concentration and modernising change. Secondly ,the right-wing opposition was divided and discredited by the legacy of the past. Thirdly, these new, or recently reconstructed parties had grown up around their leaders. Consequently the leadership was able to exert a certain autonomy from the party. Autonomy allowed them the flexibility to follow popular currents of opinion, and once in government, to adapt to circumstances uninhibited by party ideology and socialist tradition which bound the leaders of other parties. As Andreas Papandreou put it, 'I have to make a very sharp distinction between the fundamental values of the movement which I lead and the concrete policies pursued by the government in the context of present reality' (*Financial Times* 24 February 1982). Helmut Schmidt had made similar declarations, but was ultimately unable to free himself of the constraints of his party. Fourthly, and most significantly, social democratic governments in new democratic regimes were not faced by the rigid institutional and attitudinal structures of those countries where the political landscape was of a much older formation. To be sure, they faced formidable obstacles which were the legacy of decades of political and social atrophy. But in the political climate of emerging democracy, modernisation and change they had a decisive advantage, since they had been given a mandate to take action to break up the hard crust of the political structure, and to streamline and restructure economic life.

It was not that they had a mandate for socialist change. The social composition of the electoral support which had brought them to power was far too broad to be interpreted as such (Gilmour 1985, 267–8). Moreover, the economic circumstances which greeted them upon taking office were too severe to permit socialists experimentation along the lines of the Mitterrand government. During the election campaign which brought Felipe González to power, his repeated message to the electorate was that the margin for manoeuvre for a government of any party in Spain was very narrow. Economic recession and a mounting public-sector deficit rendered impossible any far reaching socialist plan. The government of Mário Soares came to power on a programme of austerity which did not seek to conceal the economic difficulties facing Portugal. The

socialist governments of Spain, Greece and Portugal were governments of national concentration and concertation, of economic and
political stabilisation, of modernisation and of progressive, but
measured reform. At most their leaders saw their task as preparing a
foundation for future developments towards socialism. Moreover,
the form of socialism which they envisaged was one for which
northern European social democracy (rather than the radical
rhetoric of their parties), provided the leitmotif. In the immediate
and medium term, their programmes were those of crisis management. However, the advantages which we have just outlined meant
that for most of the 1980's government socialism – in Spain and
Greece at least – did not suffer from the political decomposition
which crisis management entailed in Britain and West Germany.

The hallmark of government social democracy in the southern
periphery of Europe was its pragmatism, most marked in economic
policy. In all three countries the pivot of socialist governments was a
hard-headed Economics/Finance Minister – Miguel Boyer in Spain,
Gerassimos Arsenis in Greece and the non-party, independent
Ernani Lopes in Portugal. Boyer was typical of the new breed of
Spanish socialist in the government's ranks. Although he had been a
PSOE member before the party was legalised and had been
imprisoned for his political activities, he was an economic 'realist'
whose background in the Bank of Spain and private economic sector
had given him an acute awareness of the magnitude of the task the
government faced (Krasikov 1984, 191). His belief that 'the
credibility of a government is judged by its ability to face up to
unpopular decisions' (*Financial Times* 13 December 1982) was
immediately apparent as he introduced a devaluation of the peseta
and a round of price increases. His independence from party
ideology was also emphasised by his refusal to countenance the
nationalisation of the giant industrial and banking empire, Rumasa,
which the government was forced to take over in an operation to
save it from collapse early in 1983 (Harrison 1985, 184; *Financial
Times* 11 March 1983). During the next two years, Boyer established
a reputation as a supremely effective crisis manager. However, his
ambition, aloofness from Cabinet colleagues and unwillingness to
engage in dialogue with the trade unions made him a rather
awkward figure in the government, and he resigned in 1985, to be
replaced by a man of less abrasive political style.

Socialist governments in Spain and Portugal introduced austerity
programmes immediately upon taking office. Both countries had
adverse balances on external accounts, enormous public-sector

deficits and rampant inflation. The Portuguese economy was on the verge of collapse, and required substantial loan facilities from the International Monetary Fund, which were made conditional on economic discipline. Both the González and Soares governments took decisive measures to stabilise the economy. González rejected the extreme rigour of deflationary policies as practised by Conservative administrations in Britain and the USA. Nevertheless, his government took the reduction of the budget deficit and the control of inflation as priorities over reducing unemployment, which rose to 2.2. million (20 per cent of the country's workforce) by the end of the government's first year. The medicine prescribed by the Soares administration was even more bitter for socialists to swallow. An eighteen-month programme of extreme austerity involved cutting subsidies on staple commodities, inevitably driving up basic food prices. At the same time there was a freeze on wages and a clampdown on public spending. The result was a stabilisation of external accounts, but at the cost of soaring unemployment and a 10 per cent fall in the purchasing power of wages for Europe's poorest workers. Moreover, in the interests of short-term stabilisation, essential tasks of rebuilding and modernising the economic infrastructure were postponed.

The government of Andreas Papandreou was unwilling initially to adopt the wholehearted economic discipline of the Spanish and Portuguese socialists, in spite of an inflation rate of around 20 per cent. Instead, the Greek socialists set a course for growth, with a relaxed incomes policy and high levels of public spending. They also pressed ahead with the fulfilment of costly commitments like the socialisation of health care. The financial implications of this measure provoked the resignation of Finance Minister Arsenis, who was replaced by a man more amenable to the socialist trend in economic policy. By 1984, the Papandreou administration had recognised the need to tackle inflation, introducing a tighter monetary policy and price controls. Still, though, there were warnings from the Greek central bank of further inflation and balance of payments problems looming on the horizon. The government responded by urging the trade unions to restrict their wage demands, but Papandreou continued to rule out any major U-turn in economic policy. Indeed, he reiterated his refusal to alter course until after the 1985 election, which renewed his mandate. Shortly afterwards, however, the government announced a comprehensive range of austerity measures which included a suspension of the practice of wage indexation – automatic wage adjustments in line with consumer prices – a reduction of government expenditure, and curbs on the state sector of the economy (*Financial Times* 8 November 1985).

The public sector of state-owned industrial undertakings was a particular problem for socialist governments. None of the three governments were committed to the ideology of state ownership. On coming to power, all of them made attempts to establish a harmonious relationship with the private sector. However, in each country there was an inheritance of a structurally crippled state sector dating back to the years of statist dictatorship. Moreover, the Portuguese public sector had been swollen by the nationalisation programme of the immediate post-revolutionary period. De-nationalisation and the rationalisation of the remaining public sector became important elements in the industrial restructuring plans of governments in both Spain and Portugal. González's intentions in relation to the giant state holding company, the *Instituto Nacional de Industria*, had been signalled by the appointment of Enrique Moya, head of an élite private-sector business association, as its chairman. However, the major surgery on the state sector fell to his successor, Luis Croissier, a pragmatist with a background as an economist and civil servant. Croissier proceeded to draw up a major programme of privatisation, closure and rationalisation in an attempt at *saneamiento* – the purging of the state sector. Commercial market criteria were introduced into its operation as a first step towards the integration of the public and private economic sectors (*Financial Times* 1 December 1984).

The Portuguese public sector was a particular target of Soares' austerity programme. Subsidies to and investment in nationalised industry were slashed in an attempt to contain the accumulation of public-sector debt which in 1983 ran to $9 billion, more than the national budget. Enterprises were closed, returned to the private sector or slimmed down in a sustained effort to reduce overmanning and ease the strain on the national budget.

As was the case with overall macro-economic management, Greece went against this trend towards the curtailment of the state sector. Although there was some attempt at rationalisation, Economics Minister Arsenis rejected large-scale privatisation, aiming instead at a 'flourishing state sector which leaves room for private initiative' (*Financial Times* 6 July 1983). In some area of the economy – like import and export – new public-sector enterprises were created. In other areas of economic life – wholesaling and retailing – a network of state controls was imposed upon the private sector, to the considerable chagrin of the trade associations.

Socialist governments in Spain and Portugal then eschewed 'short-cut' routes to economic development via Keynesian policies of state-led growth. In both countries, a tight monetary policy, incorporating reductions in government expenditure and wage discipline, was geared to reducing inflation, budget overload and external deficits, with a view to creating a strong and competitive private sector. In Greece, Papandreou refused to follow this deflationary path during his first term of office. However, after the election of 1985, the Greek attempt to combine economic stabilisation, measured growth and welfare reform gave way to an austerity package on Spanish and Portuguese lines. In all three countries, economic discipline created tensions with the trade unions, which we will examine in a subsequent chapter.

Socialist governments dealt with this conflict by trying to establish a 'stability pact' with business and the trade unions. They invoked the fragile nature of infant democratic regimes in an appeal to all major forces in society to show restraint and responsibility in difficult economic and political circumstances. The Spanish and Greek governments were quite successful in defusing the conflict arising from economic discipline and from controversial U-turns in defence and security policy (see chapter 6). The Portuguese socialist government, on the other hand, fell in 1985, although Soares went on to win the Presidency the following year.

The continuing success of socialist governments in Spain and Greece was reflected in the electoral victories of 1986 and 1985 respectively. These examples of socialist parties winning elections from a position of government incumbency were, with the sole exception of the Swedish party, unparalleled in the 1980s. By the end of the decade, however, government socialism was losing its gloss in both Greece and Spain. The Greek party (PASOK) suffered a crushing electoral setback in June 1989, bringing to an end eight years of government under Papandreou. In October the same year, the Spanish socialist government was re-elected by only the narrowest of margins. González's announcement that he intended to stand down after his third term as Prime Minister added further uncertainty to the future of government socialism in Spain.

CONCLUSION: THE IMPACT OF SOCIAL DEMOCRACY IN POWER

So far, we have outlined the course of government social democracy in the postwar period – from the reconstruction years, through the era of growth and affluence, to the recession. We are now in a position to assess its impact on the economic and social order and its influence on the mainstream of historical development. Nowhere was government social democracy system transforming. Reconciled to the foundations and ground-rules of capitalist liberal democracy, its prescriptions were aimed at effecting structural reform within this economic and social order. It has been observed that 'social democracy is not a force that can or wants to act fundamentally differently from the other important forces of Europe: it is a force that makes policy somewhat differently and that changes society a little' (Pelinka 1983, 90-1). Moderate incrementalism, (slice by slice or 'salami'-style reform) was part of the credo of government social democracy. It was based on the belief that the accumulation of small steps would in due course bring about significant socio-economic change. It is therefore appropriate to consider whether this has in fact been the case.

The evidence is conflicting. Clearly there have been changes in the socio-economic structure of liberal capitalism which might, on a superficial view, be associated with government social democracy. We might, for instance, cite the growth of mixed economies, the welfare state, or a modest evening out in the structure of income distribution. However, it would be facile simply to identify these developments in the postwar order with social democratic government. It should be borne in mind that there is a well-established school of thought which regards public policy decision, (and therefore socio-economic development) as emerging out of an 'inner logic' of industrial society (Kerr 1962). According to this view, the growth of the state sector within the mixed economy owed more to economic rationality than to political ideology or party government. The experience of France, Italy and Franco's Spain would support this interpretation. Here the State intervened, under non-social democratic governments, primarily to compensate for the weakness of private capital. In Austria a state sector was created and consolidated (by a coalition government of which the SPÖ was a member) in order to guarantee the viability of the national economy. Here again was a response to doubts about the ability of capital to sustain itself independently of the State. Even in Britain, where nationalisation was seen by many in the Labour Party (and amongst its opponents) as a step towards the socialist commonwealth, economic rationality lay behind the undertaking.

The emergence of the welfare state might also be seen in terms of a broader logic of industrial society. Social democrats have often regarded the welfare state possessively as 'their own' property, looking to it as a vehicle for their egalitarian philosophy. However, the origins of the welfare state predate government social democracy, and it is a common feature of all capitalist countries, irrespective of their experience of party government.

> It is not in the least something peculiar to social democratic parties, but also characterises the policy which is pursued by conservative, reactionary or even fascist government. *(Larsson and Sjostrom 1979, 168)*

> As regards the welfare state, the trend in capitalist countries over the last century or so is quite unmistakable. The 'nightwatchman state' has been superseded by some form of welfare state everywhere.
> *(Mishra 1977, 101)*

Moreover, the social democratic character and 'equality function' of the welfare state has been questioned by those who argue that:

> On the one hand the welfare state represents the interests and the achievements of the Left. It is a means of imposing non-market considerations upon a capitalist economy, of making society somewhat more humane. Therefore the great mass movements for reform in all of the capitalist countries seek to control the welfare state and to impose their, the peoples' priorities on it...On the other hand the welfare state exists within a capitalist economy and is...permeated by the values of that society. *(Harrington, cited Daudt 1977, 92)*

That the secular postwar trend towards a more even structure of income distribution can be ascribed to the impact of government social democracy is most unlikely. The long-term tendency for wages and salaries to rise in relation to income from capital and property appears to stem from demographic trends and changes in the structure of capital (Feinstein 1968). The rather modest levelling of income distribution which took place between occupational groups resulted from changes in the structure of the workforce – a more general spread of skills and a generally higher level of education. Neither of these tendencies owes much, if anything to direct political intervention.

However, although it is clear that developments in the mixed economy, welfare state and structure of income distribution have run broadly parallel in all the modern industrial countries of western Europe, it is nevertheless possible to identify some distinguishing 'trademarks' of countries which have experienced periods of government social democracy. A generally higher level of the public-sector budget relative to national income, is one such characteristic. At the end of the 1970s, state consumption in Sweden (28.9 per cent of national income), Denmark (24.3 per cent) and Britain (20.3 per cent), was significantly higher than that of France (15.1 per cent) or Italy (16.5 per cent) where social democracy had only a tenuous hold on government in the postwar period (Pelinka 1983, 87).

In terms of welfare state expenditure, the 'social democratic countries' did not stand out dramatically (Mishra 1977, 95). However, the crude figures do not give the entire picture. They gloss over the institutional form of welfare state structures and their underlying principles. It has been argued persuasively that 'the social democratic welfare states were...qualitatively different from either the liberal-dominated welfare systems of the United States, Australia or even Britain, or the conservative variety seen in Germany, Italy or France' (Esping-Andersen 1985, 154). Having been introduced systematically they were contained within unified structures. They were institutionalised and comprehensive in that they were financed out of taxation or through compulsory contributions. Moreover, they incorporated the principles of universality and free entitlements on the basis of social citizenship rights. In contrast, the Italian welfare provision, for instance, operated on the basis of a sprawling and disparate bureaucracy with a large number of unincorporated insurance schemes outside the state's jurisdiction. State welfare was entwined with the clientele networks of the christian democratic party machinery. In France, welfare revolved around the traditional concern with supporting the family as a social institution. The 'social state' in West Germany contained echoes of the tradition of state paternalism and the christian ethic of social solidarity. Only in the social democratic welfare states (notably Sweden and Norway) was there a systematic attempt to supplant market forces by citizenship entitlement in the distribution of welfare.

No such clear-cut conclusion can be drawn in respect of the structure of income distribution. In the countries where social democratic parties had held a prolonged tenure on government, income distribution remained similar in structure to that imposed by the logic of the market. Indeed there was a sharp dilemma here for social democratic parties, since the egalitarian impulse came into collision with the labour movement principle of free collective bargaining on the labour market. Britain, in the immediate postwar years of Labour government saw a reduction of 30 per cent in the pre-tax incomes of the highest earners, but the beneficiaries were those in the upper-middle income bracket rather than the less well off. The share of both pre-tax and post-tax income accruing to the bottom third of the income ladder remained steady from 1945 to the mid-1970s (Drucker 1979, 60–1). Although if incomes and benefits are included the 1964–70 Labour government made some modest progress (Stewart 1972, 91–107), the pattern of income distribution went largely unchanged. Under the Callaghan government 'major plans for the redistribution of wealth were systematically postponed, diluted or abandoned' (Coates 1980, 83–4).

Similarly, during the prolonged period of social democratic government in Sweden, there is no evidence of any consistent trend towards income equalisation (Royal Commission 1977, 147). In general, cross-national studies suggest no discernable correlation between an egalitarian structure of pre-tax income distribution and social democratic government. However, cross-national comparison does indicate a modest redistribution through taxation where government social democracy made its mark. In Sweden and Norway the progressive impact of taxation on income distribution was quite significant. By comparison, in France and West Germany tax structures appeared to be much more neutral in their impact (OECD 1976, 16–17).

In the postwar period the liberal capitalist countries of western Europe followed parallel paths – to a much greater extent than they had done in the interwar years. Similar trends appeared – a tendency towards a more intensive involvement of the state in national economic life, the emergence of mixed economies, the expansion of the state's welfare rôle, a more broadly based distribution of income and consumption. It would be quite wrong to attribute these developments directly to the decisive intervention of government social democracy. They should be seen rather as part of an unfolding process of economic development in mature capitalist societies. However, the form which these developments assumed, their timing and the extent to which they took root in the institutional and attitudinal fabric of political life was related in no small measure to the degree of hegemony of government social democracy. Put differently, social democracy made a significant, though not decisive contribution to the development of the economic and social order in these years.

CHAPTER FIVE

Relations with Organised Labour and Business

RELATIONS WITH ORGANISED LABOUR

Historical background

From their inception the social democratic parties of northern Europe had a natural affinity with the trade unions, born of their common roots as Siamese twins of the labour movement. An organic relationship developed, based on a division of labour in which 'the party was to carry on politics in the state while the union conducted politics in society – harmonised and complementary' (Pelinka 1983, 99). Drawing support from the same social strata, oriented towards common objectives, and with an overlapping leadership and membership, a strong party union axis was in the interests of both. Ideologically the unions mirrored the parties, their philosophy of class accommodation matching the social democrats' reformist parliamentarianism. In short, they were social democratic unions, Over most of northern Europe, labour movements were cohesive and politically homogeneous. Trade unions based on single industries, or on the lines of craft or skill, came together to form centralised and disciplined confederations which mediated relations between labour movement and party. The dominating concern of the unions was to help the party win political power in order to create favourable conditions for them to fulfil their objectives in the economic sphere.

Southern Europe shows quite a different picture. Labour movements here tended towards fragmentation along the lines of the diverse strands in the socialist tradition. Social democracy had to compete with anarcho-syndicalism, revolutionary socialism, and, after the First World War, communism, gaining only a weak foothold in the trade union movement. Organisationally weak and politically divided, the labour movement in these countries was headed by a multiplicity of confederations each with its own social and ideological characteristics. After 1945 in both France and Italy the communist parties succeeded in 'capturing' the largest of these. Even with the non-communist confederations, the socialists remained distant cousins rather than close fraternal allies.

The close alignment between the parties and labour movements in northern Europe had two important effects. Strong, cohesive and party-aligned unions had the effect of structuring the electorate, reinforcing voting ties between manual workers and social democratic parties. In the Scandinavian countries, and Austria where these conditions were present, the parties dominated the political system and enjoyed long periods of government. Where the conditions were only partially fulfilled, as in Britain, West Germany and the Netherlands, the parties were less able to act as representatives of organised labour and consequently tended to suffer electoral reverses and periods in opposition. In France and Italy, where labour movements were organisationally weak and politically divided, the parties were excluded from government most of the time (Cameron 1984, 67). The postwar experience, then, points to the inescapable conclusion that a close party – union alignment greatly increased the party's electoral potential.

The second effect concerned the capacity of social democratic parties for government and their ability to 'order' capitalist society. A pronounced orientation towards government in the parties was reflected in a 'social partnership' posture on the part of the trade unions. As one observer has put it, 'the fundamental conflict typical of the capitalist order, expressed in the confrontation of trade unions and employers' associations, is in no way eliminated by [social democracy], but is mitigated'; (Pelinka 1983, 103). 'Social democratic' trade unions showed a readiness (indeed often a positive urge) to accept a rôle as pillars of the economic and social order. Their inclusion within that order took place on the basis of an 'exchange' (Gourevitch et al. 1984, 364–5) by which trade unions accepted a measure of responsibility for the maintenance of stability in the national economy in return for a social order which guaranteed the economic security of their members. As we have seen, social democracy played a part in shaping such a social order, thus creating the conditions for the exchange. Moreover, the exchange often took the form of tacit or formal deals between social democratic governments and labour, which became cornerstones of the liberal corporatist state. Thus the mutual embrace between the parties and organised labour in northern Europe enabled the former to ply the rôle of indispensable brokers in the postwar capitalist order. In southern Europe, by contrast, the parties retained an opposition mentality which had its counterpart in the labour movements' rejection of class accommodation. Here the parties experienced either total exclusion from government or marginalisation within coalition governments. For their part, the unions spent a quarter of a century after 1945 on the margins of the social order.

Models of party – union relations

Sweden Scandinavia, and particularly Sweden, offers the clearest example of the 'social democratic model' of party–unions relations. The relationship between the Social Democratic Party (SAP) and the trade union confederation (LO) is one of unparalleled intimacy, with party and unions inseparably entwined. The LO makes no effort to disguise its alignment with the social democrats. Indeed, many of its constituent unions are affiliated at branch level to the party, with affiliated members making up some 60 per cent of total party membership. In addition, a large part of party finance comes from union sources (Korpi 1978, 301–5). At leadership level there is an overlap between party and unions, and most union officials identify with the SAP. Amongst the membership, too, there is a considerable overlap, and in the electorate at large between 60 and 75 per cent of LO members vote for the social democrats (Gourevitch et al. 1984, 191). The mutual embrace with the trade unions is an important source of strength for the social democrats, particularly in view of the formidable organisational capacity of the trade union confederation.

The organisational density of the Swedish trade unions in the labour force is quite unique. With membership at around 90 per cent of all manual workers, the LO can legitimately claim to be the authentic voice of labour. Moreover, in its cohesion and internal discipline the LO is peerless. The Swedish confederation is highly streamlined, being composed of twenty-three industrial unions. Member unions cannot initiate any industrial action without the express permission of the LO Executive. In wage bargaining, too, the confederation dominates its constituent unions to an unusually high degree. For most of the postwar period bargaining has been

179

conducted on solidaristic lines, involving centralised negotiations between the LO and the employers' confederation, the SAF. Within the framework agreed between the peak organisations, the industrial unions have negotiated their own settlements. It is customary, however, for the LO to exercise its rights to be represented in these negotiations (Jones 1976, 60–1). Its ability to structure the labour market and to orchestrate wage bargaining has made an indispensable ally of social democratic governments. Indeed, as we saw in the previous chapter, the wages policy of successive SAP governments carried the imprint of the LO economist Gösta Rehn. Moreover, its importance in the implementation of pay policy has given the LO a powerful influence over party and government in a wider policy sphere. It has even been argued that 'the LO has come to be the dominant partner in the LO–party relationship, particularly in the framing of social and economic legislative proposals' (Esping-Andersen 1985, 69). There is some support for this view. Even when the party has regarded trade union policy proposals as an electoral gamble it has steered clear of any outright disavowal of the LO position: 'whatever risks the party leadership might have seen in going along with the LO's position ... it undoubtedly considered the risk involved in an open breach with the unions as far greater' (Gourevitch et al. 1984, 285).

West Germany and Austria   The West German and Austrian variants of the social democratic model of party–union relations have some features in common with the Swedish case. As in Sweden, the trade union confederations are highly streamlined in the lines of a small number of industrial unions. The Austrian trade union confederation (the ÖGB) is also highly centralised and disciplined, exerting substantial control over its member unions in all aspects of their activities. Its financial weight, (over three-quarters of union income accrues to the confederation) gives the ÖGB considerable power over industrial action on the part of its member unions. Moreover, there is a formal requirement that the ÖGB must be consulted at the beginning of a strike. The confederation enjoys legal or informal recognition by the state, adding to its prestige and power. It is recognised as an agent of wage bargaining under the law, and while negotiations are usually delegated to the industrial unions, no agreement is valid without the consent of the ÖGB (Steiner 1972, 298–9).

The situation in West Germany is rather different. The constituent unions have jealously guarded their autonomy and the confederation (the DGB) has often been subjected to centrifugal forces stemming from the exertion of this autonomy. In the 1970s, under the strong leadership of Heinz Oskar Vetter, the DGB became a more authoritative institution, 'respected by the individual unions, the political parties, the employers and the state' (Markovits 1986, 114). However, the member unions continued to exercise autonomy in wage bargaining and, periodically, in industrial action, in sharp contrast to the Austrian and Swedish cases.

Both the DGB and ÖGB are formally supra-partisan – entirely independent of the respective social democratic parties. They neither contribute to party funds nor campaign openly for the social democrats in elections. There are certain legal restrictions on the trade unions in these matters, but quite apart from these, the display of independence stems from the need to recognise and accommodate the presence of non-socialist elements within their ranks. The German trade unions' open support for the Social Democratic Party in the Bundestag election of 1953 precipitated a crisis within the confederation, with Christian Union supporters threatening to break from the confederation. Subsequently the DGB refrained from declaring its support for the SPD, relying instead on the device of issuing a statement of its policy positions and inviting its members to compare this with party policy statements. The Austrian trade union confederation has links with both the social democrats and the conservative rivals. To be sure, the social democratic connection is dominant, and the presidents of the ÖGB and its members unions are invariably well-known socialists, but still the confederation has maintained a formal neutrality in deference to its non-socialist minority. In 1966, for instance, when the SPÖ went into opposition, the ÖGB emphasised its supra-partisanship, making clear its readiness to cooperate with the non-socialist government.

Formal neutrality, however, does not convey a complete picture of union–party relations in West Germany and Austria. Both the DGB and ÖGB have maintained a close *informal* alignment to their social democratic allies. Trade union leaders have occupied positions in the party élite and have not been slow to involve themselves fully in internal party life. There have been considerable numbers of union representatives in Parliament and when the parties have held power there has almost invariably been a trade union presence in government. Ideologically the social democratic parties and trade unions are close, having developed along parallel lines. Additionally there is an overlap between union membership and party electorate, although the intervention of the confessional variable has meant that the overlap is not as pronounced as in Sweden. Both parties have remained conscious of their labour movement roots, although the SPD in particular has had to recognise that with the increasing diversity of the party's membership, its affinity to organised labour has weakened. Indeed, it was felt necessary in 1973 to reinforce the party's identification with organised labour, and the response was the establishment of a Working Group for Employee Affairs (Kastendiek 1984, 431). Subsequently the group has acted as a trade union pressure group within the party.

A relationship of formal independence but with close informal ties has allowed the West German and Austrian parties a certain flexibility while at the same time supplying them with an important supportive resource. In Austria, the formidable organisational strength of the ÖGB, and its strong social partnership orientation, has turned the confederation into a quasi-state organ, acting out a rôle within the framework of liberal corporatism and reinforcing the social democratic presence in political life. In West Germany the DGB did not go so far down this road, but nevertheless the axis between trade union 'barons' and the SPD élite was an important element in Helmut Schmidt's crisis management machinery (Markovits 1986, 148–9).

Britain   The relationship between the Labour Party and the trade unions in Britain is unique in that the unions are formally affiliated to the party. Affiliated union subscriptions are a vital source of party finance, in addition to the large-scale contribution of trade unions to Labour's election campaign funds. Through affiliation, trade unions are represented at every level of the party. Labour Party conferences are dominated by the unions' block vote, which heavily outnumbers that of the constituency parties. Trade union representatives are also in a majority on the National Executive Committee. The practice of union sponsorship means that the trade unions are well represented also in the Parliamentary Labour Party. Although there is no formal relationship between the Trades Union Congress (TUC) and the Labour Party there are strong informal ties (mediated since the early 1970s by a Liaison Committee) and the TUC is unambiguous about its political allegiance.

Ironically, though, the relationship between the Labour Party and the trade unions is much less cohesive than in the countries where relations are not institutionalised. The British trade union movement is highly fragmented and politically diverse. In order to accommodate this diversity, its peak organisation is an exceedingly loose-jointed confederation. In relation to its continental counterparts the TUC is puny in all respects, in spite of the fact that it encompasses some 90 per cent of all organised workers in Britain. The postwar period has seen no significant change in the organisational structure of the TUC. A review in 1968 considered *inter alia* the adoption of the industrial union principle but concluded that no drastic restructuring of the union movement was practicable. The TUC remained much weaker in terms of finance and personnel than its constituent unions, on which its decisions are in no way binding. The jealously guarded autonomy of the member unions meant that 'the TUC possessed, in fact, no independent existence but was, officially speaking, simply the tool of its affiliates' (Gourevitch et al. 1984, 27). In terms of policy generation the TUC has been inert, and its gestures towards economic analysis amount to little more than its annual *Economic Review*.

In pay bargaining and industrial action the member unions are almost wholly autonomous, and the TUC has only rarely made the fullest use of those scanty powers which are available to it (Martin 1980, 313–14). Even within the member unions, bargaining is often devolved to the local or plant levels. The myriad bargaining structure has almost invariably rendered abortive the periodic attempts of the TUC to orchestrate pay policy on behalf of Labour governments. However, if the trade unions have not always been a useful ally of Labour governments over pay policy, then it is equally true to say that the Labour governments have often failed to deliver their side of the deal. The poor performance of the British economy in the 1960s and 1970s meant that Labour was unable to pursue a consistent course for growth and employment but had to resort periodically to sharp bouts of deflation which vitiated the terms of programmes which had been agreed between party and unions. Moreover, unlike their Swedish counterparts, Labour leaders were not always sensitive in their management of party–union relations.

The failure of Labour governments to meet the aspirations of the labour movement, and conflicts over industrial relations and pay policy, set in motion a chain reaction of developments which did Labour profound harm. As Labour governments came into conflict with the union rank and file, the leaders of the big trade unions (who had traditionally mediated government–labour relations) lost their authority. Trade unions which had previously backed the Labour leadership were no longer reliable allies. The consequences were three-fold. Firstly, Labour lost its capacity to govern. Secondly, since the trade unions held the key to Labour's decision-making bodies, their increasing volatility had a dramatic destabilising effect on internal party life. Thirdly, the capacity of the trade unions for structuring the electorate weakened, with increasing numbers of trade union members voting against Labour. The umbilical cord had turned from a source of succour into an encumbrance. Whilst Sweden shows the positive side of the social democratic model of party-union relations, then, the British case illustrates its negative aspects.

France and Italy   In the countries with which we have just dealt, bad party–union relations had one particular feature in common – a close formal or informal alignment between the social democratic party and the dominant trade union confederation. France and Italy deviate from the social democratic model in that in both countries the labour movement is highly fragmented, with the dominant trade union confederations closely aligned to communist parties. Moreover, in both countries smaller non-communist confederations chose not to align themselves with the socialist parties but to maintain relations with a number of parties. Socialist parties, then, were denied the mutual embrace with organised labour. In the 1970s, however, the position changed to some extent. The non-communist confederations, both under socialist leadership for the first time, began tentatively to align themselves with the socialist parties.

In France the main division in the labour movement was between the larger communist-aligned union confederation, the CGT, and the smaller politically independent CFDT. With the formation of the Socialist Party out of the old SFIO, the CFDT began to relinquish its political independence in favour of an alignment with the socialists. The move was a recognition of the new electoral potential of the Socialist Party and was greatly facilitated by a progressive ideological convergence between the party and the CFDT (Hayward 1986, 63; Lange, Ross and Vannicelli 1982, 41–4). The new alignment was signalled by the union confederation's elections of its first socialist leader, Edmund Maire, and by its support for Mitterrand in the presidential election of 1974. By the time the Left took office in 1981, the CFDT had moderated the industrial militancy characteristic of the French labour movement, assuming in some respects the identity of a social democratic union confederation. It made only moderate demands upon the government and was cooperative in some matters – such as the question of wage compensation for the reduced working week – in which the other confederations were intransigent (Lauber 1983, 192–3). In short, it emerged as a 'responsible' union ready to accommodate a socialist government even in difficult circumstances. The government's programme of austerity and *rigeur* after 1982 might have been expected to sour relations with the trade unions, yet Maire expressed his support for the government's 'economic realism' and was rewarded by re-election with an increased majority at his unions's 1982 congress.

Nothwithstanding the convergence between the CFDT and the PS, union–party relations in France still differed from the 'social democratic model'. Firstly, the low level of trade union penetration in the labour force (variously assessed at 15 per cent (Hayward 1986, 58) and 23–25 per cent (Pelinka 1983, 102) prevented the French confederations from fulfilling the rôle ascribed to the trade unions in Britain and Scandinavia. Secondly, the syndicalist tradition, and strategic considerations involved in inter-union competition, prevented even the sympathetic CFDT from openly identifying with the socialists. The mutual embrace between party and unions was entirely missing. Even the socialist Maire took care not to involve himself in party life. Thirdly, whilst the CFDT went further than the other union confederations towards cooperation with the government, its organisational weakness and residual conflict orientation ruled out any neo-corporatist 'social partnership' agreement (Hayward 1986, 53–4).

A similar pattern of labour movement fragmentation characterised the labour movement in Italy. The largest confederation, the CGIL, was under communist domination, while cross-party pressures in the two smaller confederations meant that they remained relatively autonomous from party politics. In the 1970s the Socialist Party made a sustained effort to 'capture' one of these. It was partially successful, the UIL confederation electing its first socialist general secretary – Giorgio Benvenuto – in 1976 (Pasquino 1986, 123).

The union confederations were from time to time drawn into the complex bargaining process which was an intrinsic part of the tangled web of Italian political life. When they identified with one of the parties in government, they were prepared to participate in economic management programmes. However, their structure – strong centralised hierarchies which were remote from the shop floor – served to limit their effectiveness as instruments of wage restraint. Moreover, the ideological and confessional cleavages in the Italian labour movement meant that the trade unions did not serve to structure the electorate favourably for the socialists.

SOCIAL DEMOCRACY AND ORGANISED BUSINESS

A relationship of 'critical partnership'

Having accepted the pluralist society, and subscribing to the doctrine of the mixed economy in which the private sector continued to play the central rôle, social democrats had little choice but to come to terms with organised capital. Their orientation towards and entry into government, moreover, accelerated the process of rapprochement between the parties and business and employer associations. As government parties they had to be able to establish a *modus vivendi* with powerful interest organisations – even those with which they had little or no natural sympathy. Rarely in a sufficiently strong position to suppress or marginalise antagonistic interests, they had to make the pragmatic adjustments necessary to reach an accommodation with capital. For its part, business adopted an equally pragmatic approach, recognising the necessity of coming to terms with democratically elected governments. Outright mutual hostility was quite rare. An expedient relationship of critical harmony, or at least of critical coexistence, has usually prevailed, although the terms of coexistence have differed from country to country.

A number of factors contributed to this relationship of critical harmony. Firstly, social democrats usually recognised the prerogatives of capital – property rights, the right to manage, and market freedoms. To be sure, social democracy sometimes made incursions into these prerogatives in the form of nationalisation, worker participation in management, and state controls. However, the basic principles at stake were never abrogated outright. Moreover, such incursions were usually accepted by capital as part of a wider 'social settlement' in which ultimately their interests were preserved. Thus in Britain, the employers' and industrial associations 'accepted the challenge implied in Labour's (1945) manifesto', demonstrating a sense of responsibility in their judicious attitudes over such issues as credit control and wages and prices control' which enable them 'without undue trouble to defend their right to manage'. In return, Labour acknowledge that 'under increasingly professional management large firms are on the whole serving the nation well' (Middlemas 1979, 397). A relationship emerged in which 'a private sector responsive to national considerations was treated as an appropriate and necessary partner for Labour government' (Howell 1976, 161). In not dissimilar fashion an understanding was reached in Sweden over co-determination (worker participation in management) and restrictions on employers' rights over hiring and firing. These came to be seen as the (acceptable) price of social partnership and, it may be supposed, as a *quid pro quo* for the 'hands off' policy of successive SAP governments towards the private sector. In Sweden more than in most countries, organised capital has been prepared to give ground in compromises with social democratic governments, since organised labour is exceptionally strong and the 'industry friendly' parties of the right are divided and weak.

A second factor in the relatively harmonious relationship was that social democrats accepted without question the necessity for consultation with employer organisations, trade associations and large firms. In Britain the war had intensified consultative relations. The Labour governments of 1945–51 maintained the channels of consultation as a vital element in the drive for economic reconstruction. 'On almost every issue which involved increasing production, productivity and exports there was the utmost cooperation ... many industrialists continued to maintain close relationships with Ministers and civil servants' (Blank 1973, 108). The interventionist character of government social democracy in the 1960s brought closer contacts with business and industry. Existing networks were consolidated and new channels created. The attempt by government to steer and harmonise economic activity involved institutionalised or quasi-institutionalised consultation which usually took the form (as we shall see shortly) of forums for tripartite meetings between government, organised business and trade unions. Austria, the Netherlands and Belgium evolved commissions or councils on these lines, promoted in each case by coalition governments containing social democrats. In Sweden, a less institutionalised framework emerged in the 1950s with frequent meetings between government, employers' organisations and trade unions at Harpsbund (the Prime Minister's country residence) and later at Haga Castle (Gourevitch et al. 1984, 292). Helmut Schmidt was to adopt a similar informal style, meeting industrialists and bankers on a regular basis in the chancellery and at his private residence (Webber 1984, 248, 278). Consultation was most successful where there were strong, unitary employers' associations, as in Sweden, West Germany and Austria. It was in recognition of this fact that George Brown (Minister for Economic Affairs in the 1964–66 Labour government) took the lead in advocating a single, unitary industrial confederation with which his department could deal, and it was partly in response to his call that the CBI was created.

Only rarely have social democrats in government deviated from the dominant orthodoxies of economic management. The accord which has usually existed between government leaders and business interests is the third factor in the relationship. Accord over the fundamentals of economic management has enabled them to bridge the breaches which have periodically opened up over less essential issues. Thus, in spite of the 1964–70 Labour government's introduction of an array of irksome controls on the financial institutions of the city of London, relations remained relatively harmonious since 'contrary to expectations, the government ... endorsed the City's order of priorities' (Longstreth 1979, 183), top of which was the defence of the pound sterling on international money markets. In somewhat similar fashion, the French socialist government of Pierre Mauroy won the cooperation of business through its reversion to the monetarist orthodoxies of the 1980s after a year of the 'socialist experiment' (Lauber 1983, 219–20). However, in this instance, business had withheld its cooperation until the socialists had shifted to accommodate it. The French experience reveals a dilemma which has often faced government social democracy. Organised capital represents a cohesive and powerful force, strategically placed to undermine a government which threatens it. Social democrats have often had to consider how far they could go with policy commitments in the face of business opposition. Seldom have they risked confrontation. Their reluctance to provoke the displeasure of business and industry has frequently meant shelving or diluting 'radical' measures. A case in point was the industry policy of the 1974–79 Labour government, when a campaign of attrition by the CBI succeeded in 'taming the tiger' (Grant and Marsh, 1977, 208). The appointment to key economic posts of figures commanding the trust of the business world has also played a part in stabilising relations. The new socialist government in Spain in 1982, for instance, appointed as chief of the state holding company a former secretary general of an élite business association (*Financial Times*, 1 December 1984).

Conflict and confrontation

It would be a mistake, however, to give the impression that relations between social democratic governments and business organisations have been uniformly harmonious. Inevitably conflicts have occurred, particularly where social democrats or socialists entered power after long periods of government by parties of the Right. Thus in West

Germany, business organisations mobilised against the new Brandt government's reform programme, which they saw as an attack on capital. The metal industry association report for 1968–70 summed up the climate of open hostility. 'Various plans and announcements about codetermination, tax reform and the reduction of private profit to increase public wealth are crucial knots in a general web which threatens to strangle all entrepreneurial initiative and leads many to wonder whether it still makes sense to undertake risks and continue competing in the market' (cited in Markovits 1986, 213).

Brandt, for his part, responded to attacks from organised capital by threatening a 'trial of strength', although he simultaneously attempted to limit the damage to relations with industry by referring to the need to maintain government–industry relations (Webber 1984, 68). The deterioration of relations was the product of a general polarisation in political life. Brandt's successor, Schmidt, was markedly more 'employer oriented' and quickly consolidated relations. One leading industrialist was moved in 1975 to a personal commendation of the social democratic chancellor: 'I know that a good many of my colleagues...in industry, banking, commerce, believe that as far as economic insight is concerned we could not wish for a better Federal Chancellor' (Webber 1984, 71).

The accession to power of the French socialists in 1981 was also the signal for confrontation. Initial hostility on the part of business was manifested in manoeuvres to avoid nationalisation and a flight of capital abroad. Moreover, businessmen made a show of studied pessimism, painting reality in excessively dark colours and thus discouraging hiring and investment. However, within the first year the peak French business organisation, the so-called *Patronat*, had entered into dialogue with the government, cooperating in measures to reduce the working week. Capital remained somewhat divided in its attitude to the Mitterrand/Mauroy administration, but the election of Yvon Gattaz to the *Patronat* leadership in December 1981 signaled a victory for the accommodationists, and 'rebels' against the government were ostracised by the business community. With the *'pause Mauroy'* of 1982 business became still more cooperative, 'prepared to play its rôle with a certain amount of loyalty' (Lauber 1983, 220).

Both the West German and French cases indicate that the readiness of business to come to terms with socialist governments depends in large measure on the governments' willingness to conform to economic orthodoxy, to adopt policies of 'economic realism' and to play down party commitments to structural reform in the interests of stability in the economy. The experience of incoming socialist administrations in the new Mediterranean democracies tends to confirm this. The Spanish socialists sought from the outset to cultivate business confidence and cooperation, with González stressing his commitment to the private economic sector (*Financial Times*, 31 May 1983). As the government's tough measures imparted some stability to the crisis-torn Spanish economy, its relations with business improved steadily. In Greece, on the other hand, relations remained conflict laden for the first four years of socialist government, with frequent clashes between ministers and the private sector. Conflict came to a head in 1984 with bitter protests from trade organisations over market regulation and state encroachments in the private-sector economy. Hitherto only weakly organised, business announced the launch of a new body – a Greek *Patronat* – to represent its interests more forcefully against the government (*Financial Times*, 26 July 1984).

The experience of West Germany, France and Spain suggests that, given time, relations between social democracy and business settle down to a pattern of 'critical cooperation' reinforcing the conclusions drawn from countries where government social democracy has a longer history. It should be kept in mind, however, that business almost always prefers governments of the Right, and that their cooperation with leftist governments rarely stems from anything more than expediency. With the economic recession, even in countries with a long tradition of social partnership and coexistence between organised capital and government social democracy, relations deteriorated as business took up a more aggressive political standpoint (Peper 1982, 102–3; Fitzmaurice 1983, 206).

SOCIAL DEMOCRACY AND CORPORATISM

The conditions for corporatist development

Corporatism can be defined as the interlocking network of relations between the apparatus of government and the state on the one hand, and organised interests on the other. It should be emphasised that under liberal democracy these relations are essentially voluntary, and that organised interests retain the full measure of their autonomy. These features distinguish the democratic variant of corporatism from its fascist forerunner. Under the fascist regimes in

Germany and Italy corporatism represented an attempt to subordinate society to the state by establishing a hierarchy of official corporations, to which industry and workers were compelled to belong. Interest organisations were thus converted into the apparatus of party or government.

The rise of liberal corporatism coincided with the emergence of the interventionist state, a development which has been traced back to the First World War or beyond. As we have seen in the previous chapter, the interventionist ethos was strengthened by the experience of economic mobilisation in the Second World War. After 1945 there ensued a conflict of policy and doctrine between interventionism and market liberalism. The postwar settlement in which this conflict was resolved saw the institutionalisation of Keynesianism in government thinking, and the establishment of the mixed (public/private) economy. The state assumed wide responsibilities in national economic life, over *inter alia* employment, wages and prices, investment, credit, technology. However, the market, and the forces operating within it, retained a large part of their autonomy. Corporatism arose out of an attempt to reconcile the political management of the national economy with the autonomy of market forces. The increase in the scope and complexity of the state's activity had multiplied and intensified its contacts with economic interest organisations. A form of collaboration developed between governments and business on the one hand, and between governments and labour on the other, as governments sought to harmonise the interests of each with the broader 'national interest'. The growth of the state bureaucracy in the economic sphere, and the institutionalisation of channels of collaboration and harmonisation between the state and the 'social partners', saw the emergence of the liberal corporatist state.

The rapidity and extent of these developments depended on national circumstances. Historical antecedents inevitably played a part. Some countries – Germany for instance – had a history of state involvement in economic and social life. Here, liberal corporatism had a head start (Crouch 1979, 17). Elsewhere, as in Britain, a tradition of liberal individualism retarded the development of corporatist relations. A 'corporatist bias' has been identified in Britain (Middlemas 1979, 391), intensifying after 1945, but it lacked popular legitimacy and failed to take institutional form. Another prerequisite of corporatist development was social harmony and political consensus. Corporatism reflected a social theory in which 'the interests of society as a whole transcend narrow sectional interests' (Cawson 1978, 179). In societies like Italy which were deeply divided along the lines of class and ideology, it proved impossible to arrive at a consensual view of the national interest, an essential foundation for the collaboration which in turn was the keystone of corporatist relations. Austria, on the other hand, with a history of interest-group accommodation reaching back to the Habsburg Empire, was much more amenable to corporatism (Steiner 1972, 173–4).

The emergence of corporatist institutions and attitudes, then, was conditional upon the mosaic of national culture and history. However, it often fell to social democrats to shake the kaleidoscope and rearrange the pieces in a corporatist formation. The values and style of social democratic politics were highly conducive to corporatist development.

> Certainly,the strong presence of reformist social democracy is a major encouragement to corporatist participation in consensual regulation... The existence of a powerful social democratic movement should in the course of things accompany the development of corporatist tendencies. Social democracy itself testifies to acceptance of an ideology and comportment that views state and market as already woven together. Social democracy was built upon the premise of continuing bargaining between class actors for political and social gains. Hence it is only natural that corporatist structures should emerge easily in countries with strong social democratic traditions. *(Maier 1984, 49)*

Indeed, the circumstantial evidence linking social democracy and the rise of corporatism is very compelling. Of the seven countries in which, according to one authoritative observer (Schmitter 1979, cited Cameron 1984, 175), corporatism took root most strongly, five had experienced sustained periods of government social democracy – Sweden, Austria, Norway, Denmark and Belgium. These were also countries where the organisational strength of labour was considerable, and where a firm axis existed between organised labour and social democracy. The organisational strength and cohesion of labour movements was the most important of the preconditions for the development of corporatism. Corporatism flourished where there was a strong, centralised trade union confederation capable of articulating the interests of labour with a single voice and of binding its members to agreements concluded with capital and the state. Scandinavia and Austria, as we have seen, provided the model of this type of labour organisation. Labour movement weakness, or divisions between competing and politically opposed union confederations, tended to thwart the emergence of tripartite corporatist relations. In France, for instance, there emerged a formidable axis between business and the state from which trade unions were almost entirely excluded.

The origins of postwar corporatism

The foundations of the modern corporatist state were laid during the Second World War and in the immediate postwar years. In some countries – notably Scandinavia, Austria, the Netherlands, and Britain – the wartime experience had bred a new accord between capital and labour in which they expressed a readiness to reach a *modus vivendi* with each other and to cooperate with government in the tasks of reconstruction. There was at least the basis for a consensus over a definition of the tasks and over how they were to be achieved. Out of this new understanding, quasi-contractual agreements were reached. Government undertook to manage the economy in such a way as to maintain full employment, rising standards, business profitability and stable prices. In return for undertakings which conferred legitimacy upon their respective interests, organised labour and capital allowed themselves to be coopted into the reconstruction effort, accepting the responsibilities which cooption implied. Trade unions would act with restraint in articulating wage demands; capital, for its part, undertook to exercise the right to manage in a responsible and humane manner, with due consideration for national economic needs. In short, there was an attempt to merge sectional interests into an overarching 'national interest' to which all could subscribe.

In the Scandinavian countries this exercise in interest harmonisation was under way before the war. Trade unions and employers' associations had reached agreements in which each had formally recognised the other's legitimate interests and powers. The *Saltsjobaden Agreement* (Sweden 1938) and the *Main Agreement* (Norway 1935) had taken root in national life as 'social contracts alongside the constitution' (Hodne 1983, 96). In the Netherlands the accord between capital and labour was embodied in the Labour Federation, and in Belgium an 'Agreement on Social Solidarity' was drawn up (Van den Brande 1987, 109). In Austria the interest organisations of business, commerce, agriculture and labour rapidly developed a cooperative bargaining style which was to characterise the postwar era. In all these countries the immediate postwar years saw the crystallisation of an ethos of 'social partnership'. Having resolved their major differences, the peak organisations of capital and labour were in a position to accept cooption into the economic policy-making apparatus.

In Britain corporatist relations had been given an enormous boost by the experience of the war years. Trade union leaders had occupied positions of responsibility in wartime Cabinets and in the administration of the war economy. Equally, the representatives of the employers' and industrial confederations had been drawn into government ministries and into the panoply of wartime production boards. Under these circumstances a kind of industrial concordat emerged, incorporating a vision of the postwar order shared by both sides of industry and anticipating Labour's programme of 1945 (Middlemas 1979, 293–5). In short, wartime Britain appeared to offer the prototype of the liberal corporatist state, and it was widely envisaged that the triangular relationship between capital, labour and government would carry over into peacetime. However, for reasons, which will shortly be explained, corporatist relations did not become institutionalised in Britain as they did in Scandinavia and Austria.

Corporatist relations emerged out of attempts to resolve the central dilemma of governments in the early postwar years. We have referred in the previous chapter to the problem of reconciling full employment and growth on the one hand with wage and price stability on the other. As we have seen, the response of social democratic governments was to maintain employment through budgetary policy, to boost production through planning and to check wage and price inflation through statutory controls, persuasion or concerted labour market policies. The regulation of production, wages and prices thus entailed cooperation between government, capital and labour, and in Scandinavia and Austria tripartite cooperation assumed institutional form. This institutional apparatus was the foundation of the liberal corporatist state.

Scandinavia The structural shape of corporatism differed from country to country. In Norway the centrepiece was production planning. The immediate postwar years saw the creation of a three-tier planning pyramid, headed by an Economic Coordination Council and reaching down through sectoral Branch Councils to plant-level production committees. The Coordination Council contained representatives of the trade unions and employers, and developed as a forum of consultation and consensus building. Consultation boosted the self-esteem and political confidence of the interest organisations, feeding their appetite for political influence.

Hence, although relations were not entirely free of conflict – the government's statutory price controls, for instance, aroused business hostility – corporatist channels became a permanent feature of the political process (Hodne 1983, 142). Swedish governments, on the other hand, were less *dirigiste* and the planning exercise was more limited than in Norway. Here, too, organised interests were represented on a planning directorate, but it was the Labour Market Board which emerged as the most important forum for the regulation and concertation of economic forces. With the exception of the government-appointed chairman and deputy chairman, the Board was constituted by the nominees of the major interest organisations. As 'labour market policy' acquired a wider definition, the Board's functions were expanded to include investment decisions, industrial rationalisation and aspects of social policy. Moreover, administrative boards along the lines of the Labour Market Board proliferated in the Swedish public administration. Consequently the organised interests became intimately involved in almost every area of public policy.

Austria   In Austria the initial impetus behind the institutionalisation of corporatist relations was wage control. As a response to the inflation of 1947 a series of wage–price agreements was concluded between the interest organisations representing capital and labour. The forum in which the agreements were negotiated was known as the Economic Commission, a body which acquired the status of a quasi-official organ of government in spite of its dubious constitutional legality. In 1957 a step was taken towards institutionalising tripartite relations in the Joint Commission for Prices and Wages. Its importance was underlined by the status of its membership – chancellor, senior ministers and the leaders of the organised interests. The Joint Commission subsequently developed a dual rôle – as an organ for the voluntary self-control of prices and wages on the one hand and as an advisory and consultative organ of economic policy-making on the other. Out of this body, which was the prototype for a number of other policy commissions, there emerged a sort of 'para-coalition' between the employers and trade unions, a nexus of relations which mirrored, and were interwoven with, the Socialist Party/People's Party coalition government (Steiner 1972, 311). The integration of organised interests and government was further strengthened by the presence of the interest organisations on the Coalition Committee. It was here where the government parties negotiated coalition policy, and the presence of trade union and employers' organisation representatives conferred on these organisations the status of 'insiders' in the political process. The institutionalised integration of organised interests into the political process on these lines was the basis of Austrian corporatism – the most highly developed in Western Europe.

Britain The institutionalisation of corporatist relations in Britain was, at best, partial. Here, as we have seen, a foundation existed for the development of corporatism after the war. Moreover, the policy orientation of the 1945–51 Labour governments was conducive to corporatist relations. The commitment to full employment, and its corollary, the need to seek wage restraint, and the government's inclination towards production planning might have led down the road to institutionalised corporatism. In addition, the trade unions were willing, indeed they were anxious, to be coopted into economic policy-making. In spite of these favourable circumstances, however, corporatism failed to take root in Britain in the early postwar years.

It was the weakness of the peak organisations of capital and labour which, above all, prevented the institutionalisation of corporatist relations in Britain. As we saw in an earlier section of this chapter, neither the Federation of British Industry on the employers' side, nor the TUC for labour, measured up to the strength and cohesion of their Scandinavian or Austrian counterparts. On neither side of industry were the peak organisations capable of fulfilling the functions required of them in a corporatist system. The TUC was usually reluctant to allow the cherished nostrums of free collective bargaining to be breached by broad and binding pay agreements. The Federation of British Industry lacked the discipline and resolve to stand firm against the upward wage drift of the immediate postwar years. For its part, the Attlee government distanced itself from both sides. At their closest, relations were restricted to consultation on an informal and not institutional level. Often, however, even information consultation was missing.

The incomes policy White Paper of 1947 was drawn up after consultation with the TUC, but there was no such participation in the following year's exercise. Loyal to the government, the TUC's General Council lent its support to the 1948 White Paper despite its exclusion from the drafting process. However, that year's TUC Congress expressed its opposition to pay restraint in a sharply critical resolution. Moreover, the unwillingness of significant sections of the labour movement to accept government pay policy was expressed in a series of industrial disputes. The General Council's inability to carry the Congress and the trade union rank and file with it was symptomatic of the incapacity of the peak organisations on both sides of industry to commit their members to government policy. This, in turn, undermined the ability of the Attlee administration to fulfil the terms of the postwar settlement (full employment, stable prices, rising standards) as set out in the 1944 Employment White Paper. Failure here vitiated the terms of the wartime 'contract' between capital and labour, exposing what one observer has called 'the dismal logic of integration' – that class harmony could be achieved only if government was able to reconcile the (ultimately incompatible) objectives of full employment, stable prices and rising standards (Middlemas 1979, 417). Without such harmony, tripartism in Britain meant little more than periodical *ad hoc* attempts to avoid conflict.

Social partnership

The policy orientation of social democratic governments in the immediate postwar years drew organised interests into decision-making. Production planning, and the wage/price policies which often became necessary to suppress the inflationary pressures inherent in full employment economies, required the cooperation of organised labour and capital. Where labour movements were strong (and labour strength was very often the background to social democratic government), their cooperation was even more essential for successful economic management. Given certain conditions (which, as we have seen, were not present in postwar Britain), there was a seemingly ineluctable tendency towards the institutionalisation of such cooperation in the political process. With the incorporation of organised labour and capital in the political process there emerged a triangular structure of consultation and decision-making – a framework for a sustained dialogue between 'social partners'.

The growth of corporatist institutions was accompanied by the behavioural codes of corporatism – essential for the smooth functioning of the triangle. Here, too, government social democracy played an important rôle. Firstly, trade unions were more ready to adopt the cooperative ethos of 'social partnership' with a 'friendly' government of the Left in power. Secondly, business interests usually responded pragmatically to social democratic governments. Accepting that they would have to give ground, they were prepared to relinquish some of their own autonomy, and to recognise the trade unions as legitimate social partners. Finally, the social partnership philosophy which underlay corporatism reflected the politics of accommodation which the social democratic parties of Scandinavia and Austria had embraced more or less fully by 1945.

Where non-socialists dominated government, as in Italy, West Germany and France, the employment/inflation dilemma was solved by essentially different formulas, and corporatist relations failed to develop. Governments tended to rely on the encouragement of market forces rather than on production planning to induce growth. Less committed to full employment, they followed 'neutral' or balanced budget policies, less likely than 'employment' budgets to produce inflationary consequences. In the event of inflationary pressures they turned for their preventative measures to tight monetary policies instead of direct intervention in the labour market. Weak labour movements (often the counterpart of conservative or christian democratic government) were not in a position to exert wage pressure. Their cooperation was, in consequence, not essential to economic stability. Governments in these countries were able to exploit labour weakness, marginalising trade unions in the policy-making process. Where economic coordination did take place, as in France, it took the form of bilateral relations between government and capital from which labour was almost entirely excluded. In any event, trade unions here were generally ideologically disinclined towards cooperation with government and the employers.

Corporatism in the 1960s and 1970s

The rapid advance of corporatism in the early postwar years was halted in the 1950s. In the 'end of ideology' decade of sustained market-led growth, relative class harmony and labour movement quietude, there was little need for new initiatives in economic intervention and consensus building. However, in the two decades which followed, the pace of corporatist growth quickened sharply, driven by the downturn in economic growth, the resurgence of distributional conflict and the reappearance of the employment – inflation dilemma. Once again, though, patterns of development were uneven. In those countries where corporatist relations and institutions had taken root after the war, the machinery was consolidated and extended. Where conditions had not been propitious in the 1940s, the 1960s saw little change.

The impulse behind corporatist development in the 1960s was the twin threat of stagnating growth and inflation. Governments began to look towards some form of coordinated, systematic economic policy to restore vitality to national economies. One of the principal aims was to bring the determination of wages within the broad remit of economic coordination. In those countries where corporatism was highly developed, the response was to widen the framework of economic concertation and consensus building. In Austria, for instance, the Joint Commission for Price and Wages was extended by the addition of a sub-committee for Economic and Social Questions in 1963. This consisted of a body of experts drawn from the major organised interests and 'authorised to deal with economic and social policy from the viewpoint of the economy as a whole' (Steiner 1972, 86). It is indicative of the Austrian inclination towards corporatism that the sub-committee was the initiative not of the coalition government but of the leaders of the trade unions and business associations. Sweden's well-developed system of interest mediation and its institutionalised network of corporatist relations provided ready-made answers to the economic challenges of the 1960s. The Investment Funds were mobilised to stimulate economic activity in 1962/63 and again in 1967/68 (Lindbeck 1975, 100). In a joint report of 1968, the trade unions and employers' confederations agreed a formula for balancing wages against productivity. A further agreement, on economic rationalisation and employment, was concluded in 1972 and a Rationalisation Council was set up in 1966 to augment the work of the Development Council (Jones 1976, 81–3). At government level it became the practice to hold daily lunch meetings between union leaders and ministers concerned with trade union affairs (Shonfield 1984, 144). With its cohesive and centralised interest organisations and underlying philosophy of social partnership, Swedish corporatism adapted to the new circumstances of the 1960s with a minimum of political and social conflict.

The institutional apparatus of corporatism developed on similar lines in Norway. As in Sweden, wage bargaining was conducted on solidaristic lines, guided by an expert committee staffed by employers' and trade union representatives. In Denmark, corporatism did not take such firm root. An Economic Council had been established in 1962 as a forum for consultation between government, industry and the trade unions. However, a labour movement fragmented along craft lines made consensus difficult to achieve, and in its absence, an incomes policy was the only viable instrument for economic stabilisation (Esping-Andersen 1985, 211). The situation was similar in the Netherlands. Here, a highly developed form of corporatism had emerged by the early 1960s, focused on the Economic and Social Council. A pay explosion in 1963–5, however, exposed the fragility of the government's control over wage guidance. Increasingly, Dutch governments turned to direct forms of wage control.

West Germany For historical and ideological reasons, the West German case was rather different from the countries we have just discussed. To be sure, there was a legal framework organised on quasi-corporatist lines for the regulation of industrial relations and wage bargaining. Moreover, since the 1950s a system of co-determination meant that in the *Montan* industries at least, the trade unions were involved in company decision-making. In relations between government and business, the behavioural codes of corporatism were well established; the principle of consultation between the industrial associations (*Verbände*) and government ministries had been sanctified in the Basic Law (Shonfield 1969, 242–3). Yet for all these corporatist tendencies, in macro-economic policy formation at the national level there was by the mid-1960s still no institutionalised tripartite forum such as those we have observed in Scandinavia, Austria and the Netherlands. There were three main reasons for this. Firstly, with its doctrine of *laissez-faire*, the christian democratic government was resistant to this style of policy coordination. Secondly, the Federal Chancellor, Konrad Adenauer, refused to accept the legitimacy of trade union participation in this or any other sphere of the political process. Thirdly, the labour movement itself was deeply divided on the question of participation. Whilst the 'social partner' wing of the trade union confederation (DGB) hankered after a more positive rôle in the ordering of economic life, the 'activist left' categorically rejected such a rôle, regarding itself as a *Gegenmacht* (opposition force) in the economic order (Markovits 1986, 83–93).

The entry of the social democrats into government in 1966 saw important new developments in state–economy relations. An Economic Growth and Stability law created a legal framework for a more interventionist style of government. 'Global steering' of the economy involved the coordination of economic activity and the 'orientation' of the national economy in relation to consensually agreed objectives. Economic coordination along these lines was given institutionalised form. *Konzierte Aktion* (concerted action) was a regular series of meetings between the Economics Ministry, the trade unions and the employers' associations in which to discuss issues of mutual concern and to arrive at consensual formulas for the orientation of the economy (Clarke 1979, 242–58). Within the DGB the balance between the 'social partner' unions and the 'activist left' had by now swung to the former. The Düsseldorf Programme of 1963 was a milestone for the labour movement. Representing 'the victory of Keynes over Marx' (Markovits 1986, 101), it set the West German trade unions on the road to accommodation with capital and the state. Clearly recognising the legitimacy of the Federal Republic, the new programme indicated the DGB's readiness to play a positive rôle in the economic order.

With a government more disposed towards economic intervention and a labour movement more amenable to accommodation, the political landscape was now much more favourable to a corporatist approach to economic management. However, a number of factors conspired to undermine the effectiveness of concerted action. The first of these concerned the character of the trade union confederation. Divisions remained within the DGB, and whilst its social partner wing seized eagerly on what it saw as a long-awaited opportunity for participation, the Left was highly apprehensive, fearing that it would tie the trade unions to government economic policy, and in particular to government pay guidelines. The reservations of the Left were reinforced by an unprecedented wave of spontaneous grass-roots industrial action in 1969. A hardening of attitudes on the part of union representatives in meetings with government and the employers was the inevitable consequence. From the outset, the principle of *Tarifautonomie* (freedom of collective bargaining) militated against the smooth functioning of concerted action. A further weakness was the decentralised structure of the DGB and the autonomy of the larger unions within the confederation – *IG* Metall and *IG* Chemie. One authoritative commentator has observed how the leaders of these unions 'politely attended meetings, then left and pursued their own interests in the bargaining rounds' (Markovits 1986, 27), underlining the weakness of the DGB as a pillar of economic concertation.

The ambivalence of the DGB and its member unions towards the government indicates a second source of weakness which undermined concerted action. In Scandinavia and Austria a corporatist approach to economic management developed out of an axis of mutual support between the labour movement and social democrats in government. In the West German case the rapport between the trade unions and the SPD in government was sometimes uneasy, particularly in the Brandt administration between 1969 and 1974. Brandt was not, personally or politically, close to the leaders of organised labour. Nor was his government able to 'deliver' measures in response to trade union demands. In the Grand Coalition, the SPD had been able to satisfy at least one major DGB demand – for the introduction of a positive employment policy. After 1969, in the social–liberal coalition, SPD ministers found the Liberals exercising a virtual veto over measures for which the trade unions were pushing – vocational training programmes, employee share-holding schemes and an extension of co-determination in industry. The co-determination legislation of 1971 and 1976 fell some way short of DGB demands, and their dissatisfaction contributed to disharmony in concerted action.

The third factor which undermined concerted action was the industrial conflict and political polarisation which accompanied the formation of the social–liberal coalition. Confrontation between capital and labour, and a mistrust of the Brandt government on the part of the employers (Wessels 1987, 149), created an unfavourable environment for concerted action. Business interests viewed Brandt's reform programme with suspicion. Indeed, it was their resistance to the 1976 co-determination legislation which precipitated the withdrawal of the DGB from concerted action, and its subsequent collapse. However, long before its ultimate dissolution, this experiment in institutionalised corporatism had, to all intents and purposes, ceased to function.

Ironically, though, the demise of the formal apparatus of concerted action coincided with a marked improvement in tripartite relations. Helmut Schmidt quickly established an axis of mutual trust with trade union leaders. 'Before or immediately after almost every important set of economic and social policy decisions taken by his government, Schmidt met top trade union leaders to justify the coalition's course of action' (Webber 1984, 248). In addition to these bilateral meetings, Schmidt held regular and informal 'fireside chats' with the leaders of industry, banking and labour. This forum proved much more successful than the highly publicised, quasi-institutional forum of concerted action. Schmidt also benefited from a recognition on the part of some of the trade unions of the constraints imposed by the international recession. There was a shift to the Right in the DGB as IG Chemie, hitherto identified with the activist Left of the confederation, now threw its considerable weight behind the 'social partner' bloc. The leaders of these unions (the so-called gang of five) formed a close political alliance with the right wing of the SPD, giving unconditional support to the chancellor. Schmidt encouraged this new axis further by repudiating Brandt's strategy of cultivating the radical young and reasserting the SPD's traditional identity as the party of organised labour. The new orientation was consolidated with the *Zukunftsinvestitions programm* (programme of investment for the future) of 1976. This represented the fulfilment of a tacit bargain by which the government committed itself to a positive labour market policy in return for pay discipline on the part of the trade unions. It was part of the 'stability pact' – a sort of informal contract for economic stability and jobs – with which Schmidt successfully steered the West German economy through the international recession of the late 1970s. In the new atmosphere of 'economic realism' which prevailed in the Federal Republic in these years, informal corporatist arrangements provided the model framework for crisis management.

Britain While relations between government and organised economic interests were being consolidated in other countries, they reached new peaks of instability in Britain. British corporatism had never, in peacetime, meant more than an informal and tenuous *modus vivendi* between government and the relatively weak organisations of capital and labour. In the conditions of political, economic and industrial life of the 1960s and 1970s it was no longer possible to sustain even this. This was in spite of the fact that Labour governments were in power for eleven of the fifteen years between 1964 and 1979, and that Labour was committed to the idea of economic concertation and a partnership between government and the trade unions. In the event, however, partnerships were short lived. Voluntary wage discipline, the governments' ultimate goal, alternated with attempts to impose statutory restraint, and this, in addition to an abortive attempt to reform industrial relations, brought government into sharp conflict with organised labour.

Economic concertation was built into the strategy for 'planned growth' with which Labour entered government in 1964. 'The policy and the machinery to apply it were established within six months. It was the most ambitious attempt so far to solve the problem of maintaining full employment and controlling wage-push inflation' (Barnes and Reid 1980, 56). The centrepiece of the policy was the *Joint Statement of Intent on Productivity, Prices and Incomes*, signed by the government, TUC and employers' organisation: a 'partnership agreement' expressing a general willingness to cooperate in voluntary wage control. The failure of this agreement, and the subsequent degeneration of relations between the government and organised labour, reveals the shortcomings of corporatist solutions under British conditions. The underlying weakness of the British economy and its susceptibility to international pressures on the pound placed intolerable strains on tripartite relations, defying consensual solutions. It was apparent by 1965 that monetary stability, growth, full employment and free collective bargaining were mutually incompatible. With the introduction of statutory instruments for wage control, the tightening of pay guidelines and the sharp deflation of 1966, the government moved outside the terms of the statement of intent, which had been based on voluntary restraint and a commitment to maintaining the level of employment.

In the atmosphere of heightening economic crisis in 1967, the TUC leadership continued to endorse government policy (although they had not been consulted in its formation), accepting a rôle as 'wages watchdog'. In the rank and file of the labour movement, however, there was a growing militancy expressed in industrial unrest, a dramatic loss of leadership authority and a shift to the Left in which government sympathisers were swept aside by more left-wing leaders. The emergence of a new breed of TUC leaders, such as Jack Jones of the Transport and General Workers Union and Hugh Scanlon of the Amalgamated Engineering Union, signalled a new assertiveness towards government on the part of the TUC. Relations deteriorated still further with the publication of the Donovan Report, the 'In Place of Strife' White Paper and the subsequent Bill (eventually withdrawn under intense pressure from the trade unions) to reform industrial relations. The government now faced a three-fold crisis: in the economy, in industrial relations and in the axis between the Labour Party and the trade unions. As Harold Wilson put it: 'what we are talking about is a deep and fundamental split between the two wings of the movement. This is serious – extremely serious in any circumstances. We all recognise and approach it with that degree of gravity. I believe it means something more – whether this Labour Government or any Labour Government can continue' (cited in Barnes and Reid 1980, 124).

The demise of the traditional relationship between Labour and the trade unions was part of the wider breakdown of corporatism in Britain. The collapse of both originated in the same syndrome: economic sclerosis, the consequent inability of the government to meet the political and economic aspirations of the labour movement, and the exhaustion of the will and capacity of the trade union leadership to rein in wage demands within a decentralised and anarchic system of free collective bargaining.

The corporatist partnership having broken down, government had tried to impose its own solutions. However, in the confrontation which followed it had been forced to back down. Confrontation also characterised the administration of Edward Heath (1970–74), and the failure of the government to prevail brought about its downfall. The social contract with which Labour returned to power in 1974 was an attempt to restore the relationship between the party and the trade unions which Wilson had identified as the *sine qua non* of effective Labour government. One observer called it Labour's penance for the breach with the unions (Middlemas 1979, 445–6). For the first twelve months the leaders of the big trade unions (notably the TGWU) were able to exert an influence on government which went far beyond the usual political rôle of organised labour. They offered voluntary pay restraint on condition that government refrained from statutory income regulation and in return for the satisfaction of their demands on a wide range of policy issues. (Foremost among these, of course, was the repeal of the Heath government's Industrial Relations Act). The TUC had now become more than merely a pressure group acting out its rôle within the penumbra of government. Its leaders (notably Jones, the principal architect of the social contract) made a decisive entry into the domain usually reserved for Cabinet ministers. The corporatist equilibrium had been violently disturbed and with its restoration, the balance was skewed towards the trade unions (Middlemas 1979, 449).

A more 'normal' balance was established after 1975. With voluntary restraint proving a hopelessly inadequate instrument for controlling inflation (equivalent to an annual rate of 37 per cent at the start of the year) and the economy standing on the edge of an abyss, the trade union leadership began to retreat from the uncompromising attitudes they had struck earlier. Tightening up its own pay guidelines, the TUC was now prepared to accept a parallel system of government control. Its change of heart was due to a recognition of the crisis facing the government, and of the danger of the trade unions themselves being implicated in an economic catastrophe. The initiative returned to the government, with the unions cooperating closely in Chancellor Healey's successful rearguard action which restricted inflation to single figures by 1978. Three years of crisis management, however, imposed severe strains on the TUC's ability to hold back wages and to absorb economic militancy, particularly in the public sector where wage discipline had bitten deepest. The TUC Congress of 1978 rejected the principle of pay policy, calling for a return to free collective bargaining, and the cry was echoed at that year's Labour Party Conference. In view of these unmistakable indicators of labour movement militancy, the government's announcement of a 5 per cent pay guideline was unwise. In the winter of 1978–79 the dam burst. Amid paralysing public-sector strikes and the capitulation of the government in pay settlements which made a mockery of its targets, the corporatist answer to Britain's chronic economic problems suffered apparently terminal collapse. Significantly also the 'winter of discontent' signalled the end of Labour as a viable party of government. Its association with the trade union movement wedded it to an informally articulated, consensus-seeking corporatism which for all its inherent instability had been characteristic of Britain for the quarter-century after the war. As in other matters, Labour found it impossible to respond positively when this mode of government was discredited after 1979.

The corporatist bargain

Some observers have identified, at the heart of corporatist relations, a systematic and long-term political exchange between government and trade unions (Gourevitch et al. 1984, 364–5), the basis of which is a trade-off between wage moderation on the one hand and, on the other, economic and labour market policies aimed at fostering growth and sustaining employment. In Austria and Scandinavia a political bargain along these lines was built into the institutional fabric of the political–economic order as it had evolved in the postwar years. It was embodied in the Scandinavian Labour Market Boards and the machinery of solidaristic wage negotiation, and in the Austrian *Paritätskommission*. The axis between social democratic government and strong, centralised and accommodationist trade union confederations had played an important part in establishing and maintaining this institutional framework.

In West Germany corporatist relations were not fully articulated. The attempt to institutionalise tripartism – in concerted action – had failed. Schmidt's 'stability pact', however, represented an informal and tacit bargain on the basis of a similar trade-off. Successive cuts in employment programmes testified to the tenuous nature of the 'corporatist bargain' in West Germany, with government retaining a considerable freedom of manoeuvre. Moreover, the fact of coalition government and the existence at the heart of economic policy-making of institutions (principally the *Bundesbank*), which were entirely outside the government's domain, tended to undermine corporatism still further. In the British case, and especially under Labour governments, there was a pronounced inclination towards corporatist solutions to economic problems. Here, however, it proved quite impossible to maintain stable relations along corporatist lines.

France and Italy: the failure of corporatist initiatives

In France and Italy the basic conditions required for political exchange between governments and trade unions were absent. Labour movements were neither organisationally equipped nor ideologically predisposed to participation in tripartite relationships with government and capital. For the first two postwar decades they had been almost entirely marginalised in the political process. In the 1960s, however, attempts were made in both countries to draw the unions into the machinery of economic coordination (Lauber 1983, 7–8; Hayward 1986, 59–61; Lange, Ross and Vannicelli 1982, 24–5). In France the exercise was orchestrated by Jacques Delors, a one-time trade union leader, now an official in the Planning Commis-sariat, and later to be Economics and Finance Minister in the socialist government of 1981–86. Delors' initiative in social demo-cratic corporatism was at first attractive to trade unions such as the CFDT, which was already committed to the democratisation of the planning process. The union was prepared to countenance wage restraint within the framework of a concerted labour market policy (Delors' objective), but it became increasingly frustrated at its marginalisation and impotence within the planning structure. Ultimately by the end of the 1960s, 'militancy seemed a better bet than statesmanlike discussions at the [Planning] Commissariat' (Hayward and Watson 1975, 166).

The Italian initiative fared little better, in spite of the fact that the Socialist Party was part of the centre–left coalition. The socialists' links with the labour movement were tenuous, and it was incapable of acting as a 'consensus broker' on the lines of the 'social democratic model' in northern Europe. From the outset the trade union confederations were, at best, lukewarm towards the Five Year Plan which was at the heart of the economic concertation exercise. Only the socialist-oriented trade union confederation, the UIL, accepted outright. The communist-aligned CGIL equivocated

(Lange, Ross and Vannicelli 1982, 121–2). While they were both interested in the reform potential of the Plan, neither confederation was prepared to accept any form of incomes policy as its counterpart. Indeed, the PSI itself was torn over this issue. The socialist architect of the Plan, Giolitti, appeared to have a conception of a social contract not dissimilar from its north European form.

> I had in mind a relationship with the trade unions which would have led them to a position ... of self regulation, in which the weight of trade union action would be focused more on reforms than upon wage demands. I hoped that the unions might have been willing to accept – as a counterpart to their relinquishing certain wage demands – the reforms proposed in the 5-year plan.　　　(*Giolitti, cited in Hine 1978, 247*).

However, his overtures were rejected. To the extent that the union confederations participated in the Plan, they did so directly through the National Commission on Economic Planning and its myriad subcommittees. Their participation was unmediated by political parties. Indeed, the trade unions had come to believe that 'the government was not the centre of power [but that power] ... was diffuse throughout political and civil society' (Sassoon 1986, 129). Thus they distanced themselves from political parties, seeking instead to establish themselves independently in the political life of the state. However, as in France, 'the failure of planning ... led the unions to try to take matters into their own hands at the end of the decade' (Hayward and Watson 1975, 15).

The wave of worker militancy which swept through France in 1968 and Italy in 1969 showed up in stark relief the disparity between the potential of labour on the shop floor and its weakness in the political arena. In France the old equilibrium was quickly restored as Gaullism reasserted itself, and the long-term impact of 1968 on labour politics was slight. In 1969 Delors (now personal advisor to Prime Minister Chaban-Delmas) renewed his attempt to introduce corporatism into France with the *contrat de progrès* – public-sector pay settlements which embraced wider social issues such as the distribution of income and the low paid (Hall 1986, 247; Hayward and Watson 1975, 169). Again the CFDT was initially receptive, but again the exercise was abortive and it collapsed in 1972. The Italian trade unions, on the other hand, emerged from the 'hot autumn' of 1969 as a renewed political force. Firstly, the *Carta dei Lavorati* (Workers' Charter) of 1970 strengthened the legal rights and bargaining powers of the unions, reflected in an unprecedented upward movement of wages in the early 1970s. Secondly, there was new scope for participation in economic and social policy-making. Finally, the factory council movements of 1969 had expressed a will for labour unity to which the big three trade union confederations were forced to respond (Spotts and Wieser 1986, 202–5; Sassoon 1986, 129–32). In short, the Italian political landscape had changed, freeing the unions from the pessimism and torpor of the previous era.

After 1969, with the political balance tilted against capital and with the christian democrats no longer serving the employers' interests (Sassoon 1986, 77), industry began to seek a consensual framework within which to solve national economic problems. The progressive disintegration of the centre–left coalition in the mid 1970s lent the task an even greater urgency. However, it was to the Communist Party (PCI), not the socialists, that industry looked as an agent for social integration. The reason for this was that the communists had a much closer relationship to the dominant CGIL. It was under the influence of the PCI (now anxious to end its isolation from national political life) that the CGIL took the lead in advocating a form of institutionalised collaboration with government. In return for their cooperation in the Pandolfi Plan for economic stabilisation, the trade unions were granted inclusion in the public administration of the economy (Spotts and Wieser 1986, 207). In this short-lived rapprochement between industry, the trade unions and the government, the Italian Socialist Party (PSI) was effectively sidelined, illustrating again the historic inability of the party to play the rôle of consensus broker familiar to the northern European parties. This rôle, then, fell to the PCI, but with the rapid reversals in this party's political strategy it was not suited for the rôle of mediating a sustained and stable political exchange between government and organised labour. Its reversion to an opposition stance in 1979 brought a withdrawal from the 'social contract' on the part of the CGIL.

The Italian unions went further in their willingness to enter a contractual exchange with government than did their French counterparts. However, long-term exchange is ruled out in Italy by the fact that the one party capable of mediation (the PCI) is permanently excluded from government. The PSI cannot play this rôle. As we shall see, Craxi's solution in the 1980s was to go over the head of the CGIL in a broad popular appeal, via a referendum, to win political endorsement for his strategy for economic management.

THE EBBING OF SOCIAL DEMOCRATIC CORPORATISM

The challenge to the corporatist system

The international economic recession seriously undermined corporatist arrangements in most western European countries. Its institutions were marginalised, no longer able to contain the multiple conflicts which accompanied the loss of economic performance. A malign interaction of circumstances was at work. Firstly, the failure of 'social contract politics' in the 1970s had discredited this approach to economic management. Corporatism came under attack from business interests and the bourgeois parties who argued that the institutionalisation of corporatist systems had limited the flexibility of the economy in the face of new circumstances. In particular it was argued that it inhibited the adoption of new technologies and created rigidities in wage and social benefit structures, imposing burdens on business and damaging its competitiveness in international markets (Wilson 1985, 111). These attacks were part of a wider offensive against trade union power, which was identified as the enemy of economic efficiency. Dismantling the machinery of corporatism was thus a step in the restoration of the unconditional hegemony of capital over labour.

Secondly, the collapse of the postwar Keynesian vision of full employment and economic growth had destroyed the foundation for political exchange between organised labour and government. Exchange had taken the form of trade-offs, either explicit or tacit, from which both sides could extract advantage. Economic constraints now ruled out such mutually advantageous bargains. Thirdly, the conditions of the 1970s and 1980s had bred labour movement fragmentation. Divisions arose between the growing white-collar sectors (in some countries organised in separate and independent confederations) and the manual-worker unions. Differences of ideology and strategy arose between unions in the sunrise industries and those associated with the 'rust belt' of industrial decline, driving accommodationists and militants apart. Labour movement cohesion – a principal precondition for corporatism – had broken down. Finally, and as a consequence of these developments, the mutual embrace between social democratic parties and trade unions was weakened. Unions were now much more ambivalent towards social democratic government, their capacity or inclination to deliver wage discipline greatly reduced. Where the parties were in opposition and engaged in the exercise of programmatic reappraisal in a bid to return to power, the unions inevitably became embroiled in inner-party feuds and faction fighting, weakening the union/party axis still further.

Sweden   Even the hitherto exemplary Swedish model suffered from these developments, leading to speculation over its possible demise (Gourevitch et al. 1984, 288–98; Walters 1987, 64–77). Key precepts of industrial relations and wages policy, which had been cornerstones in the model, now came into question. Tension over wage negotiations, periodically erupting in major strikes and lockouts, cast doubt on the relevance of the classic Swedish model of harmonious labour relations (Walters 1987, 71). Attempts by social democratic governments in the 1970s to 'bridge' the crisis, by concluding bargains with the trade unions involving tax cuts for wage restraint, had merely served to postpone its effects. The bourgeois party government of 1976–82 had embarked on a reorientation of policy away from the old model, in line with the increasingly aggressive posture of the employers who saw bourgeois government as an opportunity to redress the balance of economic power to their advantage. Returning to government in 1982, the Social Democratic Party (SAP) tried to re-establish old principles, but a question mark hung over the will and ability of the political and economic élites to respond to the new problems posed by social and economic change (Walters 1987, 75). Two problems stood out particularly starkly. The first concerned the structure of the labour movement itself. The white-collar, non-party-aligned confederations had grown in strength relative to the 'social democratic' LO. Much less centralised and disciplined than the LO, these confederations were less willing and able to conclude binding wage agreements in line with government policy. A major element in Swedish corporatism – labour movement cohesion – had been eroded. Secondly, both employers and unions adopted a more aggressive stance towards each other in the 1980s. The employers favoured a less centralised (and therefore more flexible) framework for wage bargaining in which some of the larger unions in the LO also saw advantages. Pluralism in the labour movement and the fragmentation in wage bargaining threatened to undermine the Swedish model, and led to tensions between organised labour and government.

An attempt was made to revitalise the corporatist model, albeit in a modified form, incorporating the 'economic realism' of the 1980s. To legitimise the new emphasis on discipline and the necessity of restoring business profitability, the government introduced, though in a toned-down version, the LO-inspired plan for the collective ownership of share capital. However, the wage earner funds proposal illustrated the weakening of some key elements of the Swedish model. Although there had been some political convergence between the LO and the white-collar unions (Gourevitch et al. 1984, 322–8), the latter remained somewhat ambivalent to the proposal. Even more ominously, business greeted the proposal with outright hostility and street demonstrations. The ideological counter-offensive on the part of the employers and the parties of the Right underlined the demise of the politics of consensus – the foundation of the Swedish model. The LO accepted the wage earner funds as a *quid pro quo* for wage restraint. Nevertheless, in 1986 Sweden came to the brink of labour crisis, with the white-collar confederation and the LO member metalworkers' union both threatening paralysing industrial action (*Financial Times*, 8 April 1986; 28 May 1986). In the event the crisis was averted, but the reprieve was only temporary. In response to the economic crisis of 1990 (see chapter 3) the government took decisive steps towards liberalisation in the economy, provoking an unprecedented revolt on the part of the LO trade unions. The growing distance between the SAP and the LO underlined the fragility of the Swedish model of social democratic corporatism.

Austria Austria alone bucked the European trend towards the decomposition of social democratic corporatism. The transition from Austro-Keynesianism to Austro-Austerity which we observed in the preceding chapter took place 'within the existing institutional structures' (Gerlich et al. 1988, 214). Corporatism here proved more resilient and adaptive than elsewhere. At the core of the Austrian model, the system of wage and price regulation through institutionalised cooperation between the social partners remained intact. The most commonly cited explanation for its persistence was the continued strength and cohesion of the large interest organisations (particularly the trade unions) and their close ties to the political parties. However, other factors contributed to the hyper-stability of Austrian corporatism, notably a political culture in which the predisposition to negotiated compromise was second nature, and the deep entrenchment of the institutional and legal framework of interest group bargaining (Gerlich et al. 1988, 214–18). Nevertheless, stability did not mean that the terms of the corporatist exchange, and relations between the social partners, remained stationary.

The most important of the changes within the corporatist model was a progressive decoupling or loosening of ties between the Socialist Party (SPÖ) and the trade unions, expressed in a reduction (under way since the 1950s) of union representation in the Cabinet, and a growing independence of the SPÖ from organised labour in respect of economic expertise and policy-making. These tendencies were exacerbated by the end of single-party social democratic government and the entry of the SPÖ into coalition with the Austrian Freedom Party (FPÖ) in 1983 (Gerlich et al. 1988, 218–20). The latter was not party to the postwar corporatist contract, and so its entry into government had the effect of breaking up the established relations of corporatism. Thus the Austrian experience was not entirely at variance with European trends. The gradual distancing of social democracy and organised labour in Austria was part of a European-wide movement to which we shall return at the end of this chapter.

France and Italy The ebbing of social democratic corporatism was underlined by its rejection in those countries like France and Italy where left governments were newly in power in the 1980s. As we have already seen, labour movements in these countries were neither organisationally nor ideologically suited to corporatist relations. Moreover, in both countries governments ultimately found them-selves confronting communist opposition, with which the major union confederations fell into line. In these circumstances it was not surprising that neither Mitterrand nor Craxi made any serious efforts to promote corporatist relations. To be sure, a number of ministers in the socialist administration in France had trade union connections, but Mitterrand repeatedly emphasised the govern-ment's autonomy. For their part, the trade unions remained sceptical about their influence. As one leading figure in the CFDT put it, 'we are listened to politely, but are we really heard? ... The officials of our industrial federations often have a great deal of difficulty obtaining serious discussions with their corresponding Ministers' (cited in Hall 1986, 220).

In its relations with business, industry and agriculture, the government was equally assertive of its autonomy. While preserving a dialogue with business interests, the socialists sought initially to end the privileged status which certain organisations had enjoyed under governments of the Right. As part of this exercise, a variety of previously unrecognised organisations were given access to government in a bid to end the monopoly of the *Patronat* (Hall 1986,

221). Ultimately, though, the antagonism which resulted forced the socialists to reverse this course, mending its fences with the *Patronat* and effectively restoring the *status quo ante*. Thus, 'far from introducing the kind of neo-corporatism that social democrats had sought elsewhere, the Mitterrand Government reinforced the plurality of competing interests. Instead of fostering social peace, it intensified many of the underlying divisions in French society' (Hall 1986, 221–2).

The Craxi premiership in Italy saw a disintegration of those corporatist arrangements which had developed in the 1970s but which had already begun to unravel by the end of the decade. Union expectations had not been fulfilled, and there was a general feeling that the bargain struck with government and the employers had debilitated them. In the words of UIL leader Giorgio Benvenuto, Italian unions were 'A paralysed force ... a force that lives on its memories of the past and that will not tolerate renewal.' (Cited in Spotts and Wieser 1986, 208). This sense of frustration and impotence exacerbated the fragmentation which had begun when the CGIL followed the PCI into opposition. The communists now 'hammered away' at any sign of rapprochement with capital or government and it was clear that the fleeting period of labour unity was at an end (Hellman 1986, 65). Craxi's own political style was not conducive to rapprochement. The logic of his rhetoric of 'governability' and decisiveness led towards confrontation with the unions.

A catalyst for both labour movement disunity and confrontation with government was the issue of the *Scala Mobile* or wage indexation ladder. Symbolic of the advance of labour at the beginning of the 1970s, the *Scala Mobile* now came under increasing attack for its inflexibility from the industry association, Confindustria. The trade unions had agreed in 1983 to cuts in levels of indexation, but the following year saw Confindustria adopt a more radical and intransigent position and the unions divided and in disarray over their response (Lange 1986, 32–3). Attempting to cut through the complex deadlock, the Craxi government issued a decree which sought to impose a compromise settlement, but succeeded only in polarising the issue and dividing the union confederations still further. The campaign for the referendum which ensued in 1985 saw socialist and communist confederations set against each other and the largest of them, the CGIL, split between the two tendencies. Conflict now broadened in scope; ultimately the question was 'who can decide, on what basis and in whose interest how to govern the political economy ?' (Lange 1986, 39). Victory for the government answered this question unconditionally, establishing a new balance of power in political and economic life. Although the socialist-inclined confederations had backed the government, they could take no satisfaction in the outcome which effectively left the trade unions marginalised. The government's use of decree and referendum signalled the demise of the politics of neo-corporatism in Italy.

The new Mediterranean democracies The situation in the new Mediterranean democracies was somewhat different. Here, authoritarian variants of corporatism had flourished under dictatorship, with compulsory workers' organisations run by the state. In the transition to democracy, free trade unions were legalised and the machinery of corporatism reformed along liberal lines. In Spain the new constitution contained provision for the institutionalisation of liberal corporatism in the form of an Economic and Social Council. By the time the socialists came to power, moreover, experiments in tripartite economic cooperation – the Moncloa Pact (1977) and the National Employment Agreement (1981) – had already been launched. Both capital and labour were amenable to the extension of these initiatives in a formal 'social pact'. However, in spite of these favourable circumstances, the González government rejected any move in this direction. 'They feared that a neo-corporatist policy which would have required them to make even minor concessions to union demands would have met with the opposition of business and...fostered political polarisation' (Roca 1987, 263). Instead, economic policy was made unilaterally and any consultation with organised labour took place on the government's terms and only after the main lines of policy had been determined. Although the socialist-aligned trade union confederation, the UGT, was generally cooperative, its acceptance of the government's austerity programme and unemployment standing at two million strained the loyalty of its members. In order to maintain UGT support, therefore, the government was forced to make periodic gestures of conciliation towards it (*Financial Times,* 11 March 1983) but still remained *at a distance* from organised labour. After 1986 relations deteriorated rapidly, culminating in the general strike of December 1988.

Relations between the Papandreou government and the Greek labour movement were more conflictual. Weak, fragmented and militant, organised labour was ill equipped and disinclined to play the rôle of government ally. Additionally, the major confederation was divided between PASOK supporters and communists. Unable to rely on voluntary labour discipline, the government often took recourse to the methods of the past, especially after the U-turn towards economic austerity in 1985. The new course involved the truncation of wage indexation (introduced early in the Papandreou government) and a statutory incomes policy, both introduced unilaterally without union consultation. A split emerged with the labour movement between government loyalists and opponents which in turn led the government to intensify its intervention in union affairs. The expulsion of union dissidents from PASOK, and the reversal in the courts of decisions taken by legally elected trade union bodies (Mouzelis 1987, 279–81), precipitated a crisis within the unions and in their relations with government (*Financial Times,* 28 May 1986). In any event, with only one in three workers unionised and in an economy dominated by small businesses, liberal corporatism was never on the agenda in Greece.

The loosening of party–union ties

In all the countries we have just discussed, then, socialist parties in government found it hard, or indeed impossible, to sustain the mutual embrace with organised labour which was at the heart of the social democratic variant of corporatism. Adjusting to the new circumstances of late twentieth-century capitalism meant relinquishing the goal of full employment, lowering wage expectations, deregulating the labour market and liberalising the economy.

Inevitably this meant a shift in the balance of power between capital and labour at the expense of the latter. Only where the party–union axis was exceptionally strong and the labour movement disciplined and cohesive did it prove possible to *negotiate* these changes with the unions within the framework of a modified form of corporatism. These conditions applied in Sweden and Austria, where additionally the strength of social democracy and organised labour meant that labour could be compensated or its interests somehow safeguarded. Elsewhere, labour movements adopted an oppositional or even confrontational rôle. Not that social democratic parties in opposition were immune from disharmony with organised labour. Electoral defeat forced them to undertake programme reappraisals posing serious questions concerning their identity, purpose and electoral strategy which defied easy or consensual solution. For their part, confronted by bullish and hostile governments of the Right, the unions faced a similar syndrome of disorientation. Their beacon was the return of 'their' party to government, but internal differences and conflicting *perspectives* between unions and party stood in the way of a concerted drive for power.

Britain The syndrome was at its strongest in Britain. During Labour's first term in opposition after 1979, joint union–party policy-making was based on the assumption that a relatively speedy return to power would restore the postwar political economy which the Conservatives had overturned. Policy was geared to a restoration of full employment, with a programme of public investment and a 'national economic assessment' embracing wages, prices and profits (Taylor 1987, 115–20). It was implicitly acknowledged that pay discipline would be essential for the success of the programme, but although some TUC and Labour leaders pressed the unions to make a definite commitment to restraint, it was not forthcoming. Once again the inability of the TUC to commit its member unions to corporatist agreements was exposed, undermining the credibility of Labour's economic strategy. Pay policy remained a divisive issue in party–union relations (Taylor 1987, 117–22), compounding divisions over the amendment of the party's constitution.

The success of the campaign to change Labour's constitution (see p.97–101) signalled the culmination of a steady advance of the Left in the party, made possible by fissiparous tendencies within the trade unions which prevented them from playing their usual 'anchor rôle'. A bitter schism in the labour movement between supporters and opponents of constitutional change reflected the gulf in ideology and perspective between the activist Left and the traditionalists. The latter saw an activist-dominated party, obsessed with ideology, becoming 'an electoral dinosaur limping towards extinction'. For them, the Labour Party was above all else a party of power, since only as such could it advance union interests as they saw them. They believed that to regain power Labour had to return to the 'sensible middle ground' of popular socialism, and that it fell to the unions to steer the party back in this direction (Taylor 1987, 135–40). Electoral defeat in 1983 strengthened this view but also raised issues which went to the heart of the unions' own identity. New patterns of voting behaviour underlined the negative attitudes of many union members to the political and industrial practices of British trade unionism. Broad questions of internal reform, union dialogue with the Conservative government, and policy in relation to the new industrial relations legislation dominated the TUC Congress later that year.

The miners' strike of 1984 stopped the 'new realism' in its tracks, exacerbating divisions in the labour movement. The issues which it had raised, however, were unavoidable, never far beneath the surface of union life and a constant source of internal conflict. Consequently, when in the wake of a third successive electoral defeat in 1987 Labour entered a major organisational and policy review, the trade unions – a pivotal force in its outcome – were in disarray and low in the public's esteem. Once a source of stability and strength, the party's links with the unions now appeared to many as a complicating factor impeding policy change, an organisational millstone and an electoral liability. Yet the Gordian knot and cash nexus which bound the two branches of the labour movement in their tangled relationship severely limited the ability of party and union leaders to resolve the urgent issues which confronted them.

West Germany The German social democrats and their trade union allies also faced an entrenched government of the Right, but for all its rhetoric the Kohl administration did not usher in such a fundamental rupture with the political economy of the past as did the Conservative government in Britain. Additionally, both the party and the unions were more disciplined than their British counterparts, and in any case had long since come to terms with most of the issues at stake in the TUC and Labour Party. Consequently, in relative terms the equilibrium of union–party relations remained intact. Indeed, the early years of Kohl government saw a *Schulterschluss* or closing of ranks between the social democrats and organised labour, in which the acrimony of the declining years of the social–liberal coalition was buried (Padgett 1987, 334–6). Nevertheless, there were still differences of perspective between the accommodationists and the activist Left in the DGB which were bound to impinge upon the party. These ranged over attitudes to the new government and the employers, unemployment and the thirty-five-hour week proposal, but centred on two related issues – the SPD's road back to power and the party's relations with the Greens.

Accommodationists in the DGB inclined to the view that in the long run, a Grand Coalition with the christian democrats provided the best prospect for a return to power. Their attitude to the Greens was one of undisguised contempt, accusing them of being 'naive dreamers, subversive revolutionaries or significantly ... anti-growth reactionaries', and regarding their environmental concerns as 'antithetical to an industrial society' (Markovits 1986, 445). The accommodationists were therefore intransigent in their opposition to any rapprochement between the SPD and the new party, or any 'greening' of SPD policy. For the activist Left, on the other hand, talk of a coalition with the christian democrats was anathema. They found themselves in cautious agreement with the Greens and the new social movements on a number of issues, and were prepared to explore formulas for reconciling economy and ecology. Although the leaders of the two tendencies in the DGB made some attempt to reconcile or play down their differences in the run-up to the 1987 election (*Frankfurter Rundschau*, 2 May 1985), defeat placed the question of SPD–Green relations high on the agenda. Herman Rappe, leader of the accommodationist chemical workers' union, became principal spokesman of the opponents of the 'open door' to the Greens' strategy, bringing him into conflict with a growing majority in the party. The issue exposed conflicting perspectives not only within the labour movement but, perhaps more significantly, between the party majority and an important section of the labour movement. It is hard to see a rapprochement between the SPD and the Greens without a corresponding distancing in party–union relations.

CONCLUSIONS

The experience of the western European social democratic parties in their relations with organised labour point to some general, if tentative, conclusions. Firstly, the Swedish and Austrian cases indicate that labour movement solidarity remained an important component in social democratic success, buttressing the collectivist ethos on which social democracy thrives, reinforcing the parties' electoral performance and consolidating contractual agreements with social democratic governments. However, even here there was a loosening of corporatist relations, originating in Sweden from a fragmentation in the labour movement, and in Austria from a distancing in party–union relations. Secondly, and pointing us in a somewhat different direction, in southern Europe charismatic and populist leaders spearheading a drive for national integration were substituted for labour solidarity as the foundation for socialist success. Parties in government in France, Italy and Spain conspicuously spurned the solutions offered by social democratic corporatism. In previous chapters we have argued that the southern European parties had been progressively assimilated into the social democratic tradition. In this respect, however, they remained for the most part outside the mainstream, having made the autonomy of the party from organised labour no longer a hindrance but a positive virtue. Thirdly, where labour movement solidarity was badly compromised, as in Britain, the mutual embrace turned at times into a poisoned kiss. Discredited in popular perceptions, restrictive of party autonomy and serving to impart or exacerbate disintegrative tendencies in the party, the party–union machine took on an increasingly undemocratic and anachronistic appearance. Even in West Germany, where a greater 'distance' was built into party–union relations, some of these adverse effects were at work.

The common strand running through all these experiences is a tendency towards a 'decoupling' of social democracy and organised labour, with the parties exerting greater autonomy. Since party–union relations were built on different lines, the process of decoupling took different forms in each country. In southern Europe, where relations were traditionally tenuous, the process went furthest. Elsewhere historical, institutional and informal ties restricted the pace of change, particularly in those countries (notably Britain) where those ties bound most tightly. In general, though, the mutual embrace, once one of the defining characteristics of social democracy, had ceased to be unconditional. The aura of sanctity, in which the relationship had been bathed, had been lifted. Looking to the future, this development carries portents of the utmost significance for social democracy. It may well be that the changing relationship with organised labour will bring about change within the parties on a scale rivalling the ideological reorientation of the 1950s.

CHAPTER SIX
Foreign Policy

The policy attention and theoretical concern of social democratic parties has been overwhelmingly concentrated on domestic policy. Social democratic parties were essentially concerned with altering the terms of rule within national societies and their interest in foreign policy was markedly less than that of communist parties, whose Marxist analysis excluded the possibility of an exclusively domestic focus. Before the Second World War, when the social democratic parties took a stand on foreign policy issues, they were guided (Rose, 1960) by certain principles which included a belief in international cooperation, class consciousness in foreign affairs, supranationality and anti-militarism. In short, the social democrats rejected the conventional analysis of interstate relations which focused on the centrality of power relations. As social democratic parties rarely constituted the sole governing party (except in Scandinavia), it was possible for them at least to appear to abide by these principles, most of the time.

THE SOCIALIST INTERNATIONAL

As socialist parties developed in the late nineteenth and early twentieth century they evolved a loose set of principles on foreign affairs, stressing internationalism, class consciousness, supranationality and anti-militarism. These ideas were articulated and disseminated by the Second International. They were to prove no match for power politics in the prelude to the First World War when the main socialist parties were to a large extent swept along on the nationalist currents.

221

Despite the weakness of the International in 1914, socialist parties have been very unwilling to abandon the idea that an international grouping of socialist parties can have an impact on international events. This idea has naturally been held much more strongly by communist parties, given their interest in revolutionary transformation. The Comintern was founded in 1919 and was intended to coordinate the activities of all communist parties.

This organisation was intended to serve as a controlling agency of the revolutionary proletariat. Thus it insisted on conditions of membership which would have taken away much of the power of the national parties and committed them, in theory at least, to a policy of revolution.. This proved unacceptable to the socialist parties of Britain and Germany. These then took the lead in reviving the Second International (the Berne–Geneva International) in July 1920. For some time there was also a third organisation, the International Working Union of Socialist Parties, the so-called 'two-and-a-half' International. This body was founded in 1921 by representatives of minority socialist groups in Austria, France and Germany, and by delegates from the Swiss and other Left-inclined socialist parties, its aim being to stop the polarisation of the socialist movement between reform socialists and communists. In May 1923, when this objective seemed unattainable, it merged with the reformist Second International. This new association, known also as the Labour and Socialist International, was more homogeneous than its prewar counterpart. It had thirty-five affiliated parties and six million members and was a centre for liaison and information rather than an instrument of political leadership. The Labour and Socialist International faced the same kind of problems at an international level as its member parties did at the domestic level, namely the Comintern, the onset of the great depression, the rise of fascism, and finally Hitler's military victories which led to its dissolution in March 1940.

The Socialist Labour International was not reconstituted after 1945, but a series of international socialist conferences were held largely at the behest of the British Labour Party, who also provided the organisational framework. The main issue initially was the question of whether or not the SPD should be allowed to participate in these meetings as a full member. Full SPD participation was fiercely resisted at a series of meetings in Clacton (1946), Bournemouth (1947) and Zürich (1947) by a number of parties, especially those of Eastern Europe. Schumacher attended the Zürich conference however and a Commission was set up which prepared the way for SPD entry in the Antwerp Conference 1947.

The formation of Cominform as a successor organisation to Comintern, and the snuffing out of the social democratic parties in eastern Europe pushed East–West relations to the centre of the agenda and lent urgency to British and Belgian efforts to reconstitute the Socialist Labour International, which was reconstituted as the Socialist International at Frankfurt in 1951. The choice of Frankfurt was to prove prescient since, although the organisation is based in London, by far the greatest rôle in its evolution has been played by the SPD which has been the principal provider of financial and infrastructural support.

The Socialist International has a global membership but its overwhelming centre of gravity lies in the traditional centres of social democracy in western Europe. It has a tiny permanent staff and its resolutions do not bind member parties. It is essentially a forum of discussions. This may have an impact. It used always to be said during Golda Meir's lifetime that the thought of meeting her at subsequent Socialist International meetings was always in the mind of policy-makers such as Willy Brandt when they contemplated a change of policy towards Israel.

Socialist International discussions in the 1950s and 1960s were largely concerned with East–West relations. The presence of non-voting members from the exiled social democratic parties of eastern Europe meant that in framing its resolutions the Socialist International was always conscious in these years of the cost of Soviet rule in eastern Europe. East–West relations have remained an important theme in the 1970s and 1980s, but the new policy of the SPD, Brandt's position as president and the rôle of Egon Bahr, both as Brandt's interlocutor and on his own account, have made the Socialist International an important forum for ideas on detente.

The Socialist International has also consistently pressed for a more equitable distribution of global resources. It also played a major rôle in the maintenance in exile and support in the early years after their return of the Greek, Spanish and Portuguese parties, and aspires to play an important rôle as social democratic parties resurface in eastern Europe.

DEFENCE AND SECURITY IN POSTWAR EUROPE

NATO

Initially, it looked as if the social democratic parties might be able to maintain their traditional principles. Social democratic parties were now, for the most part, in government, but it still appeared possible to operate on the old principles. The United Nations had been established in New York and it was hoped that it would be much better able than the League of Nations to deal with security questions. The Labour Party had as one of its slogans in the 1945 election campaign, 'Left can speak to Left'. But the optimistic views of 1945 could not be sustained in the second half of the 1940s, when Europe was split into two halves, one dominated by the USSR and the other by the United States. In this bipolar Europe, western European social democrats overwhelmingly supported US policy, especially after the communist take-over in Czechoslovakia in 1948. It is true there were dissenters in each party, such as those in the 'Keep Left' group in Britain, but they were very definitely a minority except in Italy, where the socialist party split and the larger part, the PSI, under Pietro Nenni favoured a policy of neutrality.

On the European side the key rôle in the formation of NATO was played by Ernest Bevin, the British Foreign Secretary, and the central rôle of the British Labour government in the creation of NATO undoubtedly helped to secure the support of European social democratic parties.

Acceptance of NATO as the main instrument of western European defence was almost universal among social democratic parties by 1949. Seven out of the twelve governments who signed the North Atlantic Treaty in 1949 were either social democratic or coalitions including social democrats. Parties which had formerly espoused neutralism had changed under the shock of the German invasion; Norway wanted the proposed defence union to be compatible with an American alliance, while Sweden favoured neutrality between the two blocs. The talks broke down in 1949 and Norway, Iceland and Denmark joined NATO. The Nenni socialists in Italy were, of course, unable to agree. NATO did not initially include West Germany and, when the question of West German rearmament arose, it was in the context of a European Defence Community. Schumacher and the party leadership were not at first opposed to German rearmament, provided Germany was given an equal status in the proposed Defence Community and provided NATO adopted a 'forward strategy', i.e. to concentrate on pushing the battle-ground as far east as possible. Such a strategy would have entailed a large increase in allied troops. After Schumacher's death the tone of party pronouncements became increasingly neutralist and anti-militarist. This development reached its zenith after the collapse of the European Defence Community proposals in August 1954, when it was proposed to integrate West Germany into NATO through the Western European Union (WEU). The SPD and the trade unions took to the streets in 1955 in the *Paulskirche* movement to try to prevent German entry into NATO. After a period of uncertainty the party, or more accurately, its defence spokesmen, Fritz Erler and Helmut Schmidt, adopted a position of qualified support for NATO. The wholehearted acceptance of the SPD of NATO was signalled in a speech by Herbert Wehner on 30 June 1960.

Acceptance of the NATO framework had become by then a secondary defining characteristic of social democratic parties. Social democrats not only accepted the mixed economy and the welfare state, but differentiated themselves from all other parties and factions on the Left by their acceptance of NATO and the American nuclear umbrella as the focus of their security aspirations. This was even to prove true of the Nenni socialists. When Nenni was Foreign Minister of Italy in the 1960s, he based his policy firmly on the NATO commitment, rejecting demands by his own backbenchers for the expulsion from NATO of Greece and Portugal and criticising Russian intervention in Czechoslovakia much more forcefully than American involvement in Vietnam.

Despite the general agreement over NATO, two issues had provoked dissension within the social democratic parties of Europe. German rearmament was viewed with alarm by almost all of them and, as in the case of the Labour Party, it was often extremely difficult to get agreement on this issue. The French socialist deputies divided fairly evenly on the issue, and the party was threatened with a major split when Guy Mollet, the party leader attempted to impose sanctions on dissident deputies (Criddle 1969, 56–77). In a number of parties there was even more serious disagreement over the nuclear weapons issue. The SPD leadership participated in the *Anti-Atomtod Bewegung*, the movement against atomic death, but quietly dropped out in late 1958 when it no longer appeared electorally rewarding. In Britain, which had an independent nuclear deterrent, the issue provoked even more intense intra-party discord, when Hugh Gaitskell, mindful of the need for Labour to appear credible as a potential government, accepted the logic of the Bevanite dictum about 'not going naked into the conference chamber'. Consequently, he defied, and eventually reversed, a 1959 conference resolution ('There are some of us Mr Chairman, who will fight and fight again to save the party we love', Williams 1983, p.358) which appeared to favour nuclear disarmament. This victory caused considerable resentment on the left wing of the party and the issue was to resurface at regular intervals throughout the following decades.

The commitment of the social democratic parties to NATO was based upon a shared perception of a continuing Soviet threat. This perception began to blur slightly in the 1960s. The successful resolution of the Cuban missile crisis in October 1962 paved the way for a superpower detente which was then reflected in Europe, most notably in the *Ostpolitik* of West German governments. The development of detente was not without interruptions, most notably the Soviet invasion of Czechoslovakia in August 1968. However, the general thrust was in favour of relaxation of tension and the NATO strategic policy of massive retaliation began to appear a less convincing response, especially to many members of social democratic parties. NATO made some adjustments to its nuclear strategy. In particular, it agreed to the siting of a significant number of battlefield nuclear weapons to make the transition to a policy of flexible response. The worries of social democratic parties were more specifically addressed in the adoption by NATO of the Harmel Report in 1967. This coupled the existing alliance deterrence policy with the goal of relaxing tensions and improving relations with the Soviet bloc.

Deterrence versus detente

The inherent tension between a security policy based on the maintenance of military capabilities (deterrence) and one stressing intentions, confidence-building measures and arms reduction (detente), was one which those responsible for the security policies of the social democratic parties were able to bridge fairly easily until the 1970s, since the priority of deterrence over detente was accepted in all the major parties by a majority of supporters given the continued perception of a Soviet threat. In the 1970s these tensions became much harder to manage.

The first crisis arose over the enhanced radiation weapons, often called the 'neutron bomb'. The proposal to deploy these weapons was made by President Carter, who was keen to reinforce the alliance's tactical nuclear capability. The British Prime Minister, James Callaghan, and the German Chancellor, Helmut Schmidt, who were equally concerned to maintain the credibility of the alliance deterrent and to prevent American decoupling from western Europe, supported the proposal. It provoked tremendous opposition within both the SPD and Labour parties, where it was seen as a major threat to detente. Opposition from within the parties was not now confined to left-wing factions. In the case of the SPD, it included the party chairman, Willy Brandt, and Egon Bahr, a principal security policy spokesman. Alarmed by the amount of opposition in western Europe, President Carter unilaterally decided to abandon the neutron bomb proposal in April 1978, thereby inflicting significant damage on the standing of Prime Minister Callaghan and Chancellor Schmidt with their respective parties.

The INF episode

The tensions between the social democratic governments and their followers on defence issues, manifest on the neutron bomb issue, sharpened visibly over the stationing of intermediate-range nuclear missiles. In a speech to the International Institute of Strategic Studies in London in 1977, Helmut Schmidt drew attention to a growing imbalance between the capacities of the Warsaw Pact and NATO in medium-range nuclear systems and suggested that steps be taken to remedy this. Schmidt's initiative was taken up by NATO, and in 1979 NATO adopted the so-called twin-track resolution. This resolution envisaged negotiation with the USSR to persuade them to remove their SS20 missiles from eastern Europe, with the threat that, should these negotiations fail, then NATO would deploy inter-mediate-range missiles in western Europe.

In initiating the modernisation of theatre nuclear weapons policy, Helmut Schmidt had been pursuing the two central goals of NATO security policy: the maintenance of the credibility of the alliance deterrent strategy and the prevention of American withdrawal from Europe. These goals took precedence over the pursuance of detente. The Soviet Union did not respond at that time to the NATO offer and Cruise and Pershing missiles were stationed in West Germany in the early summer of 1983.

The priority of deterrence over detente, while still commanding majority support in West German society, now faced its first sustained challenge from a burgeoning Peace Movement. The threat posed by the Soviet Union, which had been a central experience for the postwar generation, seemed much less real to a younger generation which had grown up in a period dominated by *Ostpolitik*. The radical Left, who had broadened their support through sponsorship of environmental movements, built upon that experience to play a key rôle in the Peace Movement.

More immediately worrying for Schmidt was the fact that this opposition was now widely shared inside the SPD. The SPD had opposed nuclear weapons in the late 1950s, but the new opposition, by significant sections of the SPD, had a novel character. In the 1950s the SPD protest was largely a moral one against nuclear weapons. The opposition to the enhanced radiation weapons and, even more clearly, to the stationing of Cruise and Pershing II missiles, was clearly linked to the preservation of detente. It was felt that by stationing the weapons, the Reagan Presidency had brought detente to an end. Opposition thus continued to increase particularly as negotiations proved fruitless and plans for deployment went ahead. A demonstration in Bonn against the imminent stationing of the missiles in October 1981 was the largest in the history of the Federal Republic and was supported, much to Helmut Schmidt's anger, by almost a quarter of the SPD parliamentary party.

A possible defeat for government policy at the Munich Conference of the SPD in April 1982 was staved off by a compromise which left the decision to a special conference in November 1983. The collapse of the Schmidt government put enormous pressure on the official SPD policy of support for the twin-track decision. At the special party conference on 18–19 November 1983 in Cologne the delegates voted overwhelmingly to reject the deployment of the new missiles in the Federal Republic. The isolation of Helmut Schmidt on this issue by then became brutally apparent. Despite what many considered to be his finest speech, his arguments in favour of deployment were rejected by 400 votes to fourteen.

Social democratic opposition to NATO modernisation

Opposition to the twin-track policy was even more pronounced in the smaller European social democratic parties. This was true both in the case of the Netherlands, where there was a very fierce and polarised debate on the siting of the missiles and in the Scandinavian alliance members, where there had always been a non-nuclear policy in the sense that they would not act as sites for nuclear weapons. Paradoxically, the strongest support for the twin-track policy among socialist parties came from the *Parti Socialiste*, the French Socialist Party, although France was not itself a full member of NATO. President Mitterrand caused much offence in the SPD by speaking in favour of the twin-track policy in a speech to the Bundestag just before the 1983 election. *Parti Socialiste* support for the twin-track policy was motivated by two principal factors. The *Parti Socialiste* shared general French fears of German neutralism and was alarmed by the boost that rejection of the twin-track policy might give to such forces. It was also suspicious of the marked influence of the French Communist Party in the French peace movement, and was intent on trying to constrain the influence of its rival and adversary partner. The opposition of the social democratic parties of Scandinavia and the Low Countries led to the setting up of Scandilux in 1980. Scandilux was intended as a forum where these parties could discuss issues of arms control and disarmament and where they could coordinate their opposition to the stationing of Cruise and Pershing missiles as envisaged by the twin-track policy. The British Labour Party, the PS and the SPD were invited to take part in their meetings. Over time, Egon Bahr, owing to his knowledge and unrivalled contact with the superpowers, especially the USSR, came to play a dominating rôle in a body which was opposed to the official policy of the Schmidt-led SPD government. It suffered some loss of impetus after the stationing of the missiles but has remained an important forum for the discussion by social democratic parties of proposals on arms control.

The retreat from Atlanticism

The support of the British Labour Party and the SPD has been crucial to NATO. To demonstrate their centrality one needs only to mention Ernest Bevin's rôle as a principal architect of NATO and Helmut Schmidt's crucial rôle in NATO councils both as West German Defence Minister and West German Chancellor.

In opposition in the 1980s both parties have retreated somewhat from their former unequivocal support of NATO. The strength of the Peace Movement and the success of the Greens in securing parliamentary representation in the March 1983 election placed the SPD under severe electoral pressure to align the SPD much more closely with the Peace Movement. Pressure to do so had been visible since 1979 but had been constrained by Helmut Schmidt's position and the SPD's electoral dependence on him. His retiral to the backbench and his total failure to secure support at the so-called 'rockets conference' in Cologne on 18/19 November 1983, where the delegates rejected the deployment of Cruise and Pershing missiles totally eroded his capacity to inhibit policy change. The waning support for Atlanticism in western European social democratic parties was not simply a reflection of changes within the parties but changes within the American foreign policy-making élite. In the United States political power appeared to be moving away from the east-coast liberal élites, who had played such a profound rôle in shaping postwar US policy towards western Europe. They had a close knowledge of and many contacts with European social democratic parties. The newly dominant forces in American politics were increasingly southern and western, conservative rather than liberal, and orientated towards the Pacific Rim rather than western Europe.

The effect of the changing focus of American foreign policy was particularly marked during the Reagan Presidency (1980–88). Acute differences arose over policy towards Central America and what Americans called the Crescent of Conflict which stretched from Afghanistan through the Gulf and the Arabian Peninsula to the Horn of Africa. There was a great deal of sympathy in western European social democratic parties for the Sandinista regime in Nicaragua, and much anger was caused by the attempts of the Reagan administration to destabilise it. The American bombing raid on Tripoli in Libya in April 1986 aroused similar feelings of alienation.

The general picture of increasing distance and tension between the European social democratic parties and the United States in the 1980s has to be modified somewhat in relation to southern Europe. Whilst the northern parties were largely in opposition in the 1980s, the southern parties enjoyed unprecedented success and were in government for much of this period. In opposition and exile the Spanish and Greek parties had been vehemently opposed to NATO. The Spanish government took no position on the dual track policy after Felipe González became prime minister in October 1982. However, the Spanish government was under intense pressure from socialist party activists to take Spain out of the NATO framework and press for the removal of American bases. González agreed only to a referendum on membership, and in the referendum, held in March 1986, he played a crucial rôle in persuading the Spanish people to vote in favour of NATO (52.5 per cent), against the opposition of the bulk of party members. González was helped by the fact that the leader of the Left faction in the socialist party, Pablo Castellano, indicated that they would not campaign publicly against González' position. One important factor for González was the hope that a Spanish army genuinely integrated into NATO would be less prone to undertake coups because it would no longer be exclusively focused on Spain. It would also justify higher military spending, a policy which he hoped would pacify the officer corps.

Greece   In Greece the Papandreou government (1981–89) was much less hostile to the alliance than it had been previously in opposition. It was pledged to remove all American military bases from Greece but by the end of the Papandreou era little had been done towards achieving that goal. For Greece and the other southern members of the alliance, Portugal, Spain, Italy and Turkey, NATO is not only a security system but a development and aid system.

The Papandreou government bridged the gap between financial dependence and the anti-American views of party activists by continually attacking American policy in the Middle East. This was a nuisance rather than a major threat to American policy.

The impact of Gorbachev

Changes in the perception of the other superpower, the USSR, were perhaps even more influential in moving western European social democratic parties from an Atlanticist orientation. The Soviet Union had always been perceived as a neighbour. For most of the postwar period this proximity only heightened the sense of threat felt by western European social democratic parties. The new face of Soviet policy under Mikhail Gorbachev, altered this perception and reinforced suspicion of the United States. The Soviet Union was no longer seen as a clear threat to the security of western Europe, and the attention of social democratic parties became much more concerned than in the past with working out a *modus vivendi* with their large European neighbour, rather than seeing relationships with the Soviet Union as almost exclusively the preserve of the United States. The changing perception of the Soviet Union also had a major impact on the vexed question of the extent to which social democratic parties would continue to support a policy based on nuclear deterrence.

One major result of the Gorbachev era in Soviet foreign policy was the conclusion of the Soviet–American agreement on the scrapping of intermediate-range nuclear missiles in early 1988. This agreement was welcomed by all the social democratic parties in contrast to Mrs Thatcher and Helmut Kohl who initially reacted by expressing fears that the INF Agreement might presage an American decoupling from western Europe. In the wake of the agreement, there has been some divergence in the policy responses of the major parties. In Britain the conclusion of the INF Agreement has been used by the party leadership to move away from a policy based on unilateral disarmament. Many Labour Party members were members of the Campaign for Nuclear Disarmament which maintained a continuous pressure on the Labour Party to adopt a unilateral policy. From the mid 1950s a significant proportion of Labour Party members and affiliated trade unions had pressed for unilateral nuclear disarmament. This was resisted by the Labour Party leadership until Michael Foot became leader in 1982. Labour Party defence policy then changed to one of support for unilateral nuclear disarmament. The change in party policy did not command universal support, especially among senior members of the Parliamentary Labour Party, and Denis Healey indicated his lack of agreement with the policy during the 1983 election campaign. The unilateralist position was held to have contributed significantly to the defeat of the Labour Party in 1983 and 1987, and defence policy occupied a central place in the policy review of the Labour Party. Although the unilateralist position was identified as a vote loser, change was difficult, given the opposition of the Transport and General Workers Union and Neil Kinnock's own long-held unilateralist position. The conclusion of the INF Treaty and the apparent readiness of the Soviet Union to negotiate on arms control was used by the Labour leadership to argue that the unilateralist position was now inappropriate in changed circumstances. If multilateral disarmament now appeared possible, then the British nuclear deterrent should be part of this process in order to effect an even larger reduction on the Soviet Union, rather than simply being given up without a *quid pro quo*, as the original unilateralist position entailed.

While the INF Treaty enabled the British Labour Party to abandon its unilateralist position and to identify more closely with NATO policy, it had the opposite effect in relation to the SPD. The SPD's position, until the resignation of Helmut Schmidt, had been more firmly supportive of NATO than the Labour Party. After 1983 it began to change the relative weighting accorded to deterrence and detente in its security policy. In its revised security programme for the 1987 election, it played down the Soviet threat, explicitly endorsed the 1982 Palme Commission Report on Common Security, which called for the establishment in Central Europe of a 300-kilometre-wide nuclear-free zone (150 kilometres deep on each side of the East–West German and West German–Czechoslovak borders), advocated a reduction in defence spending and the length of national service. In all its security proposals since 1983, it has given increasing weight to detente and greater European autonomy. It has talked constantly of a common responsibility for security with the East and concluded a draft agreement with the SED on a chemical weapons-free zone in central Europe.

For a non-nuclear power like the Federal Republic, unilateralism is not a relevant option, but the conclusion of the INF Treaty has raised the question of the degree to which the SPD will continue to support a NATO policy based on nuclear deterrence. After the conclusion of the INF Treaty, a number of governmental leaders, especially Prime Minister Thatcher, argued strongly that the deterrence function of the NATO alliance could best be preserved by the modernisation of short-range and battlefield nuclear weapons in Europe. Shorter-range missiles are very heavily concentrated in the two Germanies and the SPD had already called in its 1987 electoral programme for the removal of battlefield nuclear weapons. The SPD was therefore vehemently opposed to plans for the modernisation of shorter-range nuclear missiles. They were strengthened in their opposition by President Gorbachev's speech to the United Nations Assembly in December 1988, where he announced a unilateral arms reduction of 500,000 men and held out the hope that further significant reductions could be negotiated.

The SPD then argued for a so-called third zero solution, i.e. the removal of all short-range nuclear weapons. The SPD position was shared by the FDP and had some support in the CDU, and in April 1989 Chancellor Kohl called for negotiations with the Warsaw Pact for the removal of short-range missiles altogether. This move was supported by some smaller NATO allies but gravely alarmed the British and American governments who took the view that there should be no negotiations on short-range missiles until the Warsaw Pact's superiority in conventional and chemical weapons was eliminated.

The revised position of the Federal Government evoked sharp criticism from her major alliance partners and collision seemed inevitable at the Brussels Summit Conference at the end of May 1989. In the event the tension was defused by the skilful diplomacy of President Bush. The Bush compromise does envisage negotiations with the Soviet Union on the elimination of short-range missiles, but only if and when the Soviet Union has agreed to a series of assymetric reductions at the Vienna talks, which would have the effect of reducing Soviet and US forces in eastern and western Europe to 275,000 each.

The views of social democratic parties on defence now cover quite a wide spectrum. The French Socialist Party is an unequivocal supporter of the French Force de Frappe and its policies on defence and security policy are little different from those of its conservative political opponents. Indeed, on occasions, such as when the socialist

Minister of Defence ordered the sinking of the Greenpeace ship, *Rainbow Warrior*, in Auckland harbour in 1985, they seem to identify even more closely with power politics than their traditional opponents on the Right. The other western European parties show some variations. They can still be differentiated from other left-wing parties, either communist parties or a range of independent left-wing parties in Scandinavia and the Low Countries, by their continued formal adherence to NATO membership. This statement now also applies to the Spanish and Greek parties. The enthusiasm of social democratic parties declined noticeably in parallel to their perception of a declining Soviet threat and the degree of electoral pressure they were under from left-wing competitors. Within the general framework of unenthusiastic support for NATO, they showed a much greater interest than their right-wing competitors in 'non-provocative defence', i.e. seeking to deter a Soviet attack while avoiding all appearance of threat. Beyond these general similarities, differences abounded in the degree of their lack of enthusiasm for NATO and the degree of support they advocated for defence. The collapse of most of the communist governments in eastern Europe in the autumn of 1989 had led to a process of rethinking NATO policy away from deterrence towards increasingly regarding NATO and the Warsaw Pact as diplomatic instruments for bringing about very large-scale arms reductions in Europe – a process which is now enthusiastically endorsed by the social democratic parties in all the member states.

EAST–WEST RELATIONS

Social democratic parties were less ready than their conservative adversaries to immediately adopt a bipolar world view after 1945. The formation of the Comintern in 1919 had been followed by a long period of extremely bad relations between the social democratic parties and the Soviet Union and associated communist parties. The constant statements by the Comintern from the mid-1920s onwards that social democrats were 'social fascists' did enormous damage to already strained relations. Comintern policy changed in the mid-1930s, and there was a great deal of cooperation between social democratic and communist parties in popular front initiatives in the struggle to overthrow fascist governments. Communist and social democratic parties were also able to work together in the early postwar years in western and eastern Europe. They were governmental partners in France, Italy, Czechoslovakia and all other eastern European countries. Social democratic parties were, however, unable to accept the extension of Soviet control in eastern Europe and the turning point for most social democrats was the communist takeover in Prague in 1948 and the exclusion from political life of the Czech social democrats.

In the early 1950s the dominant tone in social democratic views on East–West relations was indistinguishable from that of their bourgeois competitors. They were appalled by the excesses of Stalinism in the Soviet Union and eastern Europe generally, and accorded priority to the defence of western Europe against the possibility of further Soviet expansion though they continued to hope for change in eastern Europe through the collapse of Stalinist regimes.

The disengagement phase

The death of Joseph Stalin in 1953 had a major impact on thinking in social democratic parties. His death simultaneously reduced the perception of the military threat from the Soviet Union and appeared to greatly extend the possibilities for political change in eastern Europe. In practice the opportunities for political change turned out to be extremely limited and the 17 June 1953 uprising in the GDR, and the Hungarian revolt of 1956 were brutally suppressed by Soviet troops. There was, however, a perceptible thaw in East–West relations which reached its apogee at the Geneva Heads of Government Conference in 1955. It was, however, more a question of a change of climate, of atmospherics, than a fundamental change of policies, though it was possible in this period to agree to end the Four Power occupation of Austria and detach it from the field of East–West conflict by according it the status of permanent neutral.

In this altered context, social democratic thinking crystallised around the concept of disengagement in central Europe. Disengagement was a formula which held out the hope of freedom from Soviet control for central European states and the prospect of a reunited Germany.

The most influential statement of social democratic views on disengagement was given by Hugh Gaitskell in a series of Harvard lectures which were published as *The Challenge of Coexistence* (1957). Writing against the backdrop of the Hungarian revolt, Gaitskell argued that a similar revolt in East Germany would have incalculable consequences. West Germany had by now rearmed (it had not yet done so in 1953) and might feel impelled to intervene in such a situation. This would present intractable problems to the allies.

Gaitskell suggested the evacuation of the danger area in the centre of Europe and the creation of a disengaged zone covering the whole of Germany, Poland, Czechoslovakia and Hungary and, if possible, Romania and Bulgaria. Within this zone the armed forces would be subject to inspection and control, and 'finally, together with the permanent control on arms in these territories, there should be a multilateral European security plan, in which the various states in the neutral zone would have their territories guaranteed by the Great Powers as well as by each other' (Gaitskell 1957, 54–8). In Gaitskell's view the establishment of a disengagement zone had three preconditions: (1) Germany must accept existing frontier, i.e. recognition of the Oder–Neisse line; (2) American forces would have to remain in western Europe and NATO continue in being; (3) There would have to be complete consensus among western states.

Denis Healey restated the arguments for disengagement in *A Neutral Belt in Europe* (Fabian pamphlet 1958), where he argued that the Soviet Union had a powerful incentive to agree to such a neutral belt in order to forestall the prospect of a proliferation of nuclear weapons in western Europe.

Labour Party proposals for a zone of disengagement were paralleled by those of the SPD who argued in the 1957 election campaign in favour of a reunited Germany and the replacement of existing military alliances by a collective security system which would include provisions for the limitation and control of armaments. The SPD were, however, very careful to avoid using the term neutral, given the unpopularity in the Federal Republic in the 1950s of appearing to suggest that Germany could remain neutral in the East–West struggle.

These proposals had little impact on developments. The advent of the second Berlin crisis (1958–61) and the apparently aggressive and adventurous policy of Kruschev rendered irrelevant talk of zones of disengagement in Central Europe.

The coming of Ostpolitik

The division of Europe after 1945 had its most profound impact on Germany and the SPD has therefore had a more intense and continuous interest in East–West relations than any other western European social democratic party. In the 1950s this interest of the

SPD was very largely focused, as was the case with other West German parties, on the question of German unity. This concentration and the relative absence of contacts between leading SPD figures and representatives of Eastern Europe (Carlo Schmid accompanied Adenauer to Moscow in 1955 for the establishment of diplomatic relations with the Soviet Union) meant that SPD views on East–West relations did not exert a great deal of influence on its sister parties. The ideas of the British Labour Party on East–West relations had, as we have seen in relation to discussion on disengagement, a far greater impact. This was to change in the early 1960s and, from that period, the SPD has provided the central impetus for social democratic views on East–West relations.

The erection of the Berlin Wall in 1961 had a profound effect on SPD thinking. Hitherto the West German consensus was based on the rejection of the legitimacy of the GDR regime because of its non-elected character and the hope that the regime would collapse. The erection of the Berlin Wall seemed to indicate that East Germany would not collapse and a policy of unremitting pressure by the Federal Republic would only make the GDR leadership even more defensive and repressive towards its own population. At that time, the SPD maintained an Eastern Section (*Ostbüro*) which was concerned not only to collect information about, but to destabilise the German Democratic Republic. The effect of the erection of the Berlin Wall was to cause the SPD to begin to rethink its policy away from an exclusive emphasis on reunification to policies designed to improve the conditions of those actually living within the East German state.

This response was especially marked in relation to Willy Brandt and the Berlin SPD. A year after the erection of the Berlin Wall, in a series of lectures at Harvard entitled, in a conscious echo of Gaitskell's earlier series, '*The Ordeal of Coexistence*' (1962), Brandt argued for the abandonment of a policy of confrontation. A year later, in a much-publicised speech at Tützing, Brandt's foreign policy confidant, Egon Bahr, argued for a policy of '*Wandel durch Annäherung*' (change through accommodation). The Bahr–Brandt concept envisaged transcending the status quo by accepting it. The argument was conceived in relation to East Germany where it was argued that some accommodation with the East German state would allow it to pursue a less repressive policy towards its own population. Later it became the basis for transforming policy towards East–West European relations and has been enormously influential. As Governing Mayor of West Berlin, Party Chairman and Chancellor

Candidate, Brandt was in a strong position to get the SPD behind his new policy. Brandt became Foreign Minister in the Grand Coalition of CDU/CSU and the SPD in 1966. The constraints of coalition government inhibited directly addressing inter-German relations, but Brandt did devote a great deal of attention to the fostering of detente. The advent of superpower detente after the conclusion of the Cuban missile crisis greatly increased the opportunities for detente in Europe. Egon Bahr had followed Brandt to Bonn to head the Planning Department of the West German Foreign Office. The dual constraint of coalition government and the existence of the Hallstein doctrine, which prevented the Federal Republic from establishing full diplomatic relations with countries which recognised the GDR (an exception was made for the Soviet Union), ensured that much of the activity took place at the level of concepts rather than practice. Brandt and Bahr were preoccupied with linking the problem of peace and the German Question, not only in the obvious sense of finding a framework for the solution to the German problem, but also being driven by the conviction that the German past imposed a special obligation on Germans to contribute to detente. What was needed was 'an orientation which places the German Question in its European context' which in turn required 'a concept which contains the basis of a European Peace Order' (Brandt 1969, p.85). The concept of the European Peace Order presupposed a European security system. The basis of a European security system remained unclear. In his speeches Brandt sometimes implied that it could be created on the basis of a changed relationship between NATO and the Warsaw Pact; at other times he talked of the gradual dismantling of these alliances and their replacement by a different system.

The ideas of Brandt and Bahr had a major impact on other Western European social democratic parties. Brandt was President of the Socialist International and exercised a great deal of influence, especially on the parties of Scandinavia and the Low Countries.

Ostpolitik

The major impact of the SPD on East–West relations was to come after 1969 as the principal partner in the SPD–FDP coalition. *Ostpolitik* is the name given to the policy of the Federal Republic towards eastern Europe and is especially identified with the series of major treaties between the Federal Republic and the states of eastern Europe concluded during the Brandt chancellorship.

The early days of the Brandt government in 1969 were marked by some fairly dramatic pronouncements, particularly in relation to East Germany. Perhaps the most famous of these was Brandt's reference to 'two states of one German nation', which, while stopping short of full international recognition of the GDR, also by implication ruled out, for the foreseeable future, the reunification option. Brandt's government declaration of 1969 was the first not to use the term 'reunification'. This meant that Brandt recognised that the pursuit of a policy based on the primacy of reunification had resulted in the atrophying of contacts between East and West Germany by encouraging the government of the GDR to maintain its defensive posture. Explicit acceptance of the fact that reunification was not practical policy would, it was hoped, enable the East German government to feel free enough to liberalise contacts between the two states and thus strengthen the sense of *Zusammengehörigkeitsgefühl* (feeling of belonging together). Historically, this feeling has not, as Brandt constantly emphasised, depended on living within the same frontiers. In other words, the new government, in the hope of preserving the German nation as a *Kulturnation* (nation defined by culture) refrained from stressing the pursuit of a *Staatsnation* (nation defined by citizenship). The primary goal of *Ostpolitik* was, and remained throughout, a new relationship with East Germany. The new relationship with the GDR, although central to Brandt's plans, was likely to be the most difficult to achieve and depended on the prior settlement of relations with the Soviet Union.

For Brandt, normalisation of relations with eastern Europe was an overriding priority on three main grounds. First, normal relations with eastern Europe were seen as a precondition of progress on the central plane of German–German relations. Secondly, it was part of a process of emancipation that was calculated to decrease the reliance of the Federal Republic on the western allies, who hitherto had acted as its interlocutor in eastern Europe. Finally, there was an important moral dimension symbolised by Brandt's gesture of throwing himself on his knees at the site of the Warsaw Ghetto during his visit to Warsaw in 1970. This moral imperative had already been present in Brandt's thinking in the late 1960s, and it was to become a central element of social democratic views on *Ostpolitik*. The moral argument stressed that German action in eastern Europe in the Second World War had not only fatally compromised German territorial rights in the area, but had been of such a traumatic character that it continued to impose obligations on the Germans, not only, as Brandt had argued in the 1960s, to make a vocation of detente, but to make some sort of recompense.

The basic thrust of *Ostpolitik* was not to offer the eastern European governments renunciation of force agreements, as previous CDU/CSU governments had done, but in effect to recognise postwar realities and accept the finality of existing boundaries. Negotiations were taken up immediately with the Soviet Union and Poland rather than the GDR since it was seen as presenting the greatest difficulties.

Treaties were concluded with the USSR and Poland in 1970. In these treaties the Federal Republic recognised the inviolability of existing frontiers, for example, Article I of the Treaty with Poland stated that the Oder–Neisse line 'shall constitute the western state frontier of the People's Republic of Poland'.

The recognition of existing frontiers was flanked by provisions for economic and technological cooperation and provisions designed to make it easier for citizens of German origin to leave the USSR and Poland. Ratification of the Moscow Treaty was tied to progress on Berlin, and a Quadripartite agreement was signed in 1971 which significantly improved access to West Berlin. Despite this, ratification of the treaties proved extremely problematic and led to the erosion of the governmental majority as deputies left both the SPD and FDP to join the CDU/CSU on this issue. Both treaties were ratified in May 1972, with the CDU/CSU abstaining.

Despite the prior conclusion of the Moscow and Warsaw Treaties, the principal aim of *Ostpolitik* remained the transformation of relations with 'the other part of Germany'. Priority had been given to agreement with the Soviet Union since it was seen as the ultimate repository of power in eastern Europe. The fratricidal relations between the GDR and FRG, made if anything more difficult by older historic tensions between social democrats and communists, also dictated it should not be tackled first.

Serious progress was made only after the conclusion of the Quadripartite Agreement in September 1971. The GDR was concerned to achieve international recognition while making the minimum concessions to opening up the society of the GDR. The priorities of the FRG were reversed. The Federal Government wished for the maximum contact between the two states whilst limiting the degree of recognition in order to maintain the doctrine of common nationality and the special character of the relations between the two Germanies. In the Basic Treaty which was concluded in November 1972 the Federal Republic made more concessions than the GDR. It did not accord full international recognition, but Article 6 recognises unconditionally the internal and external sovereignty of both states. Both states agreed to support each other's membership of the United Nations and to establish diplomatic relations with each other though their representatives would be known as High Commissioners rather than Ambassadors.

Social democrats had assumed in the first two decades after 1945 that the anti-communist character of the Federal Republic and popular attachment to the idea of a reunified Germany would make an accommodation with eastern Europe on the basis of existing realities an electoral liability. In fact, the desire by 1972 for increased contacts between East and West Germany was so strong that in the ensuing election of 19 November 1972, which was fought on the *Ostpolitik* issue, the SPD emerged as the strongest party for the only time in the history of the Federal Republic.

The conclusion of treaties with the other eastern European states meant that by the end of Brandt's period as Chancellor in 1974 the Federal Republic had diplomatic relations with all the states of eastern Europe. Henceforward the views of social democratic parties on East–West European relations were dominated by those of the SPD.

Helmut Schmidt consolidated rather than extended the achievements of Willy Brandt. The new *Ostpolitik* of the 1970s had been predicated on superpower detente. This period of superpower detente came to an end in the early 1980s with the Soviet invasion of Afghanistan and the declaration of martial law in Poland in 1981. Schmidt and the SPD took the lead in trying to preserve the Inner-German detente and to prevent a too steep decline in the climate of East–West relations generally.

Throughout the 1980s the social democratic parties, led by the SPD, constantly called for the maintenance of friendly relations with eastern Europe at a time when the relations between the more conservative governments, such as those of Britain and the Federal Republic, with the Soviet Union were extremely frosty. The SPD talked constantly and bravely of a 'second *Ostpolitik*', but this bore little fruit apart from draft agreements on chemical and nuclear weapons with the SED. It was to be the historic misfortune of the SPD to be out of power when a Soviet leader emerged in the shape of Mikhail Gorbachev who appeared to be seriously interested in East–West negotiations. The collapse of the eastern European governments, especially that of the GDR in Autumn 1989 caught the SPD and other social democratic parties flatfooted as their policy had been based on working through established governments.

DECOLONISATION AND THE THIRD WORLD

Social democratic parties have reflected their socialist heritage in their rejection of imperialism, they have also played a very active part in postwar decolonisation, not only in the powers, but also in the smaller countries without colonial responsibilities. In the latter they focused a good deal of attention on colonial problems through the United Nations: they reinforced their verbal commitment by providing contingents for UN peace-keeping forces, and furnished the United Nations with some of its most active servants in this area – men such as Trygve Lie of the Norwegian Labour Party and Conor Cruise O'Brien of the Irish Labour Party. Nevertheless, the main focus of endeavour has been in the colonial powers.

The British Labour Party had a well-established interest in colonial affairs and close relations with anti-colonialist movements before the outbreak of the Second World War. Its policy in government was less radical than its anti-colonialist rhetoric of the prewar period. It presided over the granting of independence to India, Pakistan, Burma and Ceylon, but the impossibility of the security situation and Britain's parlous economic position made it unlikely that any British government would have countenanced remaining where independence demands were strong. In Africa it was to prove much less radical and very little progress towards independence was made in these years. In opposition Labour was rather more radical: its biggest foreign policy disagreement with the Conservative government was over the Anglo-French invasion of Egypt – in essence a colonial question. During its second period of office, the Labour Party was increasingly on the defensive over colonial issues. The government's stand against Ian Smith's unilateral declaration of independence in Rhodesia – taken on domestic and financial grounds – was by no means as firm as most African Commonwealth statesmen wished. Relations deteriorated further when the government, relying on economic sanctions, failed to dislodge the Smith regime. Additional tension was created by the attitude of the Wilson government towards South Africa and by its legislative measures to control immigration.

The Algerian Crisis

But it was in France that decolonisation posed the most serious problems for a European socialist party. The French Socialist Party (SFIO) shared some of the responsibility for the early conduct of the war in Indo-China, although the major responsibility in that area soon passed out of their hands. In opposition from 1951 to 1956 the socialists, like their British counterparts, adopted a more marked anti-colonial tone and fought the 1956 election on a policy of peace in Algeria where French troops were already engaged in operations against the Algerian Independence Movement (FLN). After the elections a predominantly socialist government under Mollet abandoned its liberal intentions in the face of vociferous opposition from the large European majority in Algeria. French forces there were increased to a half million, the military was entrusted with the administration of the territory and France was committed to a long and costly war. Soon afterwards Mollet authorised the Anglo-French Suez expedition which was strongly opposed by the British Labour Party. Opinion in France seemed at the time strongly to favour these chauvinist and anti-Arab policies and to sympathise with Mollet's contention that the United Nations was not competent to intervene in Algeria.

Attacked by minorities within his party and by member parties of the Socialist International, Mollet and his supporters attempted to justify their policy. Given the experience of other newly independent countries, many socialists genuinely believed that only a French presence in Algeria could save the country from the ruthless suppression of political liberties that would follow a victory by the nationalists. The SFIO even tried to counter the nationalist appeal of the FLN with the principles of democratic socialism – the Algerian Moslems were being offered not independence but economic, social and political development within the framework of a French democratic state. Others held that social democracy was interested in the 'liberty of each individual, the independence of each person'; nationalism and the creation of new nations were outmoded concepts as recent developments in western Europe showed. Others, again, held that the FLN had lost its autonomy, that it was dominated by Cairo, by the Pan-Arab movement, and was a victim of Soviet and/or American imperialist designs.

Perhaps the Algerian and foreign policies of the Mollet government can best be explained by its concern with domestic economic and social reform, and its fear of losing the votes of the Right in the National Assembly – having rejected communist support the socialists had to rely on Conservative goodwill, and the Right, in return, insisted on a policy of force in Algeria. In the event the cost of the war and the consequent inflation prevented the implementation of many of the government's economic measures and forced the postponement of others. The government must, however, be credited with one major achievement. While Mollet was engaged in a policy of repression in Algeria, his colleague, Gaston Defferre, was legislating to provide for self-government in the territories of Black Africa. This enabled those territories to opt for independence in the 1960s without recourse to bloodshed. After the Mollet government was defeated in 1957, opinion in the party, as in the country, turned against the use of force in Algeria and the great majority of the socialists welcomed General de Gaulle's initiatives to bring about Algerian independence.

Once the process of decolonisation was virtually complete by the early 1970s, interest in the Third World by the parties of the colonial powers has perceptibly waned, though social democratic parties continue to be prominent in support of the anti-apartheid struggle in South Africa, and supported the Sandinista regime in Nicaragua.

In the non-colonial powers, in Scandinavia and the Federal Republic, interest in the Third World was not exhausted by the ending of the process of decolonisation. The parties in these massively prosperous and relatively homogeneous societies have switched some of their former interest in domestic redistribution to support for some move towards a global restructuring which would ameliorate the burden of Third World debt as argued in the Brandt Report (1975). The idea that the underclass was now external to western Europe and in the Third World was a prominent feature in the Irsee Draft Programme which the SPD concluded in 1988.

SOCIAL DEMOCRATIC PARTIES AND EUROPEAN INTEGRATION

There is nothing the Socialists nationalise as quickly as socialism.
Ignazio Silone

The tension between the programmatic commitment of democratic socialist parties to internationalism and the impact of national allegiances is an old one, as indicated by Silone's remark. Nationalism proved to be a far more potent force in 1914 than the internationalism of the Socialist International. This tension has again been present in the response of the social democratic parties to the process of European integration but it is only one theme in a much more complex story (Featherstone 1988; Newman 1983; Paterson 1974).

Historical background

The theoretical attachment of the democratic socialist parties to the nation state was much less exclusive than their bourgeois adversaries. They were therefore positive about the fairly vague plans for European Unity that emerged in the interwar period. There was a reference to European unity in the SPD's Heidelberg Programme of 1925: 'It [the SPD] is in favour of the creation of European economic unity, a unity which has become necessary for economic reasons, and is in favour of the foundation of the United States of Europe.' A number of parties, including the French, expressed support for the Briand memorandum on European unity in 1929, though it was rejected by the British Labour government. 'Briand's initiative was virtually bound to collapse if Britain indicated her opposition. This was almost certain to be the case, so long as the Labour Government condemned regional trade preferences and international industrial agreements, the basic tools that Briand had to hand as contrary to free trade' (Boyle 1980 p. 26).

However, even in the case of the British Labour Party, which was hostile to the major specific initiative towards European Unity undertaken in the interwar period, there were still some signs of general support for the idea. Ernest Bevin had spoken at the 1927 TUC Congress of the need to 'inculcate the spirit of a United States of Europe – at least on an economic basis, even if we cannot on a totally political basis' and his motion at the TUC Congress was carried by 2.26 million votes to 1.46 million. The Labour Party was also not immune to ideas of federal union which had a wide currency in the British political élite in 1939/40. Clement Attlee wrote in December 1939: 'In the common interest there must be recognition of an international authority superior to the individual States and endowed, not only with rights over them, but with power to make them effective, operating not only in the political, but in the economic sphere, Europe must federate or perish' (Attlee 1939, 13).

Postwar reactions

In the immediate postwar years the major task in Europe was reconstruction and European integration was largely a matter of participation in the OEEC, an organisation which was at that time primarily concerned with the distribution of Marshall Aid. The collapse of many allied and neutral European nation states in 1940 and of the belligerent states in 1945 had provoked a fairly widespread disillusionment with the capacity of the nation state to meet the needs of its citizens and there was a greatly heightened interest in European unity. This interest was most strongly expressed in christian democratic parties but it also had a major impact on social democratic parties. The parties in the Low Countries and Italy were enthusiastic supporters of European integration and played a prominent rôle at the Hague Conference called to advance the idea of a federal Europe in 1948.

Other parties were far more reserved. The priority of the British Labour Party was the transformation of British society and the implementation of the 1945 Labour Programme. The central political lesson that they drew from the 1930s was the absolute necessity of the avoidance of the recurrence of mass unemployment. They believed that this could be best avoided by a reliance on a nationally based Keynesian system of demand management – a belief which made them extremely reluctant to contemplate the abandonment of national policy instruments.

The Scandinavian social democratic parties shared this reluctance. They had adopted neo-Keynesian economic policies and were interested in cooperation rather than integration. In the immediate postwar period their energies were concentrated on Nordic cooperation, and the Nordic Council was established in 1952.

The initial position of the SPD was unclear. It was led and dominated by Kurt Schumacher. Schumacher had always held nationalistic views and he argued strongly that a stress on defending German national interests would pay rich electoral dividends for the SPD, especially since one quarter of the population of the western zones were refugees. On the other hand, the Federal Republic had not yet been created and SPD policy gave almost no attention to this issue.

Even within those parties that were less enthusiastic about European integration, there were minorities of very active proponents, such as R.W.G. Mackay in the British Labour Party, and Max Brauer, Wilhelm Kaisen and Ernst Reuter in the SPD. These minority groups established relations with each other through the Socialist Movement for the United States of Europe founded by Andre Philip in 1947.

The creation of the Council of Europe in 1949 presented relatively few problems for the social democratic parties. Those parties in favour of far-reaching integration, while disappointed by the modest intergovernmental scope of the Council of Europe in relation to the hopes that had been expressed at the Hague Congress, hoped that it might be possible to change it from within. The parties opposed to federalism were happy to have a European organisation based on cooperation. The SPD expressed mild opposition to West German entry into the Council of Europe on the grounds that the Federal Republic was initially offered only associate membership and the simultaneous entry of the Saar might be seen as legitimising the Saar's separate status and also create an unfortunate precedent *vis à vis* German lands in the East.

The Schuman Plan

The Schuman Plan to establish a European Coal and Steel Community under a supranational High Authority presented a much more difficult problem for the social democratic parties.

The Plan was supported by the social democratic parties of the Low Countries. The Italian PSI was strongly opposed to it because of the adverse effect they felt it would have on the tiny Italian coal and steel industry. They also saw it as a further example of growing American hegemony. In France the SFIO was less enthusiastic but did eventually support the treaty.

> In May of 1950, Guy Mollet saw in the Schuman proposal little more than a scheme to shore up a decadent German and French capitalism and affront the British Labour Party. Ultimately, the SFIO came to support the Treaty, but not without serious misgivings and reservations. Gouin, Lacoste, Philip and Naegelen, among others, fulsomely supported the general 'European' doctrine of free association with Germany, rising living standards through a common market and progressive industrial policies, and the need to counter the Soviet appeal by rousing a new Europe against economic stagnation, especially that of a new cartel system, yet the deep-seated national preoccupation of many socialists was equally patent. ECSC would be good only if French coal and steel can successfully compete with their German rivals. Hence, modernisation and investments – not subject to High Authority direction – must be continued, argued Robert Lacoste. Everything must be done to interpret the ECSC Treaty so as to permit special protection for French coal production during the transitional period. The absence of Britain from ECSC was deplored by all Socialists and not considered final. If commitment to 'Europe' was present, so was a determination not to allow a European rationale to interfere with the claims of French workers.
> *(Haas 1958, 116)*

British participation in the ECSC was rejected by the Labour government. The Schuman Declaration was made in May 1950 and the attitude that the government was going to take was prefigured in

the National Executive Committee's statement on European unity
which it issued in the same month.

> The Labour Party could never accept any commitments which limited its
> own, or other's freedom to pursue democratic socialism, and to apply the
> economic controls necessary to achieve it! Any changes in Britain's
> relations with Western Europe must not impair her position as nerve
> centre of the Commonwealth and banker of the Sterling Area. Close co-
> operation with Asia and America is vital to Europe's peace and prosperity.
> Until the Soviet Union allows the United Nations to function, as it
> should, the first immediate aim for British foreign policy must be to
> construct an organic unity throughout the whole of the non-Communist
> world. No socialist party with the prospect of forming a government,
> could accept a system by which important fields of national policy were
> surrendered to a supranational European representative authority, since
> such an authority would have a permanent anti-socialist majority and
> would arouse the hostility of European workers.
>
> *(Cited in Rose 1960, 279)*

The rejection by the Labour government of participation in the
ECSC led Richard Rose to comment:

> For more than 30 years British Socialists had urged a supranational
> authority to control the vested interests of the capitalist nation states.
> When the Labour Government came into office, it found that British
> workers, as well as capitalists, had a vested interest in national sovereignty.
> The electoral plea, 'Put the Nation first', [1950 election manifesto] had
> an unintended double meaning. *(Rose 1960, 280–1)*

The strongest opposition to the Schuman plan came, however,
from the SPD using arguments that were to characterise the party's
response until 1955. The SPD objected to a lack of equal status
(*Gleichberechtigung*) for the Federal Republic; to the negative impact
a tightly integrated western Europe would have on the prospects of
German unity; to the insufficiently democratic character of the
ECSC and the central rôle of a technocratic High Authority and to
what the SPD perceived as French designs to hold down Germany by
espousing European integration. To these four stock features of SPD
opposition to European integration a fifth was added in the case of
the ECSC. The creation of a European Coal and Steel Community
would exclude the public ownership of German heavy industry, still
at that time an important element in SPD policy.

The SPD was isolated in its opposition to the ECSC. At a meeting
of socialist parties on 16/17 June 1950 to frame a response to the
Schuman Plan even the British Labour party urged the SPD to
respond positively. The SPD's position was perceived as nationalist,
while that of the Labour Party did not attract adverse comment. The

experience of 1939–45 and the prestige derived from its 1945 victory meant that the nationalism of the Labour Party attracted very little adverse comment from other western European parties. Conversely, although the SPD had not been responsible for German aggression, any apparently nationalist arguments advanced by it were quite simply unacceptable to the other western European socialist parties. It is difficult, however, not to feel sympathetic to the SPD leadership, confronted as it was with the double standards of a Labour Party which criticised the SPD for not supporting German membership of the ECSC while at the same time rejecting it for Britain.

EDC and the issue of German rearmament

The outbreak of the Korean War in June 1950 had massive repercussions in western Europe. It helped to sustain an economic boom, but it also made it inevitable that the United States would press for a major German contribution to western defence. It had long been urging such a step privately, now it would press for it publicly. In a damage-limitation exercise, the French Prime Minister, Rene Pleven, suggested the creation of a European Defence Community and a European Political Community in order to contain a rearmed Germany. The question of West German rearmament and the European Defence Community was to be a very difficult one for social democratic parties until 1954.

Schumacher was not initially opposed to West German participation, provided the Federal Republic was given an equal status in the proposed European Defence Community, and provided NATO adopted a 'forward' strategy, i.e the Federal Republic should not be the main battlefield. The rank and file in the SPD and trade unions were, however, strongly opposed to rearmament and, with the onset of Schumacher's illness in 1951, the SPD became increasingly opposed to the European Defence Community. On this issue even the pro-Europeans in the party, like Max Brauer, were opposed.

EDC also proved to be a very contentious issue for other social democratic parties. It provoked very fierce debate and factional struggles in both the Belgian and French parties and, while both parties supported ratification, a very significant minority of deputies voted against (twenty-nine deputies of the Belgian PSB voted against ratification and fifty-three deputies of the French SFIO). The Labour Party was opposed to British participation in the EDC and there was considerable opposition to the whole principle of German rearmament. After the collapse of the EDC in August 1954, as a result of a procedural vote in the French National Assembly, agreement was reached on the creation of a western European Union. That there was a great deal of opposition to the idea of German rearmament quickly became apparent. It was only with great difficulty that the principle was accepted at the 1954 Labour Party Conference. Eighteen SFIO deputies voted against ratification in France in December 1954. SPD opposition reached a peak in its participation in the *Paulskirche* extra-parliamentary opposition movement to rearmament.

Social democratic parties and the creation of the EEC

The decision to create the European Economic Community and Euratom was supported by all the social democratic parties of the six states which belonged to the European Coal and Steel Community. The support of the Benelux countries was the most wholehearted and P.H. Spaak, the Belgian socialist leader, played a major rôle in turning the original Messina proposals for the creation of EEC and Euratom into reality. The French Socialist Party had been very unenthusiastic about the EDC, but Guy Mollet was now prime minister and France was very successful in the negotiations to set up the EEC, since Adenauer feared, after the collapse of the EDC, that any agreement other than one which demonstrably respected French needs would fail to command the assent of the National Assembly. The Italian PSI supported Euratom and gave a limited welcome to the EEC, where they abstained in the parliamentary vote.

The support of the SPD was, at first sight, more surprising, but much had changed since the bitter opposition to ECSC. Schumacher, who died in 1952, had been replaced as leader by Erich Ollenhauer, who was much more ready to compromise. Economically the party had started on its route to Bad Godesberg and the socialist objections of 1950/1 had lost all force after 1952. Their opposition was at its most intense when the question of European integration became identified with that of defence. When the two were separated, and when the prospects for German unity began to appear more remote, the SPD changed its attitude. Other contributory factors were the return of the Saar to Germany, the SPD's interest in Euratom, the positive experience of prominent SPD leaders, like Wehner, in the Common Assembly of the ECSC, and the failure of their previous policy to produce any demonstrable benefits.

In October 1955 the SPD was able to join the Monnet Committee for the United States of Europe as a founding member and thereafter its leaders became enthusiastic 'Europeans', their views coinciding with government policy over the whole field of European integration. Jean Monnet had always had very good relations with European social democrats, who often claim him as one of themselves, and he was able to involve all the social democratic parties in the activities of this Committee. This was of considerable importance as it was the socialist government of Mollet that was later responsible for bringing France into the EEC (Criddle 1969). In 1954 a bare majority of the French SFIO had supported the ill-fated proposal for a European Defence Community and it was therefore a notable achievement when Mollet won the full support of his party for the EEC two years later.

Social democrats opposed to entry

The social democrats in Scandinavia have traditionally followed a policy similar to that of their British counterparts: sympathy towards certain forms of European cooperation but antipathy to integration as represented by the European Communities. The original attitude taken by most social democrat leaders in Scandinavia to the EEC was one of guarded hostility; for them the Communities represented a Catholic, conservative, capitalist bloc whose policies could vitally affect Scandinavia's trading interests. The three Scandinavian social democrat governments followed Britain in her moves to create the European Free Trade Area, the 'Outer Seven' though only Denmark joined the EEC. The move for EEC membership – under consideration in Denmark from 1961 – represented a realistic response to changes, or threatened changes, in the European trade situation rather than an enthusiastic commitment to European federalism. The latter feeling was confined to only a few members of the Danish and Norwegian social democratic parties. Social democrats of all four countries have, however, been generally enthusiastic about the various postwar attempts to further Nordic cooperation and integration. An important factor here has been the tradition of cooperation among the Nordic social democrats themselves – arising from their wartime experience and encouraged by the creation of the Nordic Council in 1952; the movement also reflects the favourable attitude shown by the Scandinavian trade unions towards such cooperation.

In the 1960s and 1970s, discussion of social democratic attitudes to European integration focused of necessity on the tortuous meanderings of the British Labour Party. The nature of the party's opposition under Gaitskell has been neatly summarised by Frank Bealey: 'The chief sentiments aired were national independence, especially the right to plan one's own economy, and distrust of Europeans, the latter coinciding with a new labour interest in the Commonwealth' (Bealey 1970). In line with these arguments the Labour party established five formal conditions for British membership, which involved safeguarding the interests of the Commonwealth and EFTA countries as well as those of British agriculture. Britain would also have to retain the right to plan her own economy and pursue an independent foreign policy. Harold Wilson was returned to office in 1964 determined to strengthen the Commonwealth; but by 1967 the Labour government had applied to join the EEC, and little was heard of the five conditions. The decision was taken at a time of great economic difficulty and Stanley Henig is probably correct when he attributes the conversion to economic and technological reasons; (Henig and Pinder 1970) the political arguments for European integration seem to have weighed much more heavily with the Conservatives.

The Labour Party and British entry

Labour had opposed Britain's first application for entry in 1961/2, while in opposition. When it was in government, however, in 1967 an application for entry was made. After 1970, when Labour was once more in opposition, there was again considerable objection to entry, especially from the trade unions and certain individual party members. Support in the Parliamentary Labour Party was much stronger and a compromise was arrived at whereby the party continued to support the principle of entry but condemned the terms achieved by the Heath government. This in itself was enough to provoke the resignation of Roy Jenkins as deputy leader and the simultaneous resignation from their shadow posts of David Owen, Bill Rodgers and Shirley Williams.

In government after 1974, labour under Wilson made some attempt to renegotiate the terms – but with a conspicuous lack of success. A referendum was held in 1975 on British membership in which a majority of the Cabinet canvassed for a 'Yes' vote, while a minority, and all the most influential trade unions, supported withdrawal. The result was a majority of almost two to one for staying in. Despite this, and despite the personal preferences of both Wilson and Callaghan for British membership, the issue remained such a difficult one that the Labour government rarely gave wholehearted support to any European initiative and the anti-EEC MPs, notably Benn and Silkin, used their portfolios to make the maximum possible difficulties for the EEC.

The departure of Roy Jenkins, David Owen, Bill Rodgers and Shirley Williams in 1981 to form the SDP considerably reduced support for the EEC within the Parliamentary Labour Party. James Callaghan had been replaced as leader in 1980 by Michael Foot, a committed anti-marketeer, and the Labour Party manifesto of 1983 was considerably to the left of its predecessors on foreign and security issues. The manifesto called for British withdrawal and the introduction of a more protectionist economic policy, the so-called Alternative Economic Strategy, to safeguard British Industry. 'British withdrawal from the community is the right policy for Britain, and should be completed well within the lifetime of the present parliament'.

The catastrophic defeat of the Labour party in the 1983 election had a number of consequences, of which the swiftest was the replacement of Michael Foot by Neil Kinnock. The alternative economic strategy was also fairly quickly dropped and the emphasis now began to be placed on 'securing the best deal for Britain within the EEC'. This change also reflected a weakening of the TUC's position. In February 1982 the TUC research section produced an internal memorandum on implementing the TUC's official policy of withdrawal. Contrary to the expectations of the TUC executive, the memorandum dwelt on the negative effects on employment of a British withdrawal. Although TUC official policy did not alter for sometime, there was no longer any real support in the TUC for British withdrawal. The lack of real TUC opposition to the EC began to turn to positive enthusiasm for integration after 1985. The lack of access to the British government contrasted strongly with their treatment by the EEC Commission, especially after the French socialist, Jacques Delors, became EC Commission President in 1985. Delors sought and secured the support of the British trade unions for his vision of a social dimension to the single market; a policy that was abhorrent to Prime Minister Thatcher, who was greatly angered by the appearance of Delors at the 1988 TUC conference in Bournemouth.

By the time of the 1987 election, Labour had made its peace with the EEC and there was little talk of withdrawal or even transformation. In the intervening years, as Mrs Thatcher has become locked in conflict with Jacques Delors over a range of issues, the Labour Party leadership has increasingly identified itself with Delors, especially on the social dimension and the protection of the environment.

Scandinavian attitudes

The difficulties of the British Labour Party with European integration have been paralleled by those of the Danish Social Democrats (SD). The party was split on the question at the time of the referendum on Danish entry in 1972, with most of its members and the trade unions in favour, but the Left campaigning against entry. The impact of the Left on party policy was increased by the existence of the Socialist People's Party, a small left-wing anti-NATO, anti-EEC competitor on its left flank. Its influence was to increase in the 1970s and in the 1979 European elections this party equalled the SD and gained 21 per cent of the vote as against 21.9 for the social democrats. The SD position on defence and the EC moved to the Left in the 1980s. On defence the SD supported in 1986 the idea of a Nordic nuclear-free zone and 'defensive defence', involving a reduced naval and air commitment. The SD was very unhappy with the provisions of the Single European Act drawn up at the Luxembourg Summit of December 1985 and campaigned vigorously to secure rejection of the Act in the subsequent referendum of 27 February 1986. The SD opposition focused on the impact that the Single European Act would have on the sovereignty of the *Folketing* and on the danger of stringent Danish environmental and work safety provisions being levelled down by common Community provisions. Despite much activity, especially by the Left, in the SD, 56.2 per cent of the electorate voted in favour of the Single European Act and 43.8 per cent against. The party leadership accepted the implications of the result and now accepts that Denmark will have to work within the Single European Act.

The Norwegian Labour Party was similarly divided on the question of entry to the European Community. As in Denmark the bulk of the party leadership and the trade unions were in favour and the Left were against. Opponents of entry broke with the party and affiliated with the newly created Socialist Election Alliance, which spearheaded the anti-membership campaign. There was a majority against Community membership in the referendum and the Labour

Party immediately resigned office. The question of possible Norwegian membership has again arisen, given the prospect of 1992, but it is being handled with extreme caution in view of the party's experience in 1972.

Southern European parties

There is a major contrast within the social democratic parties of southern Europe between the unequivocally pro-Community policy of the Spanish and Portuguese parties and the policy of PASOK, the Greek socialist party. The Spanish and Portuguese parties brought their states into the community on 1 January 1986 while PASOK was opposed to Greek membership. The Iberian parties felt that their countries have suffered from a relative isolation from the rest of Europe. An attachment to a community based on democratic European states was seen as a strength in the transition from the relatively fragile democratic regimes of the post-dictatorship era to deeply rooted democracies. The fact that a relapse from democracy would lead to suspension from the EC was seen as an important constraint on the political ambitions of some of the Spanish military. The Iberian parties continue therefore to be in favour of the maximum possible integration, and Felipe González in particular has been a notably enthusiastic ally of Jacques Delors. The Italian Socialist Party under Bettino Craxi has also been a very strong supporter and withheld support from the Single European Act until it had been voted on by the European Parliament because it believed the Act did not go far enough.

PASOK PASOK opposed Greek membership in the debate leading up to accession in 1981. In the October 1981 election, nine months after Greek accession, PASOK called for a referendum with the implication that this would lead to a withdrawal. The referendum request was turned down by President Karamanlis. The PASOK government dropped the withdrawal option and concentrated on maintaining 'the possibility of ensuring the independent economic and social development of our country'. This policy, akin at that time to that of the Danish SD, has been modified. Greece has come to depend heavily on support from the EC, a development which has been heightened by the decision of the February 1988 Brussels Summit to double the structural funds to the poorer parts of the community. PASOK has accordingly modified its policy and supported the policy of the Single European Act.

CONCLUSION

Distinctively social democratic policy ideas, centred on the rejection of power politics, failed to survive the onset of the Cold War in the late 1940s. During the next three decades the dominant social democratic voice on foreign policy was associated with support for NATO and accommodation to the realities of power politics. Social democratic parties then began to move away from an unequivocal endorsement of this position and their central policy prescriptions regained a greater measure of distinctiveness. They were the pre-eminent voice of detente, but a detente which had to be constructed on the present structures. The collapse of communist rule in eastern Europe would seem to be ushering in a period of the detente, but the new security architecture had not begun to take shape at the time of writing.

Conclusion

In the 1980s social democracy lost the intellectual and political ascendency which it had exercised since the Second World War. For the first three postwar decades, social democracy dominated the political agenda in the democratic states of western Europe, even if it was not always able to translate intellectual hegemony into electoral success. It was able to do so because its prescriptions harmonised with the broad lines of socio-economic change. Social democracy was able to reconcile the fulfilment of its own objectives with the maintenance of the process of capitalist accumulation. One of the conditions of capitalist development in its dynamic and optimistic phase in the first three postwar decades was a vast expansion in the apparatus and function of the state. In many areas of social and economic life the state undertook rôles previously served by market forces. As we have seen, in the immediate postwar years social democracy was synonymous with the rise of interventionism and the challenge to *laissez faire* liberalism. The social democratic renaissance in the 1960s coincided with a 'new wave' of interventionism as the inflation – employment dilemma intensified.

The international economic recession heralded a reversal of the interventionist trend. Firstly, the state now seemed to aggravate the very problems which it sought to resolve. The failure of the French socialist experiment underlined this syndrome. Secondly, the fiscal crisis of the state meant that its resources, and therefore its capacity for intervention were severely limited. Thirdly, the bureaucratic forms which state intervention had taken came under attack for their inertia, waste and inefficiency. The new liberal era was an almost impossibly difficult one for social democracy, characterised as it was by the rolling back of the state, deregulation and the liberalisation of market forces. At first social democrats behaved as though the 'crisis' was merely a temporary interruption in an ongoing process of capitalist growth. The recognition that the economic and political environment had changed permanently led to the adoption of a 'new realism', which in practice meant concessions to market liberalism and economic discipline.

However, the parties faced a number of problems in redefining their economic purposes. Bound by their interventionist traditions they found it hard to redefine the relationship between the market and the state. Moreover, it was hard to reconcile the individualism of the market with the traditional social democratic ethos of social solidarity. Attempts to solve these dilemmas have lacked coherence, relevance and political force, leading many to the conclusion that social democracy has lost its historic rôle. 'The end of the historical strength of [the social democratic] consensus is in sight. The social democratic syndrome of values has not only ceased to promote change and new developments, but it has begun to produce its own contradictions, and it can no longer deal with them effectively' (Dahrendorf 1980, 106–7).

It has also been argued that social democratic parties belong to a party system with its roots in the class relations produced by the industrial revolution. For decades the western European party systems remained frozen along these lines. However, the erosion of class voting in the 1970s and 1980s suggests that fundamental party system change is underway. The electoral weakening of social democracy in these decades is thus seen as part of a long-term secular decline.

Superficially, these arguments bear some resemblance to those deployed in the 1950s to proclaim the demise of the socialist tradition. The 'end of ideology' debate, however, postulated a weakening of ideology as a focus for political mobilisation whilst acknowledging the continued potential of parties of the Left for organising the interests of workers and trade unions. As Seymour Martin Lipset put it with some prescience: 'The democratic class struggle will continue, but it will be a fight without ideologies, without red flags, without May Day parades' (Lipset 1959, 408). This formulation was quite different from those in vogue thirty years later, which emphasised the exhaustion of the social democratic tradition, the decline of democratic class politics or in their most extreme form, the liquidation of ideological conflict in terms of an unconditional victory of liberal capitalism over all the variants of Left politics. This was an argument which gained force after the collapse of communist regimes in eastern Europe.

Social democratic parties also experienced difficulties in their bid to respond to the movements and themes associated with the emergence of the politics of post-industrial societies. The origins of social democracy in industrial society and its close relationship to the ethos of productionism reduced its capacity for dealing convincingly with environmental issues. Moreover, an organisational tradition of centralism in most of the parties made it difficult for them to adapt to the impulse for political self-realisation which the new movements contained.

The unavoidable (but ultimately unanswerable) question is whether social democracy has exhausted its historical potential or merely entered a long phase of lassitude and disorientation. It is a question which can only be addressed comprehensively in the context of an analysis of the long-term development of the capitalist societies, a hazardous undertaking and one which is outside the scope of the present book. We shall restrict ourselves to an assessment of the potential for regeneration within the social democratic tradition itself.

What are the possible sources of internal renewal? Firstly there is the example of the southern European parties. In the 1980s the government and opposition roles of the parties have been reversed. Social democratic parties in Britain, West Germany, and the Low Countries, which had been accustomed to a government rôle experienced prolonged periods of opposition. The Scandinavian and Austrian parties found their hold on government seriously weakened. Conversely, the parties identified with opposition socialism – the French and Italian socialist parties and the parties of the new Mediterranean democracies – entered government. The new-found government vocation, and the electoral decline of communist rivals, brought them into line in many respects with the model of social democracy characteristic of the northern European parties. In other respects, however, they retained some distinctive characteristics: charismatic leadership, a distanced relationship with the trade unions and a populist appeal based on national self-renewal.

The emergence of social democracy in France, Italy, Greece and the Iberian countries has a twofold significance. On the one hand, the convergence of socialist parties here with northern European social democracy creates opportunities for solidarity within the European community. According to Maurice Duverger:

The Congress of the twelve European Community socialist parties in Brussels in March 1989 to draw up a common position for the EC parliament elections has the same significance for European social

democracy as the Bad Godesberg Congress had for the SPD thirty years
previously. European socialists are recognising an evolution which has
already been realised, one which has drawn those from the north and
those from the south together.   *(Le Monde 2 March 1989)*

On the other hand, the distinctive features of the southern
European parties might be taken as a model for their northern
counterparts.

The capacity of the southern European parties to act as the
locomotives of regeneration is however, limited by a number of
factors. The hold of these parties on power owed as much to the
weakness of the Right as it did to their own vitality. At the end of
1989 the capacity of the PSOE for government was seriously
weakened. PASOK had lost power, its image tarnished by allegations
of corruption. Moreover, the 'confused debate over the relationship
between socialism and supranationality' (Featherstone 1988, 389)
does not augur well for Duverger's blueprint for renewal from the
European Community level. And the distinctive features of the
southern parties have roots in specific national conditions and can
not easily be adapted to circumstances in Britain, Germany or
Scandinavia.

A second possible source of regeneration, and one which has in
the past provided a source of inspiration is the Scandinavian model
of social democracy, epitomised by Sweden. In government since
1982, the SAP has undertaken a revision of the model in the light of
new circumstances, and the election of 1985 was successfully fought
on the basis of 'the defence of the social democratic model'. The
British Labour Party and the SPD have both looked to Sweden for
cues in the course of exercises in programmatic renewal.

It has been argued, however, that the Swedish model is 'culture
specific' in that it is only workable in a small, cohesive and socially
organised policy, and that it relies on the cultural hegemony of
social democracy and a very strong party organisation. Moreover, at
the end of the 1980s, the essential elements in the model –
centralised and disciplined pay bargaining, the historic compromise
between capital and labour, and an ethos of social solidarity were all
under serious strain. A dramatic downturn in economic performance was blamed by many on the institutional rigidities inherent in
the model and the failure of a labour market policy hitherto
regarded as the outstanding achievement of Swedish social democracy. The discrediting of the Swedish model represents a major
setback in the reconstruction of western European social democracy.

A third strategy in the bid to restore relevance to the social democratic parties is the intellectual and political redefinition of the tradition. The SPD was in the vanguard of this process, mounting an exercise in programmatic renewal which it claimed was comparable in scope and significance to the programme revision undertaken at Bad Godesberg. However, the programme finalised in Berlin in December 1989 was in most respects little more than a restatement of the principles set out thirty years earlier, serving to underline the problems rather than generating new solutions. In one respect, though, the new programme gave an additional dimension to the social democratic value system. Under the heading 'the ecological modernisation of the economy', the programme went some way towards reconciling the potentially conflicting objectives of economic growth and environmental pro-tection in a bid to adapt social democracy to post-industrial society. Attention was also given to the 'gender gap', traditionally neglected by social democratic parties. In these areas the SPD can be expected to give some impetus to programmatic initiatives in the other European social democratic parties. Moreover, its influence is likely to be felt in the area of defence and security, where it has taken the lead in changing the emphasis from an Atlantic-based security framework to one based on Europe, and on the concepts of common security and non-provocative defence. The incoherence of its economic policies, however, limits the extent to which the SPD can act as the ideological locomotive of social democracy as it did in the 1950s.

Fourthly, the emergence of party democracy in eastern Europe might have been expected to open up new opportunities for renewal, particularly where there was an historic tradition of social democracy to build on. For the east European states, social democracy offered a third way between state socialism and western-style capitalism, and a formula for economic reconstruction which preserved some of the guaranteed minimum levels of social security built into communist systems. Elections in the German Democratic Republic and Hungary, however, quickly dispelled the idea that social democracy had a natural vocation in these countries. First indications are that market capitalism provides the leitmotif for the aspirations of the peoples of eastern Europe, and that the clamour for market-led reconstruction translates into support for the parties of the Right. Moreover, the identification of democratic socialism with remnants of the old regimes served to handicap social democrats here. If economic take-off proves elusive, social democrats

261

may recover some ground amongst social strata disadvantaged by the market. For the present though, a social democratic renaissance based on eastern Europe lacks plausibility.

It is difficult, then to envisage a dramatic intellectual or political revitalisation of the social democratic tradition in the short- to medium-term future. However, this should not be taken to imply that social democracy is in terminal decline. One of the strengths of the parties in the past has been their capacity for responding to economic change and new patterns of class formation. Ideological flexibility and an acute sense of pragmatism means that it is unlikely that the parties will succumb to extinction. Postulations which assert the exhaustion of the social democratic tradition consequent upon the 'victory' of market capitalism over socialism fail to recognise that social democracy assimilated the values of market capitalism early in the postwar era. It is mistaken, therefore, to postulate an ideological antipathy between the two value systems. The experience of the last century suggests that market forces rarely operate successfully for sustained periods without purposeful political intervention and social amelioration. Moreover, competitive markets inevitably produce winners and losers. The latter – dissatisfied social strata or economically disadvantaged regions – will continue to provide a pillar of support for social democratic parties.

Liberal democracy hinges on inter-party competition, and there is at present no burgeoning political force threatening to displace the parties from their rôle as principle competitors to Conservative and Christian democratic parties. It is also striking that in many of the European countries the Right is weakened by division, either between rival parties or factions within a single party. In no western European country has the Right been able to sustain a permanent government rôle. It could be argued that the capacity of social democratic parties to command a government rôle has almost always depended on the *incapacity* of the Right to do so, and that this will continue to be the case.

Furthermore, while the intellectual decomposition of social democracy has been accompanied by a weakening of the parties' capacity for electoral mobilisation (especially in the northern and central countries of western Europe) the trend has not been sufficiently uniform, sustained or dramatic to suggest irreversible secular decline. Uneven electoral performance has always been a characteristic of social democratic parties, and it is likely that it will continue to be so.

What has become evident from the foregoing chapters, however, is a weakening of the social democratic tradition in terms of its distinctiveness from other political forces. The postwar period has seen a progressive ideological assimilation between social democracy and liberalism. Organisationally, the parties have moved decisively away from their extra-parliamentary roots and from the ethos of the solidarity community which previously distinguished social democratic parties from the parliamentary orientation and élitist structures of their rivals on the Right. In terms of membership and electorate, the class composition of the parties has become less sharply defined. In a number of the parties there has been a tentative but perceptible distancing in party–trade union relations. It is likely that the social democratic parties of Europe will continue to be a force in the politics of Europe well into the next millennium. The qualitative diminution in the social democratic tradition which the postwar years have witnessed is, however, unlikely to be reversed.

Further Reading

CHAPTER 1

There is no comprehensive work on the ideology of social democracy in the postwar period, so reference must be made to works on the individual parties. Even amongst these it is rare to find a work devoted exclusively to the ideological dimension of party life, and it is usually necessary to read selectively in general texts on the parties. A good account of ideological development in the Swedish party in the immediate postwar years is Sainsbury (1980) whilst Tilton (1990) deals with the theoretical foundation of Swedish social democracy. For the ideological and programmatic development of the British Labour Party, see Howell (1976). Braunthal (1983) covers the German party from 1969-82, whilst Klotzbach (1982) and Meng (1985) are also useful for readers of German. On France see Bell and Criddle (1988) and on Spain, Gillespie (1989).

CHAPTER 2

The best general guide to the development of organisational structure of political parties is Von Beyme (1985). Chapters 2 and 3 are especially useful on the development of social democratic parties. On individual parties Shell's (1962) study of the SPÖ is the most outstanding. Readers of German should consult Klotzbach (1982) on the SPD. The Labour Party is well covered in Shaw (1989) and the Scandinavian parties are comprehensively and incisively covered by Esping-Andersen (1985). The two volumes by Paterson

264

and Thomas (1977, 1986) contain useful material on a range of issues.

CHAPTER 3

The electoral development of social democratic parties is a main feature of both volumes by Paterson and Thomas. It is the central theme of Przeworski and Sprague (1986) and is treated extensively in Esping-Andersen (1985). Esping-Andersen is accessible to those without a sophisticated knowledge of statistics but much of Przeworski and Sprague's argument is at a rarefied mathematical level.

CHAPTER 4

The expence of the British Labour Party in power is very well documented with Morgan (1984) and Pelling (1984) on the 1945/51 governments, Lapping (1970) on the 1960s, and Holmes (1985) and Coates (1980) on the 1974/79 experience. Braunthal (1983) deals with the German party in power. Ambler (1985), Hall (1986), Cerny and Schain (1985) and Lauber (1983) contain useful material on the French socialists in power in the 1980s, while Graham (1965) gives a detailed account of socialist participation in government in France in the early postwar years. Esping-Andersen (1985) contains an excellent conceptual account of the exercise of social democratic power in Scandinavia.

CHAPTER 5

Relations between social democracy and organised business are treated in rather summary fashion, if at all, in the literature on the parties, but see Blank (1973) on Britain in the early postwar years. There is, however, a large body of literature on the relationship between parties and trade unions. For comparative studies, see Gourevitch et al. (1984) on the northern European countries, and Lange et al. (1982) on southern Europe. There is good coverage of the politics of the British labour movement of which Taylor (1987), Panitch (1976) and Barnes and Reid (1980) give most attention to the Labour Party connection. Markovits (1986) has given a masterful account of party–union relations in Germany. For a conceptual treatment of the relationship between the labour movement and social democracy in Scandinavia, see Korpi (1978).

CHAPTER 6

The foreign policies of the social democratic parties have been covered very patchily. There is much useful material in Bullock's *Ernest Bevin, Foreign Secretary*, (1983). Much attention has been devoted to the theme of European Integration, and Featherstone (1988), Newman (1983) and Paterson (1974) are all useful. There is no adequate account of social democratic parties on defence.

Bibliography

ABERT J.G. *Economic Policy and Planning in the Netherlands, 1950–1965* (Yale University Press 1969)

ADDISON P. *The Road to 1945, British Politics and the Second World War* (Quartet 1977)

AIMER P. The Strategy of Gradualism and the Swedish Wage Earner Funds. *West European Politics* 8 (3) 1985

AMBLER J.S. (ed.) *The French Socialist Experiment* (Institute for the Study of Human Issues, 1985)

ARANGO R.E. *Spain: from Repression to Renewal* (Westview Press 1985)

ASHFORD D.E. *The Emergence of the Welfare States* (Basil Blackwell 1986)

ATTLEE C. *Labour's Peace Aims* (Labour Party, 1939)

BARKER E. *Austria 1918–1972* (Macmillan 1973)

BARNES D. AND REID E. *Government and Trade Unions: the British Experience 1964–79* (Heinemann 1980)

BEALEY F. (ed.) *The Social and Political Thought of the Labour Party* (Weidenfeld & Nicolson 1970)

BECKERMAN W. Objectives and Performance: an overall view. In Beckerman W. (ed.) *The Labour Government's Economic Record* (Duckworth 1972)

BECKERMAN W. (ed.) *The Labour Government's Economic Record 1964–70* (Duckworth 1972)

BEECHAM J. *Labour's Next Moves Forward*, in Fabian Tract 521 (Fabian Society, 1987)

BEER S.H. *Modern British Politics: a study of parties and pressure groups* (Faber & Faber 1965)

BELL D. *The End of Ideology: on the exhaustion of political ideas in the fifties* (Free Press of Glencoe 1960)

BELL D.S. (ed.) *Democratic Parties in Spain: Spanish politics after Franco* (Frances Pinter 1983)

BELL D.S. AND CRIDDLE B. *The French Socialist Party: the Emergence of a Party of Government* (second ed.) (Clarendon Press 1988)

BYRD P. The Labour Party in Britain. In Paterson W.E. and Thomas A.H. (eds) *The Future of Social Democracy: Problems and Prospects of Social Democratic Parties in Western Europe* (Clarendon 1986)

BLANK S. *Industry and Government in Britain: The Federation of British Industries in Politics 1945–65* (Saxon House/Lexington Books 1973)

BORNSEN G. *Innerparteiliche Opposition (Jungsozialisten und SPD)* 1969

BOYLE R. Britain's First No to Europe: Britain and the Briand Plan, 1929–30. *European Studies Review*, 10, 1980.

BRANDT W. *The Ordeal of Coexistence* (Harvard UP 1962)

BRANDT W. *A Peace Policy for Europe* (Weidenfeld & Nicholson 1969)

BRAUNTHAL G. *The West German Social Democrats 1969–82. Profile of a Party in Power* (Westview 1983)

BRAUNTHAL G. The West German Social Democrats: Factionalism at the local level. *West European Politics* 7, 1, 1984

BRAUNTHAL J. *History of the International*, Vol. 3, 1943–68 (Gollancz 1980)

BRITTAN S. The Economic Contradictions of Democracy. *British Journal of Political Science*, April 1975

BULLOCK A. *Ernest Bevin: Foreign Secretary* (Heinemann 1983)

BURNHAM J. *The Managerial Revolution* (Penguin 1945)

BUTLER D. AND STOKES D. *Political Change in Britain* (Macmillan 1969)

CAHM E. *Politics and Society in Contemporary France (1789–1971): A Documentary History* (Harrap 1972)

CAIRNCROSS A. *Years of Recovery: British Economic Policy 1945–51* (Methuen 1985)

CAMERON D.R. Social Democracy, Corporatism, Labour Quiescence, and the Representation of Economic Interest in Advanced Capitalist Society. In Goldthorpe J.H. *Order and Conflict in Contemporary Capitalism* (Clarendon Press 1984)

CARR R. AND FUSI P. *Spain: dictatorship to democracy* (Allen & Unwin 1979)

CAWSON A. Pluralism, Corporatism and the Role of the State. *Government and Opposition* 13, 1978

CERNY P. AND SCHAIN M.A. (eds) *Socialism, the State and Public Policy in France* (Frances Pinter 1985)

CHANDLER J., MORRIS D.S. AND BACKER M.J. *The Ascent of Middle Class Politics: The Middle Class Membership of the Labour Party*. Paper delivered at the Annual Conference of the Political Studies Association, University of Kent 1982

CHILDS D. *From Schumacher to Brandt: The Story of German Socialism 1945–1965* (Pergamon Press 1966)

CLARKE J. Concerted Action in the Federal Republic of Germany. *British Journal of Industrial Relations* 17, 1979

CLEMENT W. 'Social Partnership and the Austrian Economic Order: stabilisation versus efficiency'. *Association for the Study of German Politics, Journal* 13, 1987

CLOGG R. *Parties and Elections in Greece: the search for legitimacy* (Hurst & Co 1987)

COATES D. *The Labour Party and the Struggle for Socialism* (CUP 1975)

COATES D. *Labour in Power? A Study of the Labour Government 1974–79* (Longman 1980)

COLE G.D.H. *Europe, Russia and the Future* (Macmillan 1942)

CRIDDLE B. *Socialists and European Integration: A Study of the French Socialist Party* (RKP 1969)

CROSLAND A. *The Future of Socialism* (Cape 1956)

CROUCH G. *The State, Capital and Liberal Democracy.* In Crouch C. (ed.) *State and Economy in Contemporary Capitalism* (Croom Helm 1979)

DAHRENDORF R. *Life Chances: approaches to social and political theory* (Weidenfeld and Nicholson 1980)

DALTON H. *High Tide and After: Memoirs 1945–1960* (Müller 1962)

DAUDT H. The Political Future of the Welfare State. *The Netherlands Journal of Sociology* 13, 1977

DE VRIES J. *The Netherlands Economy in the Twentieth Century: an examination of the most characteristic features in the period 1900–70* (Van Gorcam 1978)

DRUCKER H.M. *Doctrine and Ethos in the Labour Party* (George Allen & Unwin 1979)

DURBIN E.F.M. *The Politics of Democratic Socialism* (Routledge 1940)

EDINGER L. *Kurt Schumacher, A Study in Personality and Political Behaviour* (OUP 1965)

ESPING-ANDERSEN G. *Politics Against Markets: The Social Democratic Road to Power* (Princeton University Press 1985)

ESPING-ANDERSEN G. From Poor Relief to Institutional Welfare States: the development of Scandinavian social policy. In Erikson R., Hansen E.J., Ringen S., Uusitalo (eds) *The Scandinavian Model: Welfare States and Welfare Research* (M.E. Sharpe Inc, 1987)

ESPING-ANDERSEN G. AND KORPI W. Social Policy and Class Politics in Postwar Capitalism: Scandinavia, Austria and Germany. In Goldsthorpe, J.H. (ed.) *Order and Conflict in Contemporary Capitalism* (Clarendon Press 1984)

FARNETTI P. *The Italian Party System (1945–1980)* (Francis Pinter 1985)

FEATHERSTONE K. Pasok and the Left. In Featherstone K. and Katsoudas D.K. (eds) *Political Change in Greece : before and after the Colonels* (Croom Helm 1987)

FEATHERSTONE K. *Socialist Parties and European Integration: A Comparative History* (Manchester 1988)

FEATHERSTONE K. AND KATSOUDAS D.K. *Political Change in Greece: before and after the Colonels* (Croom Helm 1987)

FEINSTEIN C.H. Changes in the Distribution of the National Income in the United Kingdom since 1860. In Marchal A. and Ducros B. (eds) *The Distribution of National Income* (1968)

FITZMAURICE J. *Politics in Denmark* (Hurst & Co 1981)

FITZMAURICE J. *The Politics of Belgium: crisis and compromise in a plural society* (Hurst & Co 1983)

FORBES I. (ED.) *Market Socialism: whose choice?* Fabian Tract 516 (Fabian Society 1986)

FRASER D. *The Evolution of the British Welfare State: A history of social policy since the industrial revolution* (second edn, Macmillan 1984)

GAITSKELL H. *The Challenge of Coexistence* (Methuen 1957)

GALBRAITH J.K. *The Affluent Society* (Penguin 1958)

GALLAGHER T. AND WILLIAMS A. *Southern European Socialism: Parties Elections and the Challenge of Government* (Manchester 1989)

GAY P. *The Dilemma of Democratic Socialism: Eduard Bernstein's Challenge to Marx* (Columbia University Press 1952)

GEORGE V. AND WILDING P. *Ideology and Social Welfare* (Routledge & Kegan Paul 1976)

GERLICH P., GRANDE E. AND MÜLLER W.C. Corporatism in Crisis: Stability and Change of Social Partnership in Austria. *Political Studies XXXVI*, 1988

GILLESPIE R. *The Spanish Socialist Party; A History of Factionalism* (Clarendon 1989)

GINER S. Southern European Socialism in Transition. In Pridham G. (ed.) *The New Mediterranean Democracies: regime transition in Spain, Greece and Portugal* (Frank Cass 1984)

GILMOUR D. *The Transformation of Spain: from Franco to the Constitutional Monarchy* (Quartet 1985)

GOUREVITCH P., MARTIN A., ALLEN C., ROSS G., BORNSTEIN S. AND MARKOVITS A. *Unions and Economic Crisis: Britain, West Germany and Sweden* (George Allen & Unwin 1984)

GRAHAM B.D. *The French Socialists and Tripartisme 1944–1947* (Weidenfeld & Nicolson 1965)

GRANT W. AND MARSH D. Tripartism: Reality or Myth. *Government and Opposition* 12, 1977

GREENLEAF W.H. *The British Political Tradition, Vol. 1: The Ideological Heritage* (Methuen 1983)

GROSSER A. *The Western Alliance: European–American relations since 1945* (Macmillan 1980)

HAAS E. *The Uniting of Europe* (Stevens 1958)

HALL P.A. *Governing the Economy: the politics of state intervention in Britain and France* (Polity Press 1986)

HANLEY D. *Keeping Left? CERES and the French Socialist Party* (Manchester University Press 1986)

HARRINGTON M. The Welfare State and its Neoconservative Critics. *Dissent*, Fall 1973

HARRISON A. *The Distribution of Wealth in Ten Countries. Royal Commission on the Distribution of Income and Wealth, background paper to report no. 7* (HMSO 1979)

HARRISON J. *The Spanish Economy in the Twentieth Century* (Croom Helm 1985)

HASELER S. *The Gaitskellites: Revisionism in the British Labour Party 1951–64* (Macmillan 1969)

HAYWARD J. Introduction: Change and Choice : The Agenda and Planning. In Hayward J., Watson M. (eds) *Planning, Politics and Public Policy. The British, French and Italian Experience* (CUP 1975)

HAYWARD J. *The State and the Market Economy: Industrial Patriotism and Economic Intervention in France* (Wheatsheaf 1986)

HAYWARD J. AND WATSON M. *Planning, Politics and Public Policy: The British French and Italian Experience* (CUP 1975)

HEADEY B. *Housing Policy in the Developed Economy: The United Kingdom, Sweden and the United States* (Croom Helm 1978)

HEALEY D. *A Neutral Belt in Europe* (Fabian Society Pamphlet 1958)

HEIDAR K. Programmatic Renewal in the Norwegian Labour Party: New Wine or Just New Labels? (Paper delivered at Annual Conference of Political Studies Association, University of Warwick 1989)

HEIMANN S. Die Sozialdemokratische Partei Deutschlands. In Stoss R. (ed.) *Parteien-Handbuch: Die Parteien der Bundesrepublik Deutschland 1945–1980*, Band II (Westdeutscher Verlag 1984)

HELLMAN S. The Italian Communist Party between Berlinguer and the Seventeenth Congress. In Leonardi R., Nanetti R.Y. (eds) *Italian Politics: a review*, Vol. 1 (Frances Pinter 1986)

HENIG S. AND PINDER J. *Political Parties in the European Community* (Allen and Unwin 1970)

HINE D. Italian Socialism and the Centre Left Coalition: Strategy and Tactics. *Journal of Common Market Studies* 13, 1975

HINE D. The Italian Socialist Party and the Centre–Left coalition: A

Study of the Effects upon the Party of Participation in the Governing Coalition (1962–1972). (Thesis submitted for the degree of D.Phil., Nuffield College, Oxford, 1978)

HINE D. The Italian Socialist Party under Craxi: surviving but not reviving. *West European Politics* 2, 1979

HINE D. Leaders and Followers: Democracy and Manageability in the Social Democratic Parties of Western Europe. In Paterson W.E. and Thomas A.H. (eds) *The Future of Social Democracy: Problems and Prospects of Social Democratic Parties in Western Europe* (Clarendon 1986)

HINE D. The Craxi Premiership. In Leonardi R., Nanetti R.Y. (eds) *Italian Politics: a review*, Vol. 1 (Frances Pinter 1986)

HMSO 1947 Economic Survey for 1947, Cmd 7046

HMSO 1977 Royal Commission on the Distribution of Income and Wealth, *The Distribution of Income in Eight Countries*. Background Paper No. 4

HODNE F. *The Norwegian Economy* 1920–1980 (Croom Helm 1983)

HOFFMAN S. *In Search of France* (Harvard University Press 1963)

HOLMES M. *The Labour Government 1974–79: Political Aims and Economic Reality* (Macmillan 1985)

HOLTON R. Industrial Politics in France: Nationalisation under Mitterrand. *West European Politics* 9, 1986

HOWELL D. *British Social Democracy: A Study in Development and Decay* (Croom Helm 1976)

HUSTER E-U. *Die Politik der SPD 1945–1950* (Campus Verlag 1978)

JOLL J. *The Second International 1889–1914* (Routledge & Kegan Paul 1974)

JONES H.G. *Planning and Productivity in Sweden* (Croom Helm 1976)

JONES B. AND KEATING M. *Labour and the British State* (Clarendon Press 1985)

KASTENDIEK H. Struktur und Organisationsprobleme, einer staatstragenden Arbeitnehmerpartei: zum Verhaltnis von SPD und Gewerkschaften seit 1966. In Ebighausen R., Tiemann F. (eds) *Das Ende der Arbeiterbewegung in Deutschland*? (Westdeutscher Verlag 1984)

KERR C. *Industrialism and Industrial Man: the Problems of Labour and Management in Economic Growth* (Heinemann 1962)

KESSELMAN M. The Recruitment of Party Activists. *Journal of Politics*, Feb. 1973.

KIRCHHEIMER O. The Transformation of the Western European Party Systems. In La Palombara J., Wiener M. (eds), *Political Parties and Political Development* (Princeton University Press 1966)

KLOTZBACH K. *Der Weg Zur Staatspartei: Programmatik, praktische Politik und*

Organisation der deutschen Sozialdemokratie 1945 bis 1965 (Verlag Dietz 1982)

KOGAN M. *A Political History of Postwar Italy: from the old to the new centre–left* (Praeger 1981)

KOHLER B. *Political Forces in Spain, Greece and Portugal* (Butterworth 1982)

KOLINSKY E. *Parties, Opposition and Society in West Germany* (Croom Helm 1984)

KORPI W. *The Working Class in Welfare Capitalism* (Routledge & Kegan Paul 1978)

KRASIKOV A. *From Dictatorship to Democracy: Spanish Reportage* (Pergamon 1984)

KUISAL R. *Capitalism and the State in Modern France: Renovation and Economic Management in the Twentieth Century* (CUP 1981)

LABOUR PARTY *Annual Conference Report* (Labour Party 1960)

LABOUR PARTY *Let Us Face the Future* (1945)

LANDAUER C. *European Socialism: a History of Ideas and Movements from the Industrial Revolution to Hitler's Seizure of Power*, Vol. 1, (Greenwood 1976)

LANGE P. The End of an Era: the wage indexation referendum of 1985. In Leonardi R. Nanetti R.Y. (eds) *Italian Politics: a review*, Vol. 1 (Frances Pinter 1986)

LANGE P., ROSS G. AND VANNICELLI, M. *Unions, Change and Crisis: French and Italian Union Strategy and the Political Economy, 1945–1980* (George Allen & Unwin 1982)

LA PALOMBARA J. Socialist Alternatives: the Italian variant. *Foreign Affairs* 60, 1981–82

LASKI H. *Reflections on the Revolution of Our Time* (Viking 1943)

LAPPING B. *The Labour Government 1964–70* (Penguin 1970)

LARSSON S. AND SJOSTROM K. The Welfare Myth in Class Society. In Fry J. (ed.) *Limits of the Welfare State: Critical Views on Postwar Sweden* (Saxon House 1979)

LAUBER V. *The Political Economy of France: from Pompidou to Mitterrand* (Praeger 1983)

LAUBER V. Reinventing French Socialism: Economic Policy, Ideology, Political Strategy. *Parliamentary Affairs* 38, 1985

LEADBEATER C. *The Politics of Prosperity, Fabian Tract 523* (Fabian Society, 1987)

LEONARDI R. AND NANETTI R.Y. *Italian Politics: a review*, Vol. 1 (Frances Pinter 1986)

LIEBER R.J. Labour in Power: Problems of Political Economy. In Brown B.E. (ed.) *Eurocommunism and Eurosocialism* (Cyrco Press 1979)

LIEBERMANN S. *The Growth of European Mixed Economies 1945-70: a Concise*

Study of the Economic Evolution of Eight Countries (Wiley 1977)

LINDBECK A. *Swedish Economic Policy* (Macmillan 1975)

LIPSET S. M. *Political Man* (Heinemann 1959)

LONGSTRETH F. The City Industry and the State. In Crouch C. (ed.) *State and Economy in Contemporary Capitalism* (Croom Helm 1979)

LOSCHE P. Ende der sozialdemokratischen Arbeiterbewegung? *Die Neue Gesellschaft*, May 1988, 453–63

LUTHER R. Austria's Future and Waldheim's Past: The Significance of the 1986 Elections. *West European Politics* 10, 1987

LYRINTZIS C. Political Parties in Post-Junta Greece: a case of bureaucratic clientelism? In Pridham G. (ed.) *The New Mediterranean Democracies: regime transition in Spain, Greece and Portugal* (Frank Cass 1984)

MAIER C. S. Preconditons for corporatism. In Goldthorpe J. H. (ed.) *Order and conflict in contemporary capitalism* (Clarendon Press 1984)

MARKS H.J. The Sources of Reformism in the Social Democratic Party of Germany 1890–1914. *Journal of Modern History* Vol. XI 1939, 334–56

MARKOVITS A.S. *The Politics of the West German Trade Unions: Strategies of Class and Interest Representation in Growth and Crisis* (CUP 1986)

MARAVALL J.M. The Socialist Alternative: the policies and electorate of the PSOE. In Penniman H.R., Mujal-Leon E.M. (eds) *Spain at the Polls, 1977, 1979 and 1982* (American Enterprise Institute, 1985)

MARSHALL T.H. *Citizenship and Social Class, and Other Essays* (CUP 1950)

MARTIN R.M. *TUC: The Growth of a Pressure Group 1858–1976* (Clarendon Press 1980)

MAYNE R. *The Recovery of Europe: from devastation to unity* (Weidenfeld & Nicolson 1970)

MENG R. *Die sozialdemokratische Wende* (Focus Verlag 1985)

MICHELS R. *Political Parties: a sociological study of the origins of the oligarchical tendencies of modern democracies* (Dover Publications Inc. 1959)

MIDDEL B. AND VAN SCHURR W.H. Dutch Party Delegates. *Acta Politica*, April 1981, 241–63

MIDDLEMAS K. *Politics in Industrial Society: The experience of the British system since 1911* (Andre Deutsch 1979)

MILIBAND R. *Parliamentary Socialism: A Study: The Politics of Labour* (2nd edn) (Merlin Press 1972)

MILLER K. *Government and Politics in Denmark* (Houghton Mifflin Co 1968)

MILLER S. *Die SPD vor und nach Godesberg* (Neue Gesellschaft 1974)

MILWARD A.S. *The Reconstructions of Western Europe 1945-51* (Methuen 1984)

MISHRA R. *Society and Social Policy: Theoretical Perspectives on Welfare* (Macmillan 1977)

MISHRA R. *The Welfare State in Crisis: Social Thought and Social Change* (Wheatsheaf 1984)

MORGAN K.O. *Labour in Power, 1945–51* (Clarendon Press 1984)

MOSS R. *The Collapse of Democracy* (Sphere 1977)

MOUZELIS N. Continuities and Discontinuities in Greek Politics: from Elefterios Venizelos to Andreas Papandreou. In Featherstone K., Katsoudas D.K. (eds) *Political Change in Greece: before and after the Colonels* (Croom Helm 1987)

MÜLLER-ROMMEL F. *Innerparteiliche Gruppierungen in der SPD. Eine empirische Studie uber informell-organisierte Gruppierungen von 1969–1980* (Westdeutscher Verlag 1982)

NARR W-D., SCHEER H. AND SPORI D. *SPD – Staatspartei oder Reformpartei* (Piper 1976)

NEWMAN M. *Socialism and European Unity: The Dilemma of the Left in Britain and France* (Junction 1983)

O'CONNOR J. *The Fiscal Crisis of the State* (St Martin's Press 1973)

OECD *Economic Outlook* (1976)

OLSEN S. Sweden. In Flora P. (ed.) *Growth to Limits: The Western European Welfare States since World War II*, Vol. 1: Sweden, Norway, Finland, Denmark (Walter de Gruyter 1986)

PADGETT S.A. The West German Social Democrats in Opposition 1982–86. *West European Politics* 10, 1987

PANITCH L. *Social Democracy and Industrial Militancy: the Labour Party, the Trade Unions and Incomes Policy 1945–74* (CUP 1976)

PASQUINO G. Modernity and Reforms: the PSI between political entrepreneurs and gamblers. *West European Politics* 9, 1986

PATERSON W.E. The SPD after Brandt's fall: change or continuity? *Government and Opposition* X (2), 1975

PATERSON W.E. *The SPD and European Integration* (Saxon House 1974)

PATERSON W.E. AND THOMAS A.H. *The Future of Social Democracy: Problems and Prospects of Social Democratic Parties in Western Europe* (Clarendon Press 1986)

PATERSON W.E. AND THOMAS A.H. *Social Democratic Parties in Western Europe* (Croom Helm 1977)

PELINKA A. *Social Democratic Parties in Europe* (Praeger 1983)

PELLING H. *The Labour Governments 1945–51* (Macmillan 1984)

PENNIMAN H.R. AND MUJAL-LEON E.M. *Spain at the Polls, 1977, 1979 and 1982* (American Enterprise Institute, 1985)

PEPER B. The Netherlands: A Permissive Response. In Cox A. (ed.) *Politics, Policy and the European Recession* (Macmillan 1982)

PERRY R. United Kingdom. In Flora P. (ed.) *Growth to Limits: The Western European Welfare States since World War II*, Vol. 2: Germany, United Kingdom, Ireland, Italy (Walter de Gruyter 1986)

PETRY R. Die SPD under der Sozialismus. In Flechtheim O.K. (ed.) *Die Parteien in der Bundesrepublik Deutschland* (Hoffmann & Campe Verlag 1973)

PIMLOTT B. *Hugh Dalton* (Cape 1985)

PHARO H. Bridgebuilding and Reconstruction: Norway faces the Marshall Plan. *Scandinavian Journal of History* 1, 2, 1976

PRZEWORSKI A. Social Democracy as an Historical Phenomenon. *New Left Review* 122, 1980

PRZEWORSKI A. AND SPRAGUE J.S. *Paper Stones: A History of Electoral Socialism* (Chicago 1986)

ROCA J. Neo-Corporatism in Post-Franco Spain. In Scholten I. (ed.) *Political Stability and Neo-Corporatism: Corporatist Integration and Societal Cleavages in Western Europe* (Sage 1987)

ROSE C. *The Relationship of Socialist Principles to British Labour Foreign Policy 1945–51* (Oxford D.Phil. 1960)

SAINSBURY D. *Swedish Social Democratic Ideology and Electoral Politics 1944–48: a study of the functions of party ideology* (Almqvist and Wiksell 1980)

SASSOON D. *Contemporary Italy: Politics, Economy and Society since 1945* (Longman 1986)

SCHARF A. *Österreichs Erneuerung 1945–55* (Wiener Volksbuchhandlung 1955)

SCHARPF F. Economic and Institutional Constraints of Full-Employment Strategies: Sweden, Austria and West Germany, 1973–82. In Goldthorpe J.H. (ed.) *Order and Conflict in Contemporary Capitalism* (Clarendon Press 1984)

SCHONAUER K. *Die ungeliebten Kinder der Mutter SPD* (Bonn, 1982)

SCHUMPETER J.A. *Capitalism, Socialism and Democracy* (4th edn) (George Allen & Unwin 1954)

SCHAIN M. AND CERNY P. (EDS) *Socialism, the State and Public Policy in France* (Frances Pinter 1985)

SHAW E. *Discipline and Discord in the Labour Party 1951–1987* (Manchester University Press 1988)

SHAW E. 'The Labour Party and the Militant Tendency'. *Parliamentary Affairs* 42 (2), 1989

SHELL K.L. *The Transformation of Austrian Socialism* (State University of New York Press 1962)

SHELL K.L. Extraparliamentary Opposition in Post War Germany *Comparative Politics*, XXI 1970

SHONFIELD A. *British Economic Policy since the War* (Penguin 1958)

SHONFIELD A. *Modern Capitalism: the changing balance of public and private power* (OUP 1969)

SHONFIELD A. *In Defence of the Mixed Economy* (OUP 1984)

SIMMONS H.G. *French Socialists in Search of a Role 1956–1967* (Cornell University Press 1970)

SKED A. AND COOK C. *Postwar Britain: a political history* (Harvester 1979)

SKIDELSKY R. The Decline of Keynesian Politics. In Crouch C. (ed.) *State and Economy in Contemporary Capitalism* (Croom Helm 1979)

SOZIALDEMOKRATISCHE PARTEI DEUTSCHLANDS *Jahrbuch 1981-83* (SPD 1984)

SOZIALDEMOKRATISCHE PARTEI DEUTSCHLANDS Die Wirtschaft Oklogisch und Sozial Erneuern. *Politik: Informationsaienst der SPD* 10, 1985

SOZIALDEMOKRATISCHE PARTEI DEUTSCHLANDS *Parteitag der SPD in Nurnberg, 25–29 August 1986 Service der SPD für Presse, Funk, TV* (Parteivorstand 1986)

SOZIALDEMOKRATISCHE PARTEI DEUTSCHLANDS *Entwurf für ein neues Grundsatzprogramm der SPD* (Parteivorstand 1986)

SPOTTS F. AND WIESER T. *Italy: a Difficult Democracy: a Survey of Italian Politics* (CUP 1986)

STEINER K. *Politics in Austria* (Little Brown & Co 1972)

STEWART M. The Distribution of Income. In Beckerman W. (ed.) *The Labour Government's Economic Record 1964–70* (Duckworth 1972)

SULLY M.A. *Political Parties and Elections in Austria* (Hurst 1981)

SULLY M.A. Austrian Social Democracy. In Paterson W.E., Thomas A.H. (eds) *The Future of Social Democracy: Problems and Prospects of Social Democratic Parties in Western Europe* (Clarendon Press 1986)

TARROW S. Introduction to Leonardi R., Nanetti R.Y. (eds) *Italian Politics: a review*, Vol. 1 (Frances Pinter 1986)

TAYLOR A.J. *The Trade Unions and the Labour Party* (Croom Helm 1987)

THOMAS A.H. Social Democracy in Scandinavia: Can Dominance be Regained. In Paterson W.E., Thomas A.H. (eds) *The Future of Social Democracy: Problems and Prospects of Social Democratic Parties in Western Europe* (Clarendon Press 1986)

TILTON T.A. A Swedish Road to Socialism: Ernst Wigforss and the Ideological Foundations of Swedish Social Democracy. *American Political Science Review* 73, 1979

TILTON T.A. *The Political Theory of Swedish Social Democracy: through the welfare state to socialism* (Clarendon 1990)

TINGSTEN H. *The Swedish Social Democrats: their ideological development* (Bedminster 1973)

TZANNOTOS Z. *Socialism in Greece: the first four years* (Gower 1986)

URWIN D.W. *Western Europe since 1945: a short political history* (3rd edn) (Longman 1981)

VAN DEN BRANDE A. Neo-corporatism and Functional Integral Power in Belgium. In Scholten I. (ed.), *Political Stability and Neo Corporatism: Corporatist Integration and Societal Cleavages in Western Europe* (Sage 1987)

VERNON R. *Big Business and the State: Changing Relations in Western Europe* (Macmillan 1974)

VON BEYME K. Policy-making in the Federal Republic of Germany: a systematic introduction. In Von Beyme K., Schmidt M. (eds) *Policy and Politics in the Federal Republic of Germany* (Gower 1985)

VON BEYME K. *Political Parties in Western Democracies* (Gower 1985)

VON BEYME K. (ED.) *Policy and Politics in the Federal Republic of Germany* (Gower/German Political Science Association 1985)

WALTERS P. Distributing Decline: Swedish Social Democrats and the Crisis of the Welfare States. *Government and Opposition* 20, 1985

WALTERS P. The Legacy of Olof Palme: the condition of the Swedish Model. *Government and Opposition* 22, 1987

WEBBER D. *German Social Democracy in the Economic Crisis: Unemployment and the Politics of Labour Market Policy in the Federal Republic of Germany from 1974 to 1982* (PhD thesis, Essex University 1984)

WEBBER D. Social Democracy and the Re-emergence of Mass Unemployment in Western Europe. In Paterson W.E., Thomas A.H. (eds) *The Future of Social Democracy: Problems and Prospects of Social Democratic Parties in Western Europe* (Clarendon Press 1986)

WEIL G.L. *The Benelux Nations: The Politics of Small Country Democracies* (Holt, Rinehart & Winston Inc. 1970)

WESSELS B. Federal Republic of Germany: Business Profits from Politics. In van Schendelen M.C.P.M. (ed) *The Politicisation of Business in Western Europe* (Croom Helm 1987)

WHITELY P. *The Labour Party in Crisis* (Methuen 1983)

WILLIAMS P. *Politics in Postwar France: Parties and the Constitution in the Fourth Republic* (Longman 1958)

WILLIAMS P.M. *Hugh Gaitskell: a Political Biography* (Cape 1979)

WILLIAMS P.M. (ed.) *The Diary of Hugh Gaitskell 1945–56* (Cape 1983)

WILSON F.L. Socialism in France: A Failure of Politics not a Failure of Policy. *Parliamentary Affairs* 38, 1985

WILSON F.L. *The French Democratic Left, 1963–69: towards a modern party system* (Stanford University Press 1971)

WILSON G.K. *Business and Politics: A Comparative Introduction* (Macmillan 1985)

WOLINETZ S.B. The Dutch Labour Party: a social democratic party in transition. In Paterson W.E., Thomas A.H. (eds) *Social Democratic Parties in Western Europe* (Croom Helm 1977)

WRIGHT J.F. *Britain in the Age of Economic Management. An Economic History since 1939* (OUP 1979)

WRIGHT V. Socialism and the Interdependent Economy: Industrial policy-making under the Mitterrand Presidency. *Government and Opposition* 19, 1984

Index